A History of
The Malthusian League
1877-1927

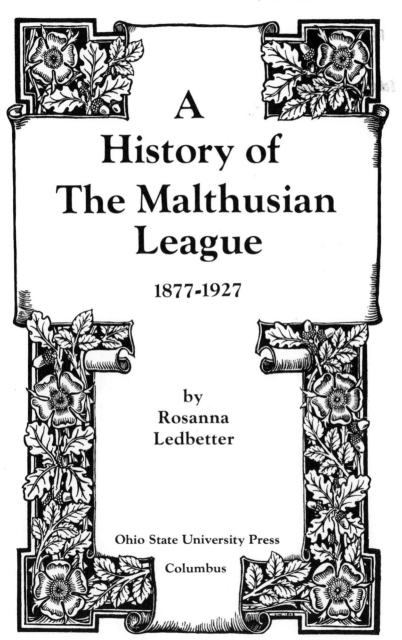

A
History of
The Malthusian
League

1877-1927

by
Rosanna
Ledbetter

Ohio State University Press

Columbus

Copyright © 1976 by the Ohio State University Press
All rights reserved
Manufactured in the United States of America

Library of Congress Cataloging in Publication Data

Ledbetter, Rosanna, 1932–
  A history of the Malthusian League, 1877–1927.

  Bibliography: p. 243
  Includes Index.
  1. Malthusian League. I. Title.
HQ763.M3L4   301.32'1   76-10822
ISBN 0-8142-0257-8

This book is dedicated to
EILEEN PALMER
and to the memory of her husband
HORACE PALMER
both of whom were so kind and helpful
to me during my researches
in England in 1970.

CONTENTS

Preface   ix
Introduction   xi
1. The Embryonic Stage   3
2. The Fetal Stage   25
3. The Anatomy of the League   57
4. Labor and the Malthusian League   87
5. The Doctors, Clergymen, and Politicians   121
6. The Neo-Malthusians Abroad   169
7. The Final Years   203
8. The Postmortem Period   237
Bibliography   243
Index   253

Illustrations
  George Drysdale   10
  Declaration Form   210

Preface

The Malthusian League was the first organization in the world to advocate voluntary family limitation as the solution to the problems of overpopulation and poverty. Its tenets were a mixture of Malthusian doctrine, early nineteenth-century liberal economics, and new scientific theories that challenged the prudish Victorian view of sexual relations. New economic theories and a growing unpopularity of Malthusian views, however, reduced the effectiveness of the Malthusian League's propaganda among the English poor. Nevertheless, its enlightened view of sexual relations continued to win acceptance and, by the turn of the century, was enforced by the work of men like Havelock Ellis and Sigmund Freud. Further, its battle to gain acceptance of family planning launched a movement that now reaches into almost all areas of the world. But the League's continued insistence upon the validity of increasingly outmoded economic theories brought the demise of the organization in 1927 after fifty years of sustained activity.

In searching for materials directly related to the Malthusian League and its activities, I am indebted to many people but particularly to the following. Mr. Samuel Huang, director of interlibrary loans, Northern Illinois University, was a most cheerful and helpful supporter in the initial stages of my research when the difficulties of obtaining materials on the league in the United States were becoming painfully obvious. Of the libraries consulted in the Midwest, the John Crerar Library at the Illinois Institute of Technology was the most helpful. Its file of *The Malthusian* and *The New Generation* is quite limited, but it provided at least a start.

I am further indebted to David V. Glass, professor of sociology at the London School of Economics and Political Science, for corresponding with me prior to my leaving for England and for his help in locating materials. It was Professor Glass who told me of the location of the C. V. Drysdale Papers in the British Library of Political and Economic Science and who led me to Mrs. Eileen Palmer and probably the best collection in existence on the Malthusian League. I shall be forever in the debt of Mrs. Palmer and her late husband, Horace, for not only access to the collection but also for the sincere kindness and friendship they extended to my daughter and me during our stay in London.

I am also grateful to the Family Planning Association in England for their assistance, particularly for running an ad in their quarterly journal, *Family Planning,* requesting information for me on the Malthusian League. Perhaps the fact that there was no response to either this appeal or a similar one in *Notes and Queries* is indicative of the extent to which the league so woefully misjudged the main currents of thought in early twentieth-century England. The organization has been almost entirely forgotten while the family-planning movement that it helped to launch has mushroomed into importance not only in England but throughout the world.

I should also like to express my thanks to Professors Marvin Rosen, Margaret George, and Richard Price of the Department of History, Northern Illinois University, for their critical observations. And finally, almost every author is indebted to those around her who exercise great patience and forbearance during the moods of exhilaration and depression that invariably accompany the task of writing. In this regard, I am eternally grateful to my daughter, Cathy.

Introduction

Poverty and starvation on a worldwide scale prompted the United Nations General Assembly to designate 1974 as International Population Year and to convene a World Population Conference in Bucharest, Romania. It quickly became apparent at the meeting, however, that there is no world consensus as to the cause of poverty and its concomitant, starvation. Representatives from the industrialized nations present at the conference expressed dismay at statistics that indicated that from the beginning of human existence until about 1830 the world's population reached one billion; in the next one hundred years, the number doubled; by 1960, it reached three billion; and in only fifteen years it was expected to increase another billion. Such numbers, the representatives argued, will outstrip the earth's resources and result in starvation for millions. Delegates from other nations, however, declared that the major cause of poverty in the world is not excessive population but rather the uneven distribution of the world's resources.

Representatives from the industrialized countries came out strongly at the conference in favor of the international dissemination of methods of birth control on the grounds that population growth must be checked before efforts at economic development can succeed. Representatives from developing and Communist countries, such as, Algeria, Argentina, Cuba, North Korea, Syria, and China, however, argued that a redistribution of resources among nations must take precedence over efforts to encourage family limitation. They reasoned that people without hope for a better future have no motivation to adopt family planning. Economic development, they insisted, must come first in order to establish such hope.

Which is the cause of poverty—overpopulation or the inequitable distribution of resources? The opposing views expressed at the World Population Conference have pretty much dominated the ongoing debate over the issue in Western society for almost two centuries. The Malthusian League would have argued with the industrialized nations. Socialists who opposed the league in nineteenth-century England would have supported the position taken by the developing and Communist nations. But the debate as to the cause of poverty predates even the Malthusian League. It has been waged at least since 1798 when Thomas Robert Malthus first published his *Essay on The Principle of Population*.[1] Eighteenth-century writers before Malthus had tended to favor an increasing population. Adam Smith, for example, reflected a common eighteenth-century belief when he wrote in the *Wealth of Nations*, "the most decisive mark of prosperity of any country is the increase of the number of inhabitants."[2] William Paley, the eighteenth-century theological reformer, proclaimed that "the decay of population is the greatest evil the state can suffer."[3] The younger William Pitt, while prime minister of England, introduced a poor-relief bill providing for liberal allowances for children. He, like most of his peers, believed that by having children citizens enriched their country and should consequently be helped. Malthus, however, challenged this laudatory view of the relationship between numbers of people and national prosperity. An ever-increasing population, he proclaimed, will inevitably experience not only poverty but starvation since a country can produce just so much food and no more. "With Malthus," wrote D. E. Eversley, "the language of population literature changes. The old, familiar assumption that a larger population was 'good' in every case, hardly ever challenged in the eighteenth century, was dropped in favour of an equally simple, but not so universally accepted view that a fast-growing population was a menace."[4] Gone was the "wonderful world of Adam Smith" and in its place a debate that waxed strong in the English Parliament, pulpit, and pub throughout the early nineteenth century. Is poverty, as Malthus claimed, an inevitable concomitant of an ever-increasing population or is it the result of an inequitable distribution of wealth brought about by an economic system created and controlled by a few to the detriment and impoverishment of the many? The two views continue to dominate the debate on the cause of poverty as evidenced by the 1974 population conference in Bucharest. Only the geographical area circumscribed in the debate has changed. We now view poverty on a worldwide scale rather than in terms of individual countries.

As the debate continued in England in the nineteenth century, both Conservatives and Liberals, the Malthusian League included, tended to accept T. R. Malthus's position that poverty is the result of an ever-increasing population. They differed, however, as to how poverty could be eliminated or at least reduced. Some said it was a dilemma that would work itself out if left alone. To others such an easy explanation was unacceptable; but what should and could be done? Some argued for reforms that would at least postpone the inevitability of population outstripping the food supply for as long as possible. These would include land reform to increase food production and emigration to relieve the immediate population pressure. Another proposal, much more radical for the early nineteenth century, called for the control of population by individuals themselves through the acceptance and practice of voluntary family limitation. Only a very few dared voice such a proposal publicly in Victorian England, and it made little headway until the latter part of the century.

The first organized effort to promote popular acceptance and, in fact, state coercion of family limitation came in 1877 with the formation of the Malthusian League. Its primary objectives were:

1. To agitate for the abolition of all penalties on the public discussion of the Population Question, and to obtain such a statutory definition as shall render it impossible, in the future, to bring such discussions within the scope of the common law as a misdemeanor.

2. To spread among the people, by all practicable means, a knowledge of the law of population, of its consequences, and of its bearing upon human conduct and morals.[5]

The league became the first organization in the world to advocate actively and publicly voluntary family limitation as the solution to poverty. Its views were secular, utilitarian, individualistic, and, above all, Malthusian, or more correctly, neo-Malthusian. The term *neo-Malthusian* was more accurate in that it allowed for a delineation between Malthusian doctrine, which did not include conscious family limitation as an acceptable check on population, and the doctrine of the league, which stressed such limitation as not only desirable but as the only workable solution to the population-poverty dilemma. The term neo-Malthusian was apparently coined in the late 1870s by Dr. Samuel Van Houten, at one time prime minister of Holland and a vice-president of the English Malthusian League for many years. Dr. Van Houten described the origin of the word while speaking before an international meeting held at the Hague in 1910. An account of his speech was included in *The Malthusian,* the monthly journal of the Malthusian League:

> Dr. Van Houten said that when the late Dr. C. R. Drysdale had spoken to him on his first visit to Holland concerning the difference between family prudence and late marriage as proposed by Malthus and known as Malthusianism, he replied, "Then you must call your proposal Neo-Malthusianism."[6]

Other terms frequently used in connection with family planning, such as, *contraception* and *birth control,* were unheard of in the nineteenth century. The former apparently first appeared in print in the early twentieth century and was probably used first by an American, Edward Bliss Foote (1829–1906), a pioneer in birth control.[7] Margaret Sanger, the leader of the first organized birth-control movement in the United States, was involved in the events that led to the coining and popularizing of the phrase "birth control." In her autobiography, *My Fight For Birth Control,* she described the procedure whereby the term was chosen to represent the drive for family limitation, an organized movement that got underway in the United States over thirty-five years after a similar movement had begun in England:

> The first thing necessary was to get a name for contraception which would convey to the public the social and personal significance of the idea. A few friends and supporters of the paper [*The Woman Rebel,* a

periodical published by Sanger in 1914] gathered together one evening in my apartment to discuss the selection of a distinctive name. We debated in turn: "Malthusianism," "conscious generation," "voluntary parenthood," "voluntary motherhood," "preventception," "the new motherhood," "constructive generation," etc., etc.

All of these names were cast aside as not meeting the demands. Then we got a little nearer when "family control" and "race control" and "birth-rate control" were suggested.

Finally it came to me out of the blue—"Birth Control!"[8]

Obviously, such terms as contraception and birth control could not have been used by the Malthusian League in describing voluntary family limitation until well into the twentieth century. Further, the league members employed the terms Malthusian and neo-Malthusian interchangeably all during the lifetime of the organization in spite of objections voiced from time to time and the confusion that the practice caused. It did, however, allow the leaders of the league to claim as supporters anyone who adhered to Malthusian economic theory whether they approved or not of "family prudence," another favorite expression for family limitation. A case in point was Thomas Huxley whose writings could be and were cited by the Malthusian League to show that Huxley subscribed to Malthusian doctrine. On several occasions, the league included in its journal a quotation from an article that Huxley had written for the February 1887 issue of the *Nineteenth Century:*

> So long as unlimited multiplication goes on, no social organization which has ever been devised, no fiddle-faddling with the distribution of wealth, will deliver society from the tendency to be destroyed by the reproduction within itself, in the intensest form, of that struggle for existence, the limitation of which is the object of society.[9]

The implication, of course, was that Huxley also approved of voluntary family limitation, when in fact he repeatedly refused all invitations of the league to attend their meetings and attempts to associate his name with the practice.

Anyone who writes on the development of the family planning movement in England would be remiss to omit mention of the Malthusian League. It was, after all, the first organized and enduring attempt to promote voluntary family limitation not only in England but throughout the world as a whole. And yet there has actually been very little written about this interesting and, in some respects, amazing organization. Its influence has undoubtedly been greater than any obtainable evidence can show. But, then, acceptance of birth control as a topic for public discussion is a relatively recent phenomena beginning, for example, hesitantly in the United States in the early twentieth century. As a consequence, sociologists have been so absorbed in the task of promoting family limitation that they have had little time to bother with its history. Professional historians appear to have ignored the development of the movement almost entirely. Those who have written on the origins of family planning have been primarily sociologists, such as Norman E. Himes, David V. Glass, J. A. and Olive Banks, or economists interested in the problems of population.

One of the earliest individuals to do research on the origins of the nineteenth-century neo-Malthusian movement was James Alfred Field (1880–1927), professor of political economy at the University of Chicago from 1908 until his death in 1927. One author has called Field "the first academic historian of the British birth control movement."[10] His essay on "The Early Propagandist Movement in English Population Theory," which appeared in the *Bulletin of the American Economics Association* in April 1911, was, indeed, one of the first pieces of research on the development of family limitation.[11] His studies dealt primarily with the movement in the early nineteenth century and more particularly with the activities of Francis Place in the 1820s. He apparently did not include the Malthusian League in his researches though he met C. V. Drysdale before World War I while in London gathering material on the birth-control movement.[12]

Until the 1960s, the most extensive research on the origins of the birth-control movement was done by Norman E. Himes (1899–1949), professor of economics and sociology at Cornell College and later at Colgate University. Unfortunately, his work was cut short by his untimely death in an auto accident in 1949. His *Medical History of Contraception,* first published in

1936, remains the standard work on the subject, though understandably now quite out of date. He was berated, however, by the editor of *The New Generation,* formerly *The Malthusian,* for dismissing "in a single sentence the forty years or more of spade-work that preceded the opening of the first birth control clinic in England in 1921," a reference undoubtedly to the work of the Malthusian League.[13] The editor suggested that at least "a passing mention would hardly be out of place of the family [the Drysdales] whose efforts inspired the organized movement for birth control, not only in England, but also in other countries in Western Europe."[14] Himes was personally well acquainted with the Malthusian League. He addressed the annual meeting of the organization in 1926, and his death was called "a great loss to the Malthusian movement" in *The Malthusian* in 1949.[15] His personal acquaintance with the leaders of the Malthusian League in the 1920s, however, may have caused him to be careless in his acceptance of their versions as to the origins of the league. His information, in this respect, is not reliable. He cites, for example, George Drysdale as the original founder of the Malthusian League in 1861 when indeed it was Charles Bradlaugh. He gives the date of the formation of the league after the Bradlaugh-Besant trial as 1878; the correct date was 1877. C. V. Drysdale often made this same error in his own writings. Perhaps Himes relied too much on C. V. as his source without checking the information himself. He appears to have done little actual research as to the origins of the early Malthusian League. He seems to have depended upon those whom he knew in the group, especially during the 1920s, for his information. This is not intended to belittle the work of Norman E. Himes. His researches into the birth-control movement have been of enormous value to those interested in the subject. This is just to say that research into the history of the early Malthusian League itself was apparently not one of his major points of interest.

David V. Glass, professor of sociology at the London School of Economics and Political Science, has been an outstanding contributor of information on the population policies and movements in not only England but throughout the world. He has been prominent on government commissions appointed to study population problems in the twentieth century and as a researcher on such issues in the nineteenth century. His work brought him into personal contact with the Malthusian League, and until recently, the accounts of the league that he included in his books dealing with broader topics provided the most accurate and complete information available on the organization in one place.[16]

A more extensive account of the Malthusian League can now be found, however, in a book entitled *The Birth Controllers*. It was written by Peter Fryer and first appeared in 1965. Mr. Fryer has done extensive research in the primary sources on the Malthusian League though, once again, the organization was apparently of secondary interest to him, being only an incident in the much broader movement of birth control as a whole.

None of the researchers mentioned have dealt with the relationship of the Malthusian League to the working class, which assumedly was to be its beneficiary.[17] Further, no full-length study prior to this one has been made of the organization. And yet no organized movement for family limitation existed prior to the formation of the Malthusian League in 1877 and none competed with it in England until the 1920s. The most important effort to promote the practice of voluntary birth control prior to the 1870s was undoubtedly the work of Francis Place in the 1820s. Others approved of family limitation before 1877 and a few made feeble efforts to encourage it, but nothing in the way of an organized movement resulted from their attempts until the Malthusian League was formed.

The most important source of information on the Malthusian League itself remains unquestionably the league's monthly periodical, *The Malthusian*, published first in February 1879. Its publication continued without interruption until 1952, in spite of the fact that the league itself, for all practical purposes, became defunct in 1927. From January 1922 until October 1949 the periodical was called *The New Generation*. It was, however, basically the same publication. The Malthusian League itself, in fact, changed its name for a short time in the 1920s to the New Generation League. Complete sets of the league's periodical are now rare, and yet it is a *must* for the history of the organization. The most complete set of *The Malthusian* that I know of is owned by Mrs. Eileen Palmer, who rescued it from a nearby home in north London during the bombings in World War II and combined it with what she had in her own possession. The set is more complete than the one located in the British Library of Political and Economic Science. In 1927, C. V. Drysdale summarized the work of the organization in an article entitled "After Fifty Years" and proclaimed: "The record of the League's work is chronicled in *The Malthusian* and the *New Generation,* and can be appraised by future historians on its own merits."[18]

In December 1940, the offices of the publishing firm of George Standring, who had published *The Malthusian* almost since its inception, were totally destroyed in a German bombing attack. In 1950, Olive M. Johnson, for many years general secretary of the organization, lamented that she could no longer get back issues of *The Malthusian* and *The New Generation* earlier than 1941, since the building in which the league's literature and library were contained had been demolished.[19] The destruction of the publishing offices has made finding information on the Malthusian League even more difficult and the sets of *The Malthusian* and *The New Generation* still in existence much more valuable as the major primary source of the organization. Some have asked what other periodicals of the day had to say about the Malthusian League, but contemporary journals and newspapers with wide readerships hesitated to include in their issues such morally questionable topics as family planning or even news of an organization that publicly advocated such a practice. This situation, unfortunately, limits still further information available on the Malthusian League.

The league's philosophical position was based on views that were present in early nineteenth-century English society and that took root in the minds of its future members long before the organization itself coalesced. The idea for such a group originally came from Charles Bradlaugh. He suggested the formation of a league in 1861 in the pages of his journal, *The National Reformer.* The idea did not catch on at that time, but Bradlaugh deserves to be recognized as the major force behind the eventual successful organization of the Malthusian League in 1877. His earlier attempt to form such a group was revived when he and Annie Besant were prosecuted in 1877 for selling a pamphlet not only advocating but describing methods of birth control. The leaders of the new Malthusian League subsequently formed set about building an organization whereby to disseminate its doctrines and direct its activities in the ensuing years of its existence.

Such an organization in Victorian England could hardly expect, however, to go unchallenged. Opponents of the group included socialists, labor leaders, doctors, clergymen, and politicians, though their reasons for opposing the league differed markedly. In spite of the opposition in England, however, the influence of the Malthusian League spread to the European continent and into other parts of the British Empire. It is the influence that the organization exerted upon the fledging family planning movement as a whole that has earned for it a richly deserved place in the annals of social history. To overemphasize the role of the Malthusian League in producing the tremendous contemporary interest in family planning in the late twentieth century would be misleading. But, at the same time, to deny it a prominent place among those who promoted the family planning movement in English society, indeed in world society, at a time when many opposed it would lead to an even more serious distortion of the development of the movement.

These, then, are some of the questions about the Malthusian League that deserve consideration. What prompted the formation of the organization, both philosophically and practically? Who was attracted to such a group? How did the members attempt to disseminate their ideas? How successful were they? Who opposed the organization and why? What influence did the group have? Finally, and perhaps most importantly, why did the Malthusian League disintegrate in the 1920s just as the family planning movement that it had helped to launch began a rapid climb to prominence in Western society?

1. The debate in its early stages has been described in detail by Kenneth Smith, *The Malthusian Controversy* (London: Routledge and Kegan Paul, 1951). Smith covers the controversy, however, only to around the time of Malthus's death in 1834. Also helpful in this regard is James A. Field's essay on "The Malthusian Controversy in England," in *Essays on Population and Other Papers,* comp. and ed. Helen Fisher Hohman (Chicago: University of Chicago Press, 1931), and Norman E. Himes's introduction to a reprint of Francis Place's economic classic, *Illustrations and Proofs of the Principle of Population* (New York: Augustus M. Kelley, 1967).

2. Charles Robert Drysdale, "Adam Smith on the Population Question," *The Malthusian* 19, no. 1 (January 1895): 3.

3. Robert L. Heilbroner, *The Worldly Philosophers* (New York: Simon and Schuster, Inc., 1964), p. 59, citing Paley.

4. D. E. Eversley, *Social Theories of Fertility and the Malthusian Debate* (London: Oxford University Press, 1959), p. 10. I am well aware that the views expressed by Malthus were not original, but his work has served as a point of reference for debate of the problem. The views he expressed in his essay on population had been expressed as early as 1753 by Robert Wallace in *A Dissertation on the Numbers of Mankind, in Ancient and Modern Times* and by Joseph Townsend in *A Dissertation on the Poor Laws* in 1786.

5. Listed in every issue of the Malthusian League's journal, *The Malthusian.*

6. "International Neo-Malthusian Conference Report of the Proceedings," *The Malthusian* 34, no. 9 (September 1910): 76. D. V. Glass suggests, however, that there is some doubt as to whether Van Houten actually coined the word. The term was used as early as February 1879 in the pages of *The Malthusian.* If C. R. Drysdale's meeting with Van Houten did not occur until later in the year, then the latter was apparently not the originator of the term. See David V. Glass, *Population Policies and Movements in Europe* (London: Frank Cass and Company, Ltd., 1967; first published in 1940), p. 425. C. V. Drysdale, C. R.'s son, felt quite confident that Van Houten first coined the term, but then he was never too accurate on information regarding the origin of the Malthusian League itself, let alone the terms it used. On several occasions, he gave 1878 as the year in which the league was formed; 1877 is the correct date. Norman E. Himes was unquestionably wrong when he said "the word Neo-Malthusianism was apparently first used in English by J. M. Robertson in the early eighteen eighties." Norman E. Himes, *Medical History of Contraception* (Baltimore: The Williams and Wilkins Company, 1936), p. 257, fn. The league itself might well have been called the Neo-Malthusian League had the term been known as early as 1877.

7. Norman E. Himes, "Notes on the Origin of the Terms Contraception, Birth Control, Neo-Malthusianism, Etc." *Medical Journal and Record* 135, no. 10 (May 1932): 495.

8. Margaret Sanger, *My Fight For Birth Control* (New York: Farrar & Rinehart, Inc., 1931), p. 83. Sanger gave no date for the origin of the term, but it first appeared in print in an article in her journal, *The Woman Rebel,* in April 1914; and in 1930, Mary Breed and Edith How-Martyn, both friends of Sanger, said: "The slogan 'birth control,' first coined by her in 1913, came to be adopted in England as expressing the purpose and aim of the movement better

than the older term, 'neo-malthusianism.'" *The Birth Control Movement in England* (London: John Bale, Sons and Danielsson, Ltd., 1930), p. 14.

9. "Report of the Council of the Malthusian League," *The Malthusian* 12, no. 5 (May 1888):35. The article is cited again in the "Report of the Council of the Malthusian League," *The Malthusian* 14, no. 5 (May 1890):35.

10. Peter Fryer, *British Birth Control Ephemera, 1870–1947*, The Collis Collection (Leicester, Eng.: The Barracuda Press, 1969), 1:9.

11. James Alfred Field, "The Early Propagandist Movement in English Population Theory," *Bulletin of the American Economics Association,* 4th ser., 1, no. 2 (April 1911): 207–36.

12. In 1922, C. V. Drysdale said: "Professor Field made an exhaustive personal research into the original records at the British Museum, and did not come into contact with the Malthusian League until after his paper was published." *The New Generation* 1, no. 3 (March 1922): 7, fn.

13. R. B. Kerr, "Review of *Medical History of Contraception," The New Generation* 14, no. 8 (August 1935):87.

14. Ibid.

15. Herbert Cutner, "Obituary of Norman E. Himes," *The Malthusian,* n.s., no. 2 (November 1949), p. 4.

16. See, for example, Glass, *Population Policies and Movements in Europe.*

17. As a starting point on the topic, one might well find it profitable to consult John Peel's article on "Birth Control and the British Working-Class Movement: A Bibliographical Review," *Bulletin of the Society for the Study of Labour History,* no. 7 (Autumn 1963), pp. 16–22. Peel, however, deals primarily with sources from the early nineteenth century and with the period of the 1920s and 1930s.

18. C. V. Drysdale, "After Fifty Years," *The New Generation* 6, no. 12 (December 1927): 138.

19. Letter to S. Namek, Esq., The University Union, Edinburgh, from O. Johnson, dated 21 June 1950. Palmer Collection. The publishing office was located at 17/18 Finsbury Street, London. The owner in 1940, A. E. Owen, moved the business to his home in Worcester Park, Surrey, but maintained the address on Finsbury Street where the firm had been located since 1850.

A History of
The Malthusian League
1877-1927

1 : The Embryonic Stage

An embryo is an organism as yet without form; but the features that will appear in its fetal period are nevertheless taking shape at this rudimentary stage of development. So it was with the as yet unborn Malthusian League in early and mid nineteenth-century England. During what could be called the league's embryo stage, the philosophical principles of its future leaders, who would determine the organization's theoretical position for all of its fifty years of existence, developed from four major currents of contemporary thought—classical economics, Malthusianism, utilitarianism, and new physiological and psychological ideas as to how the human body and mind operated.

From the classical economists, such as, Adam Smith and his later disciple, David Ricardo, came the concept of a natural law of supply and demand that applied not only to the prices of goods and services but also to the amount of wages a worker could expect for his labor. These gentlemen postulated that when the supply of labor is high and the demand for it is low, wages tend to be low. When the supply dwindles and demand increases, wages tend to rise. The former appeared to be the case in late eighteenth- and early nineteenth-century England, at least to members of the gentry, such as Thomas Robert Malthus, who sought an answer to the unrest so apparent in western Europe.

Having observed the outbreak of revolutionary violence in late eighteenth-century France, the well-to-do classes of England feared a similar revolt in their own country. A burning question of the day was how to prevent it. One did not have to wander far in London streets, or any other English city for that matter, before encountering the squalid living and working conditions of the "swinish multitude" as Edmund Burke so indiscreetly labeled the lower classes. Who was responsible for such impoverishment? Was it the wealthier classes of England as the rhetoricians of the revolutionary spirit so loudly proclaimed? The Reverend T. R. Malthus thought not. Drawing on the classical economic theory as to how wages are determined in the free market, Malthus proclaimed that the poor themselves were to blame for their impoverished condition. By having large families, he maintained, workers increased their numbers to the extent that they created an overabundance of labor, which then competed for a limited number of jobs and drove wages down. His *Essay on the Principle of Population* in which he first published his view as to the cause of poverty was warmly received in 1798. It soothed the fears and consciences of the English upper classes by shifting any responsibility for poverty and misery from their shoulders to those of the workers themselves.

At this point, the controversy that characterized the debate at the 1974 World Population Conference in Bucharest first became apparent. Malthus postulated, just as the industrialized nations tend to do today, that poverty is primarily a product of excessive population. Like the developing and Communist countries, William Godwin, an English philosopher in the early nineteenth century, challenged Malthus's conclusion and blamed a social hierarchy that allowed the few to dominate and dictate the life patterns of the many.[1] Malthus's theory of causation required the working classes themselves to take action in order to rise out of poverty. Godwin's called for a reorganization of the political and economic system. The debate on population and poverty has henceforth followed the division of opinion first expressed by Malthus and Godwin.

The Malthusian League would, of course, argue on the side of its namesake. Where the league would differ with Malthus was over the means whereby workers could limit their numbers and thus alleviate their own poverty. Malthus, being a good Anglican clergyman, recognized "preventive checks" as the only moral means of family limitation. These included either late marriage or sexual abstinence. Of those who accepted Malthus's explanation of poverty, the Malthusians as they have been called, the majority also accepted his pronouncements on the immorality of methods of family limitation. Some, however, differed with his moral injunctions. These revisionists, or neo-Malthusians, argued that it was hypocritical to believe that any young person who postponed marriage also postponed sexual relations, an imperative condition if late marriage were to be an effective check on population. In the second place, they claimed, total abstinence from or even postponement of sexual relations could produce in the individual both physical and psychic damage. This line of thinking was derived from physiological theories that presaged the work of men like Havelock Ellis and Sigmund Freud but that were new in nineteenth-century medical thought. The neo-Malthusians argued that workers should use the most effective and healthful methods of voluntary family limitation available. Not surprisingly, however, there were few who would risk their reputations by publicly discussing such methods. "There can be no doubt," said F. H. Amphlett Micklewright in his study on "The Rise and Decline of English Neo-Malthusianism," "that most . . . middle-class philosophers were inhibited from plain speech on the subject by the horror with which it was regarded by popular opinion."[2]

Among the early neo-Malthusians was James Mill, the noted early nineteenth-century English philosopher, who wrote an article for the *Encyclopaedia Britannica* in 1819 and advocated a new standard by which to judge the morality of voluntary family limitation. He wrote:

> What, then, are the best means of checking the progress of population when it cannot go on unrestrained without producing one of two most undesirable effects, either drawing an undue proportion of the population to the mere raising of food, or producing poverty and wretchedness; [this] . . . is, indeed, the most important practical problem to which the wisdom of the politician and moralist can be applied. It has, till this time, been miserably evaded by all those who have meddled with the subject, as well as by all those who were called upon by their situation to find a remedy for the evils to which it relates. And yet, if the superstitions of the nursery were discarded, and the principle of utility kept steadily in view, a solution might not be difficult to be found, and the means of drying up one of the most copious sources of human evil, a source which, if all other sources of evil were taken away, would alone suffice to retain the great mass of human beings in misery, might be seen to be neither doubtful nor difficult to be applied.[3]

5

Mill expressed the position of those in early nineteenth-century English society who followed the teachings of Jeremy Bentham and became known as utilitarians. The morality of an act, they argued, should be judged not by biblical injunctions but by the extent to which the act brings happiness or lessens evil. This is the line of reasoning adopted by neo-Malthusians to defend the practice of voluntary family limitation from attacks, particularly by the clergy.

Being neo-Malthusians, the future leaders of the Malthusian League adopted the principle of utility as a moral standard. C. R. Drysdale, president of the organization for many years, wrote: "The propriety of actions which . . . enables them to be described as right or wrong, moral or immoral, depends on their effect on human happiness; moral actions being those which tend to produce the greatest happiness for sentient beings; immoral, those which tend to produce pain and misery."[4] His son, C. V. Drysdale, put it even more succinctly in 1901: "Our goal is the definite and simple one of Bentham: 'The greatest *happiness* of the *greatest* number.'"[5]

In the defense of voluntary family limitation, the leaders of the Malthusian League often quoted still another proponent of utilitarianism, namely, John Stuart Mill. In fact, aside from Malthus, no other author provided more ammunition in the form of quotations for the league than did the young Mill. One such quotation adorned the regular heading of the league's periodical, *The Malthusian*, for decades: "Little improvement can be expected in morality until the production of large families is regarded in the same light as drunkenness or any other physical excess." Charles R. Drysdale and his brother, George, apparently both knew and admired Mill. "When Mr. Mill was a candidate for the Borough of Westminster," C. R. Drysdale wrote, "I asked him whether he meant this objection to large families to apply to the rich as well as the poor. His reply was, 'Certainly.'"[6] Drysdale's advice to a Malthusian reader was, "Read Malthus, James and J. S. Mill, Senior, Ricardo, Chalmers, Cairnes, and Fawcett: Above all, read J. S. Mill's 'Principles of Political Economy.' It is by far the most important work on the science of this century."[7] But the Drysdales, like so many, took from Mill only what supported their position and ignored what appeared to contradict it. Mill pointed out, for example, that society could redistribute wealth in an attempt to alleviate poverty if it chose to do so. Production, he argued, was indeed controlled by the economic rules of behavior outlined by earlier laissez-faire economists, but distribution was, he said, determined by society. "The Distribution of Wealth . . . depends on the laws and customs of society. The rules by which it is determined are what the opinions and feelings of the ruling portion of the community make them."[8] Poverty could be alleviated by redistributing wealth. This kind of thinking just did not mesh with that of the Malthusian League and so it was ignored.

J. S. Mill, like his father, James, subscribed to the population theories of Malthus; but like so many of his fellow intellectuals, the younger Mill shunned public discussion of methods of preventing conception. He emphasized, rather, the theoretical advantages that could be gained by the working classes if they adopted the practice of family limitation. During his adult life, Mill never publicly advocated the use of contraception appliances. Only after his death did it become known that he had, as a teenager, helped his father's friend and creditor, Francis Place, distribute birth-control leaflets.[9] His efforts brought him and his young companions before a local magistrate on a charge of promoting obscenity. After three or four days in jail, he and his comrades were released and the whole affair hushed up. The episode came to light only when Mill died in 1873 and a public memorial in his honor was proposed. Even Prime Minister Gladstone pledged his support. Mr. Abraham Hayward, however, published in the *Times* an obituary of Mill with a description of his youthful indiscretion intimating quite clearly that Mill had never wavered in his approval of family limitation practices. "Nor was this a repented error of his youth," Hayward claimed. "It was the persistent error of his mature years."[10] The result was that Gladstone withdrew his support from the project. "In my view," he wrote to the promoters of the memorial, "this painful controversy still exists. I feel that it is not possible for me, situated as I am at the present time, to decide or to

7

examine it with a view to decision. The only course open to me is to do no act involving a judgment either way, and therefore, while I desire to avoid any public step whatever, I withdraw from cooperation and request that my name may be no further mentioned."[11] Gladstone's action was indicative of the attitude of English politicians toward voluntary family planning in general in Victorian England. The subject was just too sensitive.

The two Mills along with their fellow utilitarians may have been hesitant in their public defense of neo-Malthusianism, but nevertheless utilitarian philosophy provided the moral standard whereby the Malthusian League would later claim voluntary family limitation should be judged. However, the league's arguments as to the deleterious effects of Malthus's "preventive checks" to population, that is, late marriage and abstinence, came from new nineteenth-century theories as to the operation of the human body and mind. As James A. Field observed, "historically the birth control movement is the child of utilitarian philosophy and the nineteenth-century discoveries in biology."[12] At this point, we can establish a direct contact with one of the founders of the Malthusian League, George Drysdale, a young medical student in mid nineteenth-century England. It was he who added the sanction of science to the idea that one's failure to satisfy the sexual needs of the body could cause mental and physical illness. As early as 1825, however, Richard Carlile, a social reformer in early nineteenth-century England, had called attention to the "impediments to natural enjoyment" that could "bring on the more violent paroxyms of the fit. ... . It may truly be inferred, . . . that Love is a disease: a disease delightful in its cure, but distressing and disastrous if not cured."[13] He spoke less romantically and more to the point when he wrote:

> One of our principal London physicians, in conversation on female disorder, observed to a lady, that *in nine cases out of ten of sickness, and in five cases out of six of death from consumption, among young women, the proximate cause was the want of sexual commerce. He added, the present state of society will not admit of my saying this publicly; but such is the fact, and it would be well if it were more generally known.* [The italics are Carlile's.][14]

Carlile, however, spoke without authority; he was not a member of the medical profession. "It was Dr. George Drysdale in his

'Elements of Social Science' (1854)," wrote his nephew, C. V. Drysdale, "who first put what has since been called the neo-Malthusian doctrine into definite form by demonstrating the potency of the sex instinct, the terrible evils which inevitably arose from its attempted suppression, and the fundamental disharmony of Nature—the antagonism between the satisfaction of food and sex hunger to which the greater part of human misery was due."[15]

Since George Drysdale (1825–1904) was one of the founders and leading members of the Malthusian League, his life and work are important in a history of the organization. Actually very little is known about either his personal or public life. He wrote his major contribution to neo-Malthusian theory while still a medical student at the University of Edinburgh, the city of his birth.[16] His father, Sir William Drysdale, sometime treasurer of the city of Edinburgh, was wealthy enough to give both his sons, George and Charles Robert, the advantages of a good education coupled with travel on the Continent. Both boys attended the Circus Place School, Edinburgh Royal Academy, and the University of Edinburgh. Two months of the year they were free to roam the banks of the river Nith; and George, as his brother later commented, "was as successful in all boyish sports as he was as a student. He was an excellent shot and a lover of fly-fishing."[17] George did well in academic pursuits, winning the highest prizes in his classes at the academy and drawing high praise from his professors at the University of Glasgow, which he also attended. He took his medical degree in 1855 and practiced as a physician for many years. He was apparently a person of great sensitivity, fearful less he bring pain and sorrow to those closest to him. When he finally, after much difficulty, found a publisher for the book that contained his outspoken, radical views, he was well aware that it might be received with howls of derision and censure. In the preface to the first edition of the book, he wrote: "Had it not been from fear of causing pain to a relation [his mother], I should have felt it my duty to put my name to this work; in order that any censure passed upon it, should fall upon myself alone."[18] After his mother died, however, he continued to write anonymously because, his brother claimed, "his health was getting weaker and he disliked the

George Drysdale

wordy disputes which so interfere with that philosophic tranquillity so necessary for thinking out the different problems of social life."[19] He wrote many pamphlets and articles for various journals but all were published without his name. In his own journal, *The Political Economist; and Journal of Social Science,* he was listed as "the Author of 'Physical, Sexual, and Natural Religion.'" In Charles Bradlaugh's *National Reformer,* Drysdale wrote under the letters "G. R."[20] In *The Malthusian,* the journal of the Malthusian League, he wrote as "Q."[21] It is perhaps evidence of the integrity of the publisher, Edward Truelove, a secularist and former Owenite who made a practice of publishing controversial material that coincided with his own free thought, that Drysdale's identity was never made public until after the latter died in 1904.

George Drysdale and other leaders of the Malthusian League were unquestionably children of the Enlightenment. They were convinced that just as there were laws that governed the mechanical operations of the universe so there were similar laws that governed human behavior and relationships. The mechanical laws were discoverable through new techniques being developed in science; the behavioral laws must also be discoverable through scientific techniques, or so they thought. George Drysdale adopted August Comte's name for the new study. "Now that the human mind has grasped celestial and terrestrial physics," he wrote, citing Comte, "there remains one science, to fill up the series of sciences of observation—Social physics."[22] The aim of his book, *The Elements of Social Science,* was to further the work of establishing the new area of study. The great stumbling block to nineteenth-century secularists, like Drysdale, however, was the Christian religion with its stubborn insistence that life on earth was but a trial, a preparation for the afterlife. The spirit, not the body, was of primary importance. Such a view stood as a barrier to scientific advances, particularly in medicine. "There is nothing from which mankind in the present day suffers more," said Drysdale, "than from the want of reverence for the human body." His primary argument was that to break the physical laws that govern the operation of the body was as immoral as breaking a Christian

11

principle of behavior. "The conduct of our physical life is just as difficult as that of our moral one." His appeal for a more scientific approach to the study of the body was couched in religious terminology, a practice not uncommon in the secular literature of the nineteenth century. He titled his book, for example, *Physical, Sexual and Natural Religion* in terms of its three major parts. A fourth section, entitled "Social Science," was added when the third edition was published in 1858. Perhaps Drysdale hoped to render his ideas less offensive by swaddling them in religious jargon; but there was little chance of that, since much of what he proposed was anathema not only to devout Christians but also to many secularists who still viewed such institutions as monogamous marriage as the foundation stone of a stable society.

In the first part of his book, Drysdale argued that everyone, women as well as men, should have a basic knowledge of the operation of the human body. He lamented that the medical profession was still looked upon with suspicion and considered unacceptable as employment for a gentleman, let alone a woman.

> The noble science of medicine has never yet received due reverence from mankind. This arises chiefly from the cause that has been mentioned . . . , namely, the want of reverence for the body, the special object of its attention. The physician, to the eyes of other men, appears as one apart, who is initiated into mysteries which their imagination dreads, yet dwells upon; who is devoted to studies, the materialising and debasing influences of which are still, in the light of the nineteenth century, vaguely whispered of, though society is now-a-days too polite to utter openly for coarse and irreverent accusations of our forefathers.
>
> . . . The seeds sown by our ancestors still flourish among us, and long will be the struggle before the prejudices against medicine and its followers, and the materialising tendencies of the science be totally uprooted. It is rarely that we see in the writings, even of the most cultivated men of past times, the medical profession alluded to, except with a sneer at their lowmindedness, or expressed contempt at their want of skill.

Drysdale also reflected a new trend in medical research in his insistence that the body and mind directly affect each other.

Psychology was a very new branch of science in the mid nineteenth century, but Drysdale was obviously in contact with it.

> Every physical state has its peculiar mental one, and to discover what this is, and what influence on the mind all bodily states from so-called perfect health, to hypochondria, insanity, delirium, or death, is a most essential branch of medical science. This psychology of health and disease is to be obtained only by the study of every individual's mind compared with his bodily condition, and a full knowledge of this is to be arrived at only by his own revelations.

"Sexual Religion," the second part of Drysdale's book, began with a startlingly frank, at least for Victorian England, discussion of the human reproductive system. His physiological facts, however, were inaccurate on some points. For example, following the general medical view in the nineteenth century, Drysdale maintained that the "theory of menstruation—namely, that it is connected with the *spontaneous discharge of eggs,* is one of the most recent and most important discoveries in physiology." The theory was probably based on observations of animals, which do ovulate during the menstrual period or, as it is commonly called, during "heat." The observations applied to humans served as the basis, unfortunately, of a longstanding and mistaken view that the so-called safe period occurred midway *between* the menstrual periods since the egg was believed to be released *during* the periodic flow. This was at least an advance, however, over the previous belief "that eggs are discharged from the ovaries only in consequence of sexual intercourse."

Drysdale's major objective in the second part of his book was to dispel the kind of thinking that had led Malthus to conclude that the only acceptable preventive checks were abstinence or late marriage. "It is most unwise," he said, regarding the former practice, "to suppose that our chief duty with regard to our appetites and passions is to exercise self-denial. . . . Sexual abstinence is frequently attended by consequences not one whit less serious than sexual excess, and far more insidious and dangerous, as they are not so generally recognised." All should be able to satisfy the needs of the body "especially so in the years

13

immediately after puberty." If society would allow the "natural" expression of the sexual appetite, the result, proclaimed Drysdale, would be a diminution of such "perverse" activities as masturbation and prostitution and such medical problems as syphilis, gonorrhea, and hysteria. "Unless we can remove the main cause of hysteria, namely insufficient sexual gratifications, it is totally impossible to prevent that disease." It is unnecessary, though it would be interesting, to catalogue here all of the very modern-sounding ideas expressed by Drysdale in his detailed account of the hazards of abstinence and late marriage, of sexual intercourse as treatment for certain ailments, and of the need to rid the country of prostitution by providing women with a means to gain a livelihood without having to "make a barter of their love—the only marketable commodity, on which the poorest women among us have to rely."[23] The medical authorities he cited in defense of his pronouncements were primarily French physicians and medical researchers of the early nineteenth century, such as, M. Lallemand, Professor Recamier of Paris, and M. Parent Duchatelet. Their theories were much too frank to have been formulated by medical practitioners in Victorian England.

After a detailed presentation of the need for a more scientific view of the human body, and more specifically of the sexual organs, Drysdale moved to a long and sometimes rambling exposition of the Malthusian law of population. "It may be called *the* question of the age," he explained, "for upon it, as Mr. Malthus and Mr. Mill have shown, depend the grand problems which are at present convulsing society; the wages of labour, poverty and wealth, &c." "The law of population," he proclaimed, "is as certainly true, and as clearly shown as that of gravitation." Neither emigration nor the Poor Laws nor charity nor any such artificial interference in the wages of labor could alter the operation of such a law. The poor must be taught "that they themselves are the cause of their own poverty, that the means of improving their condition are in their own hands, and in the hands of no other persons whatever, that society and the government are without any direct power in this matter, and

14

cannot assist them, however they might desire to do so." No such scheme as socialism can alleviate the situation.

> The . . . error of Socialism is, that it attributes to the constitution of society and to *competition,* (as political reformers do to forms of government, and theologians to man's original sin,) the evils, which really spring from the principle of population. It falls into the inveterate and almost universal error of ascribing the chief ills of mankind to human institutions, instead of to Nature. It vehemently urges the adoption of a complete change in our social fabric, but to what end? After all this trouble, there would not be one of the great human difficulties removed. If the preventive check to population be increased, Socialism is not needed; if not, it is useless.

This served as the stock argument employed by the Malthusian League against Socialism, particularly in the 1880s. Drysdale admitted, however, that there was extensive poverty in England. He referred to Henry Mayhew's study of "London Labour, and London Poor" and concluded "that unless this state of things can be altered, we cannot expect that our society will long hang together as it is." This became a familiar theme among both Malthusians and neo-Malthusians in the last half of the nineteenth century: reduce poverty before it causes a revolution. The solution, of course, was to get the lower classes to limit the number of their offspring by employing contraceptive devices and techniques.

Drysdale then launched into a discussion of the four available methods of contraception, the first of which he called a "natural" method; in the twentieth century it is more commonly known as the "safe period." There is a possibility that there are periods, he said, when conception is less likely to occur than at others. "In most women, conception dates from intercourse either during menstruation, or a few days before or after it. Hence it results, that in abstaining from intercourse from the second or third day before the menstrual epoch till the eighth day after it, one may be certain to diminish considerably the chances of reproduction."[24] One cannot help wondering how many women relied upon such information, much to their dismay and disappointment. Drysdale himself admitted that "on account of the rigid

15

and ruinous secrecy, that is kept upon all sexual subjects, no individual gives the result of his or her experience on these matters; and it is almost impossible to ascertain, whether such means have been tried, and whether they have been found efficacious or not."

The "unnatural," or mechanical, methods Drysdale described were withdrawal (or *coitus interruptus*), the sheath, and the sponge. The first "is physically injurious," he said, "and is apt to produce nervous disorder and sexual enfeeblement and congestion, from the sudden interruption it gives to the venereal act, whose pleasure moreover it interferes with." The second, he continued, "dulls the enjoyment, and frequently produces impotence in the man and disgust in both parties; so that it also is injurious." The sponge, he concluded, is "by far the best of these mechanical means." Francis Place had advocated and published this method in the 1820s in a two-page handbill entitled "To the Married of Both Sexes of the Working People." Drysdale mentioned one other "unnatural" or mechanical method of preventing conception, the douche, a procedure first proposed in the 1830s by Charles Knowlton, an American physician. "The injection of tepid water into the vagina, immediately after intercourse, would also be a very effectual means of preventing impregnation," Drysdale wrote.

It was unfortunate for the Malthusian League that Drysdale chose to call methods that require purposeful action on the part of the participants in the sexual act unnatural. League members were obliged to argue on many occasions against the charge that unnatural practices are contrary to nature and thus are harmful to humans who are, of course, part of nature. The league countered this argument with statements similar to the following taken from *The Malthusian:*

Some people have a strong, though vague, objection to interfering, in any unaccustomed way, with nature. . . .

Such interferences with nature as have become established, and have been shown by experience to work comfortably, excite no qualm. Even the Salvation Army wink at the useful lightning conductor, which wards nature's flashes from their noisy roofs. Even the dirtiest of us do not, in these days, object to using knives and forks to

eat with, though when first introduced, to the alleged disparage-
ment of the fingers, they were stigmatised as profane.

As to rain, we have become so familiarised with waterproofing, that
we seem to have lost all reverent curiosity as to nature having a
design to drench us. . . .

Some people still allow nature to rain babies upon them, though, for
my part, I think it is not right to do so, unless she shows satisfactory
symptoms of raining a sufficient supply of bread and butter, and
shoes and stockings also. In other words, I consider it wrong to be a
party to bringing more children into the world than I am likely to be
able to bring up comfortably.[25]

In the third part of his book, Drysdale pleaded for a "Natural
Religion" based on a scientific knowledge of natural laws. Nature, not the supernatural, should be "taken for the standard of
truth." Drysdale, like many of his fellow nineteenth-century
rationalists and secularists, believed that the mind and body or
the spirit and matter form an indivisible whole. "Mind is transient," he said, "being absolutely inseparable from transient
forms of matter; and is not a force alien from the rest of Nature,
but an entirely natural one, inseparably linked with the rest in
mutual interdependence." Such a belief formed the basis of
Drysdale's acceptance of the idea, which is the foundation stone
of modern psychology, that the mind and body are inseparably
linked and what affects one will also affect the other.

The fourth part of the book, "Social Science," consisted
primarily of a rehash of nineteenth-century classical economic
theories presented as natural laws, much as Adam Smith and
his disciples had stated them, and of the Malthusian law of
population. Taken as a whole, Drysdale's book contained almost
every argument used and every idea expressed by various members of the yet-to-be-born Malthusian League. The only major
point on which the future league and Drysdale would appear to
have possibly disagreed was over the extent to which sexual
intercourse should be socially permissible outside of marriage.
The only "true mode of sexual union," said Drysdale, is "an
agreement between two people to live together as man and wife,
so long as they love each other." Whether he meant to go so far as
to approve of such a union without the benefit of clerical sanc-

17

tion is not clear. The fact remains, however, that Drysdale's words were interpreted as such; and by recommending his book, the league became irreconcilably associated in the minds of many with the advocation of so-called free love. Consequently, it was repeatedly assailed for defending such a practice. On numerous occasions *The Malthusian* carried statements disclaiming any support among league members of such behavior:

> We have taken care to point out that, despite the popular idea to the contrary, and the misrepresentations of our traducers, Neo-Malthusianism, instead of leading to irresponsibility and irregularity in such relations, is the only way by which the ideal monogamic union can be secured for the whole community, by removing the fear of marriage and of the unhappy unions caused by the strain of too many children or by the irregularities consequent of late marriage.[26]

In her autobiography, Annie Besant, who was associated with the Malthusian League for over twelve years, gave an interesting account of how both she and Charles Bradlaugh suffered from the onus of association with Drysdale's book and his seeming advocation of "free love":

> Lecturing in June, 1875, at Leicester, I came for the first time across a falsehood that brought sore trouble and cost me more pain than I care to tell. An irate Christian opponent, in the discussion that followed the lecture, declared that I was responsible for a book entitled, "The Elements of Social Science," which was, he averred, "The Bible of Secularists." I had never heard of the book, but as he stated that it was in favour of the abolition of marriage, and that Mr. Bradlaugh agreed with it, I promptly contradicted him; for while I knew nothing about the book, I knew a great deal about Mr. Bradlaugh, and I knew that on the marriage question he was conservative rather than revolutionary. He detested "Free Love" doctrines, and had thrown himself strongly on the side of the agitation led so heroically for many years by Mrs. Josephine Butler. On my return to London after the lecture I naturally made inquiry as to the volume and its contents, and I found that it had been written by a Doctor of Medicine some years before, and sent to the *National Reformer* [which Bradlaugh edited] for review, as to other journals, in ordinary course of business. It consisted of three parts—the first advocated, from the standpoint of medical science, what is roughly known as "Free Love"; the second was entirely medical; the third consisted of a clear and able exposition of the law of population as

laid down by the Rev. Mr. Malthus, and—following the lines of John Stuart Mill—insisted that it was the duty of married persons to voluntarily limit their families within their means of subsistence. Mr. Bradlaugh, in reviewing the book, said that it was written "with honest and pure intent and purpose," and recommended to working men the exposition of the law of population. His enemies took hold of this recommendation, declared that he shared the author's views on the impermanence of the marriage tie, and, despite his reiterated contradictions, they used extracts against marriage from the book as containing his views. Anything more meanly vile it would be difficult to conceive, but such were the weapons used against him all his life, and used often by men whose own lives contrasted most unfavourably with his own. Unable to find anything in his own writings to serve their purpose, they used this book to damage him with those who knew nothing at first-hand of his views. What his enemies feared were not his views on marriage—which, as I have said, was conservative—but his Radicalism and his Atheism. To discredit him as politician they maligned him socially and the idea that a man desire "to abolish marriage and the home," is a most convenient poniard, and the one most certain to wound. This was the origin of his worst difficulties, to be intensified, ere long, by his defence of Malthusianism. On me also fell the same lash, and I found myself held up to hatred as upholder of views that I abhorred.[27]

Perhaps this explains at least in part why both Besant and Bradlaugh were never primarily neo-Malthusians and gradually detached themselves from the Malthusian League during the 1880s, after playing a major role in the creation of the organization.

Nevertheless, George Drysdale's book enjoyed a wide circulation. It was translated, under his own direction, into French (1873), German (1875), Dutch (1873 and 1875), Italian (1875), Russian, Portuguese (1876), Swedish, Hungarian, Danish, and Polish. When the thirty-fifth edition was published in 1905, a bookseller's advertisement issued by the publisher, G. Standring, claimed "nearly ninety thousand copies of the book have been sold."[28]

Drysdale wrote a number of other articles and books, primarily in the 1860s, all of which echoed the same themes found in his first and most popular work.[29] In 1856–57, he edited fifteen issues of his own eight-page journal, *The Political Economist; and Journal of Social Science,* and had it published by Edward

Truelove. The object of the periodical was explained in its opening lines: "to endeavor to explain in a clear and open manner some of the chief Principles of Political Economy, and of Social Science; the natural law on which poverty and wealth depend; and the true cause and only cure of the evils existing in our society."[30] The journal gave Drysdale a forum in which he could expand upon and defend, when necessary, the ideas he had originally presented in his book renamed the *Elements of Social Science* when the second edition was published in 1857.

One correspondent offered financial assistance should Drysdale decide to further "the dissemination of the population view" by forming a tract society. Drysdale expressed interest in such an organization and said, "I should be most happy to give any assistance in my power in promoting such an object." But he had little faith that such an effort would have any effect. "Every effort . . . which has been made in this country to spread the subject by tracts or treatises, has been a total failure." What is needed, he said, "is that a *public demonstration* should be made upon the subject," preferably by the working classes. "The grand object to be aimed at is that the population-principle should be *openly discussed* in newspapers, public assemblies, lecture-rooms, and elsewhere. A Tract Society, however, would certainly be of very great service, especially if it could be openly organized, with a steady determination to spread these truths and to obtain for them a candid hearing."[31] In the pages of George Drysdale's journal was thus implanted the seed that would develop into the Malthusian League twenty years later. The last issue of the journal appeared in April 1857, however, and the subject of an organization to advocate neo-Malthusian doctrines was closed for the moment.

1. See Kenneth Smith's *The Malthusian Controversy* for an extensive description of the debate between Malthus and Godwin (London: Routledge & Kegan Paul, 1951).

2. F. H. Amphlett Micklewright, "The Rise and Decline of English Neo-Malthusianism," *Population Studies, A Journal of Demography* 15, no. 1 (July 1961): 32.

3. *The Queen v. Edward Truelove* (London: Edward Truelove, 256, High Holborn, 1878), p. 104. Included as part of an appendix of quotations on the population question.

4. Charles Robert Drysdale, "The Utilitarian (or Happiness) Theory of Morals," *The Malthusian* 22, no. 6 (June 1898): 41.

5. Charles Vickery Drysdale, "National Life From the Standpoint of Science," *The Malthusian* 25, no. 3 (March 1901): 21.

6. Charles Robert Drysdale, "The Principle of Population Considered as a Fundamental Point in Ethics," *The Malthusian* 19, no. 3 (March 1895): 18.

7. Charles Robert Drysdale, *The Malthusian,* no. 2 (March 1879), p. 12.

8. John Stuart Mill, *Principles of Political Economy* (New York: D. Appleton and Company, 1887), p. 155.

9. The leaflet was written by Richard Carlile and was entitled *Every Woman's Book; or, What is Love?* (London: R. Carlile, 62, Fleet Street, 4th ed., 1828). First published as a booklet in 1826.

10. W. D. Christie, *John Stuart Mill and Mr. Abraham Hayward, Q. C.* (London, 1873), p. 8. James A. Field also gives a short account of the episode in his "Early Propagandist Movement in English Population Theory," *Essays on Population and Other Papers* (Chicago: University of Chicago Press, 1931), pp. 125–26. Also see Peter Fryer, *The Birth Controllers* (London: Transworld Publishers, Ltd., 1967), pp. 50–51.

11. "Gladstone, Morley, and Mill," *The Malthusian* 28, no. 1 (January 1904): 3.

12. Field, *Essays on Population,* p. 311.

13. Carlile, *Every Woman's Book,* p. 14.

14. Ibid., p. 21.

15. Charles Vickery Drysdale, "The Birth Control Movement: Its Scientific and Ethical Bases," *The Eugenics Review* 20, no. 3 (October 1928): 174.

16. Most of the biographical data given here on George Drysdale was gleaned from two sources: a "Memoir" of his brother written by Charles Robert Drysdale as an introduction to the 1905 edition of the *Elements of Social Science* (35th ed.; London: G. Standring, 7/9 Finsbury St., E. C., 1905), and an unpublished MS found among the C. V. Drysdale papers in the British Library of Political and Economic Science. The latter was written by Herbert Cutner, an active member of the Malthusian League in its last years. It was written in 1954, entitled "A Notable Pioneer Work," and may have been intended for publication in a future issue of *The Malthusian* but none ever appeared. Also see *Zeitschrift fur Sexualwissenschaft,* Marz 1908, pp. 140–41.

17. Charles Robert Drysdale, "Memoir of the Author," *The Elements of Social Science.*

18. Ibid., Preface by the author, George Drysdale.

19. Ibid., "Memoir of the Author."

20. "George Rex," a nickname given Drysdale by one of his teachers, Mr. Musgrave, at the Circus Place School in Edinburgh, stemming from the boy's apparent facility in his studies. Ibid.

21. For any who may wonder how I arrived at an identification of "Q" in the league's journal: In February, 1879, *The Malthusian,* p. 7, advertised an article

to appear in a future issue under the title "The Progress of Society" by "the author of the 'Elements of Social Science' " who, of course, could be none other than George Drysdale. When the article appeared, it was signed "Q." *The Malthusian,* no. 6 (July 1879). Drysdale never allowed his name to be used in *The Malthusian* though he wrote many articles for it; and his book was advertised in every issue well into the twentieth century as the work of "A Doctor of Medicine."

22. [George Drysdale], *Elements of Social Science,* p. x. The remainder of the quotations in this chapter are taken from Drysdale's book unless otherwise indicated.

23. During 1970, *Newsweek* reported on experiments being conducted by Dr. William H. Masters and Virginia E. Johnson. "Partner surrogates" participated in the treatment of young men with sexual problems by playing the role of "wives." When George Drysdale suggested such treatment in 1854, English scientists ignored him. It appears he has now been vindicated. "Human Sexual Inadequacy," *Newsweek,* 4 May 1970, p. 90.

24. In this respect, Peter Fryer, in *The Birth Controllers,* is wrong in saying that "Drysdale delimits the 'safe' period as from the second or third day before menstruation to the eighth day after it" (p. 124). Indeed, this is the period that Drysdale delimits as the time in which a woman is most likely to conceive. Admittedly, Drysdale seemed very unsure, with good reason, of the method. He also cites the opinion of a German physiologist, M. Bischoff, who said "sexual intercourse, *to be fruitful* [italics are mine], must take place within from eight or twelve days after the menstrual period." (*Elements,* p. 348, misnumbered in the 1905 edition as p. 343.) According to information published by the Family Planning Association of England in 1970, the twelfth to the twentieth days of a woman's menstrual cycle constitute the period when she is most likely to conceive. This is very different from what either Drysdale or Bischoff prescribed, but a more precise definition of the "safe period" had to await further discoveries in the 1930s. As we shall see, future propagators of contraceptive information reiterated Drysdale's error.

25. J. Rothwell, "Frustrating Nature," *The Malthusian,* no. 49 (February 1883), p. 390.

26. "Notes," *The Malthusian* 33, no. 1 (January 1909): 7.

27. Annie Besant, *Annie Besant: An Autobiography* (London: T. Fisher Unwin, 1893), pp. 197–98.

28. Bookseller's advertisement included in *Pamphlets on Malthusianism, 1879–1916,* Goldsmith's Library, University of London.

29. His other writings included: *The Irish Land Question* (1867), *Evils of a Hereditary Aristocracy* (1869), *Logic and Utility* (1866), *Population Fallacies: A Defence of the Malthusian or True Theory of Society* (1867), *The State Remedy for Poverty* (1904), *State Measures for the Direct Prevention of Poverty, War and Pestilence* (1885), and *State Measures for the Direct Prevention of Poverty, War and Infectious Diseases* (1905).

30. "Introductory Remarks," *The Political Economist; and Journal of Social Science,* no. 1 (January 1856), p. 1.

31. *The Political Economist,* no. 11 (January 1857), pp. 86–88.

2: The Fetal Stage

The idea of forming a Malthusian League came originally from a reader of George Drysdale's *Political Economist*. The first attempt to actually form such a group was made by Charles Bradlaugh in 1861, though his efforts remained confined to the pages of his journal, *The National Reformer*. The birth of the league came finally in 1877 but only after a number of secularist and neo-Malthusian freethinkers in English society had laid the groundwork for it. They, therefore, deserve a place in the history of the league. Among the most prominent were Charles Bradlaugh, Annie Besant, and Edward Truelove, all members of the National Secular Society, founded by Bradlaugh in 1866, and all charter members of the Malthusian League.

Secularist thought and neo-Malthusian theory developed together in nineteenth-century England. In his article on "The Rise and Decline of English Neo-Malthusianism," F. H. Amphlett Micklewright said neo-Malthusianism was "a generally accepted principle of the secularist philosophy and most secularist propaganda contained some reference to it."[1] It is no wonder, then, that when the Malthusian League was born in 1877 most of its members were drawn from the principal contemporary secularist organization, the National Secular Society. Such leading members in the league as Annie Besant, George Standring, Robert Forder, William Reynolds, Touzeau Parris, J. Symes, Edward Truelove, W. J. Ramsey, and, of course, Charles Bradlaugh, were also members of the NSS. In 1882, C. R. Drysdale, president of the league and editor of its periodical, *The Malthusian,* observed with regret that "the only really unprejudiced public in this country is to be found among the members of the National Secular Society. All other bodies of men and women, whether Protestant, Catholic or simply conventional, have an almost insuperable objection to looking a truth so fundamental as the law of population fair in the face."[2]

The prime mover of the Malthusian League was the leading secularist himself, Charles Bradlaugh. Without his initial efforts and continued support during the 1870s, it is doubtful the league would ever have been born. Like other secularists in England, he had been attracted to neo-Malthusianism as a solution to England's poverty. His own impoverished youth made him an eager recipient of ideas such as those expressed in George Drysdale's controversial *Elements of Social Science.*

Bradlaugh had grown up in the Hoxton district of squalid East London after his birth in 1833 and knew the pangs of poverty from experience, his major mentor.[3] He left school before he was eleven and earned a meager living as a general errand boy, wharf clerk, and cashier. His incessantly active and inquiring mind led him into public discussions of social, political, and theological questions in his moments of leisure. The heretical ideas that resulted from his deliberations, however, brought him dismissal from his pending confirmation in the Church of England, from his position with a firm of coal merchants, and from the humble home he had shared with his parents and sister. He was taken in by Eliza Sharples Carlile, the widow of Richard Carlile, who had died in 1843. He tried hard to earn a living by becoming a coal merchant, but by the close of 1850, he was obliged at the age of seventeen and a half to seek a livelihood in some other manner. He entered the English military forces as a member of the Seventh Dragoon Guards and served in Ireland for three years at a time when that unfortunate land was still suffering from the aftereffects of the disastrous potato famine. With the aid of a small inheritance, he bought a discharge in 1853 and returned to London to work, as his father had before him, as a solicitor's clerk. During the remainder of the 1850s, he began to lecture and write under the nom de plume, "Iconoclast," and edited the short-lived *Investigator.* The experience prepared him for editorship of the *National Reformer* and the political career that would bring him national fame.

The Reform Bill of 1867 provided the basis for the election of a number of independent working-class members to Parliament, such as Bradlaugh. He won a seat in the House of Commons representing the borough of Northampton in 1880 but fought a six-year battle to be allowed to affirm his loyalty to his sovereign without taking the usual parliamentary oath on the Bible, a practice repugnant to him in view of his secularist beliefs. He finally took the oath in 1866 and continued to sit in Parliament for Northampton until his death in 1891.

The poverty of the lower classes was of the utmost concern to Bradlaugh. "I know the poor," he insisted. "I belong to them. I was born amongst them. Among them are the earliest associations of my life. Such little ability as I possess to-day has come to me in the hard struggle of life."[4] His only solution to their poverty, however, was the panacea proclaimed by James Mill, Francis Place, and George Drysdale. As early as 1862, his Malthusian views were apparent. In one of his many lectures, he said:

> There can be no permanent civil and religious liberty, no permanent and enduring freedom for humankind, no permanent and enduring equality amongst men and women, no permanent and enduring fraternity, until the subject which Malthus wrote upon is thoroughly examined, and until the working men make that of which Malthus was so able an exponent the science of their everyday life; until, in fact, they grapple with it, and understand that the poverty which they now have to contend against must always produce the present evils which oppress them.[5]

Bradlaugh's introduction to neo-Malthusian thought may have occurred during his stay with Carlile's widow while he was still a teenager. It is more likely, however, that he became acquainted with both the *Elements of Social Science* and its author sometime during the late 1850s and was persuaded to become a disciple. He personally acknowledged his debt to George Drysdale in 1862 in an editorial for the *National Reformer*. "We are personally deeply indebted to G. R. [Drysdale's pseudonym in the *National Reformer*] for that [*sic*] he has opened to us a wide field of possible usefulness from which no vulgar insinuations

27

shall turn us away. The investigation of the cause of poverty, with a view to its removal, the endeavour to discover the source of human suffering, and to alleviate social ill; these present to us inducements of no mean order."[6]

Bradlaugh was the most active and influential exponent of neo-Malthusianism during the 1860s and early 1870s. It was he who proposed in the pages of his journal, the *National Reformer,* in May 1861, that a society or league be formed whereby Malthusians could come together "to help and encourage one another, and to defend and advance their opinions." The objectives of the organization would be twofold, he continued:

> *Firstly,* to promote the discussion of the Malthusian doctrines, and to show that the law of population is the fundamental cause of poverty, prostitution, and celibacy, the great social evils of old countries; and *secondly,* to show, in particular that poverty is caused by over-procreation, which leads to a permanent over-crowding of the labour market, and an undue depression of the agricultural margin; and that it might be radically removed, if all classes, rich and poor alike, were sufficiently to limit the number of their offspring.[7]

The group would promote these objectives through lectures, discussion, public meetings, and any other means within its power. Bradlaugh signed the article as "Secretary, *pro tem,"* and invited anyone in agreement with the goals as outlined and desirous of joining such a league to communicate with him. The response to his invitation was not overwhelming, to say the least. A letter from John F. Cookson, M.D., Edinburgh, in support of the organization appeared in the *National Reformer* in the first week in June, but apparently nothing further resulted from the proposal.[8] Both Bradlaugh, as "Iconoclast," and George Drysdale, as "G. R.," continued to write articles and letters on the neo-Malthusian topic for the *National Reformer,* but they made no further mention of a Malthusian league after the early 1860s.[9] Neo-Malthusianism needed a *cause célèbre* before it could attract enough attention to support a full-fledged organization to promote its case. The opportunity came in 1877 when Charles Bradlaugh and Annie Besant decided to challenge the Obscene Publications Act of 1857, also called the Campbell Act after its sponsor, Lord John Campbell.

The famous trial of the *Queen* vs. *Charles Bradlaugh and Annie Besant* dealt largely with the question of the morality of neo-Malthusianism and directly prompted the formation of the Malthusian League. The events leading to the trial began in the winter of 1876–77 when a Bristol bookseller by the name of Henry Cook was arrested for distributing an "obscene" pamphlet. The book in question was a work written by Charles Knowlton, a Massachusetts doctor, and published in the United States in 1832.[10] Its discreet title, *The Fruits of Philosophy,* concealed the fact that the publication contained information designed to help young people limit the size of their families, though the subtitle, *The Private Companion of Young Married People,* tended to reveal its real content and purpose. The book contained, in fact, the fullest account of contraceptive methods available at that time. It was first published in England in 1834 and was sold openly by James Watson until his retirement in 1853. He retained the plates for the book but allowed George J. Holyoake and later Holyoake's brother, Austin, to continue publishing and distributing it. In 1875, the plates for *The Fruits of Philosophy,* along with hundreds of other stereotyped plates, were sold by Watson's widow to Charles Watts who then published the book with his own imprint until he became embroiled in the prosecution involving the pamphlet in late 1876.

Just why the book should suddenly have caused such a stir in the late 1870s after being circulated for over forty years in England without challenge remains somewhat of a mystery. Marie Stopes, one of the most prominent leaders of the English birth-control movement in the twentieth century and, on the whole, an opponent of the Malthusian League, suggested in her autobiography that the explanation is to be found in the "obscene" pictures that Cook allegedly added to the book before putting it out for sale in his shop. "An unauthorized [?] Bristol bookseller [Cook] added questionable pictures to an edition which was promptly suppressed," she said. It was, she continued, "the first link in the chain of the prosecution which to us must appear otherwise inexplicable."[11] Annie Besant had been one of the first to call attention to the added pages in her own autobiography: "The book was never challenged till a disreputable Bristol bookseller put some copies on sale to which he added some improper pictures, and he was prosecuted and convicted."[12] Whether the pictures Cook added were obscene or not will probably remain unanswered since they have disappeared. They could have been pictures, for example, of feminine syringes and might well have been judged obscene in nineteenth-century Victorian England. As late as 1912, J. R. Holmes, a bookseller and distributor of pharmaceutical products, was prosecuted for including such pictures in a pamphlet that was basically an advertisement of the wares he had for sale in his business.[13] On the other hand, perhaps the illustrations Cook inserted were intentionally pornographic in nature. Besant's biographer, Arthur H. Nethercot, claims Cook "had already acquired a minor police record for offering 'obscene' works for sale."[14] Whichever the case may be, the Bristol police adjudged the book indecent, and Cook was sentenced to two years with hard labor.

As the publisher of the book in question, Charles Watts hurried to Bristol "to defend the book, believing at the time that it was a proper and legal publication." He admitted later, however, that he had never even read the pamphlet. Since the book had been sold without question for over forty years, there was, he said, no reason for him to read this particular work. "Having nothing whatever to do myself with the publishing department of my establishment, there was little chance of the said pamphlet coming under my notice."[15] But he was legally responsible for what his company published. He expressed horror when told for what purposes the book had allegedly been used, withdrew from Cook's defense, and promised the Bristol authorities that, regardless of their decision, he would publish the work no more. Nevertheless, he was arrested in London on 8 January 1877 and arraigned at the Guildhall on 12 January entering a plea of not guilty. His trial was set for 5 February 1877 in the Central Criminal Court, but before that date, Watts decided to change his plea to guilty. When the case came up, the judge accepted his altered plea and released him on a recognizance of five hundred pounds, to return for judgment when called. The case against him was subsequently dropped in late April, with only the provision that he pay twenty-five pounds in costs. At no time did Watts ever again republish *The Fruits of Philosophy* in spite of a steadily increasing demand for the book.

The whole episode brought Watts into direct conflict with Charles Bradlaugh. The two had been associated for a number of years in the publication of the *National Reformer*. Watts had served as a subeditor of the weekly periodical ever since April 1866. The two were apparently very close friends, Bradlaugh having even named the Watts's new baby in early 1876.[16] Watts's refusal to stand trial in defense of the Knowlton pamphlet, however, so infuriated Bradlaugh that he withdrew all the printing business of the National Secular Society from Watts's company, even though Watts had just invested £120 in a new set of type to be used especially for the *National Reformer*. In addition, Bradlaugh dismissed Watts from his job as subeditor of the weekly as of 25 March 1877.[17]

What was so importantly at stake, in Bradlaugh's opinion, was the struggle for a free press that had been a significant objective of the freethought movement throughout the nineteenth century. In his journal, the *National Reformer,* he wrote:

> I hold the work to be defensible, and I deny the right of anyone to interfere with the full and free discussion of social questions affecting the happiness of the nation. . . . I have no right and no power to dictate to Mr. Watts the course he should pursue, but I have the right and duty to refuse to associate my name with a submission which is utterly repugnant to my nature and inconsistent with my whole career.[18]

Words waxed hot in print between Bradlaugh and Watts in the early months of 1877, each in uncompromising tones accusing the other of deceit, cowardliness, and prevarication.[19] The breach between the two split not only their own longstanding friendship but the freethought movement as well. Bradlaugh's daughter, Hypatia, later wrote of the incident: "Mr. Watts' plea of 'guilty,' followed by Mr. Bradlaugh's indignation . . . produced considerable division amongst former friends."[20] George Holyoake broke with the *National Reformer;* and Watts joined with another disaffected freethinker, G. W. Foote, to publish the

Secular Review and Secularist. In 1879, continuing his opposition to neo-Malthusianism, Watts wrote *The Over-Population Craze: A Refutation and a Plea* and signed it simply "By Anti-Malthusian." The abrupt manner in which Bradlaugh dealt with Watts is perhaps indicative of his uncompromising and brusque way of handling those who disagreed with him. Henry M. Hyndman's description of Bradlaugh, written after the two had debated the pros and cons of socialism in 1884, seems appropriate:

> That he [Bradlaugh] was more than a little of a bully and a despot, as well as a capable and courageous leader, cannot be disputed. But this was almost inevitable, not only from his natural character but from the circumstances in which that character developed. He was an individualist of individualists. Every man must make his own way with his own right arm. That the weakest should go to the wall was a beneficial fact for the race: that he, Bradlaugh, would survive in this competition as one of the fittest he had no doubt whatever.[21]

Even though he, too, didn't particularly like the book, Bradlaugh felt so strongly about Watts's refusal to defend the Knowlton pamphlet that he decided to challenge the Campbell Act himself. "If the pamphlet now prosecuted had been brought to me for publication," he said, "I should probably have declined to publish it, not because of the subject-matter, but because I do not like its style. If I had once published it, I should have defended it until the very last."[22] Bradlaugh made it very clear that what he was defending was not so much neo-Malthusianism as the freedom of a publisher to print whatever he chose.

With the help of Annie Besant, his co-worker in the secularist movement, he organized the Freethought Publishing Company, at 28, Stonecutter Street, and began preparing a reprint of the Knowlton pamphlet. He called in his good friend, George Drysdale, to bring the medical parts of Knowlton's work up to date. A number of footnotes in the new edition subsequently contained the initials "G. R." "Physiology has made great strides during the past forty years," Bradlaugh explained in his Preface to the reprint, "and not considering it right to circulate erroneous physiology, we submitted the pamphlet to a doctor whose accurate knowledge we have the fullest confidence, and who is widely known in all parts of the world as the author of the 'Elements of Social Science'; the notes signed 'G. R.' are written by this gentleman."[23] In addition, Bradlaugh changed the subtitle of the book from *The Private Companion of Young Married People* to *An Essay on the Population Question.* Norman E. Himes suggested that perhaps Bradlaugh made the title change in order to prevent any subsequent prosecutor from arguing that the work was intended primarily for young people. But, Himes went on to say, "it would seem much more likely, however, that the sub-title was changed ... because Bradlaugh tended to consider birth-control theory as a part of general population theory; he was more interested in its wider implications that [sic] in the personal, family approach to the birth-control movement."[24] This is, of course, all speculation, Himes cautiously added. Unfortunately, Bradlaugh himself has left us no explanation. Others later tried to accuse him of changing the pamphlet substantially. In reviewing the credibility of the charge, Himes investigated several copies of Knowlton's book and concluded, "after careful collations I say that no changes of any considerable importance were made in the Bradlaugh-Besant edition of 'The Fruits of Philosophy.'"[25]

The reprinted pamphlet was ready in late March 1877. On Friday, 23 March, copies of the new edition were delivered to the chief clerk of the magistrates of Guildhall, to the city police office in Old Jewry, and to the solicitor for the city of London with the notification that the publishers, Bradlaugh and Besant, would sell the book themselves from 4 to 5 P.M. on the following day in their shop.[26] The government, however, appeared reluctant to become involved in the whole business and made no effort to arrest the two, though they continued to make themselves available between 10 and 11 A.M. each day. An organization called the Christian Evidence Society sent a deputation to call upon the home secretary in order to urge the Conservative government to prosecute the two. Whether due to the society's demands or not, warrants were finally issued for the publishers' arrest.

Just who was responsible for the prosecution of Bradlaugh and Besant for publishing the Knowlton pamphlet has never been clear. Besant's biographer, Arthur Nethercot, claimed:

No one ever was allowed to learn who had initiated the proceedings against Mrs. Besant and Bradlaugh, in spite of Bradlaugh's persistent inquiries. Denials were issued by authorities all down the line: it was not the national government, nor was it the City, though the city solicitor played a prominent role and the City paid at least £700 of the considerable costs; it was not the Vice Society, which Mrs. Besant sarcastically referred to as the Society for the Promotion of Vice; nor was it any other public agency or organization. Bradlaugh, however, seems to have suspected an alderman named Ellis, who directed the strategy of the prosecution, of having been the mask used by the unknown enemy, probably someone close to the Christian Evidence Society, through not in it.[27]

During the trial, Mrs. Besant criticized the government's buck-passing:

It is one of the principles of English justice, that those accused shall be placed face to face with their accusers, and shall understand who brings them to answer before the bar of justice. Our difficulty in knowing the aim of the prosecution is, that we don't know at the present moment who is prosecuting us. When first we were arrested and taken to the Guildhall we were kept waiting for more than two hours shut up in the cold and uncomfortable cells under the Guildhall court of justice. We were then told that we were kept there to await the presence of the City Solicitor, who had the conduct of the prosecution. Hearing that, we thought we were to fight a prosecution conducted by the city authorities. We wrote to the City Solicitor, and our belief was strengthened by his answer, because the City Solicitor, writing on the paper of the Corporation, using the stamp of the Corporation, and signing under his name "City Solicitor," has only the right to use the funds of the city to conduct prosecutions for the city authorities; we naturally then believed that we were being prosecuted by the city authorities. Imagine our astonishment on Mr. Bradlaugh asking whether that was so, we were told that "the Corporation of the City of London has nothing and never had anything to do with the prosecution against you and Mrs. Besant"! . . . We wrote to the solicitor and he wrote us telling us the Corporation had nothing to do with it, and referred us to the head of the Police of the city, who in his turn, in answer, said he had nothing to do with it, and that we must refer to the information. We found upon the information the name of William Simonds, there being no address given. We wrote for the address, which was furnished to us, and we then wrote to detective Wm. Simonds asking if he were the man responsible. We received in return merely an answer expressing his pleasure at receiving our letter.[28]

The prime suspect was an organization called the Society for the Suppression of Vice. According to Samuel Van Houten, a member of the Dutch Parliament in the late nineteenth century and a long-time supporter of the Malthusian League, the society developed in 1862 under the impetus of "certain pious bishops and nobles" to instigate the prosecution of anyone thought guilty of challenging laws which protected the Church and its doctrines.[29] Even the lord chief justice who tried the Bradlaugh-Besant case confessed ignorance as to the real prosecutor. In his summation, the judge commented that when the solicitor-general "talks of the authorities I should like to know who are the authorities and what are the authorities to whom he refers. . . . It is not a Government prosecution," he insisted, "nor have we any evidence that it is a prosecution set on foot by any authority which we should be disposed to treat with any great amount of consideration."[30]

The exact role of the Society for the Suppression of Vice in the prosecution of Bradlaugh and Besant has never been clear. Later writers in dealing with the trial, however, tended to accept the view that the society was responsible. F. H. Amphlett Micklewright, for example, merely stated without comment, "The Society for the Suppression of Vice began a prosecution, and both Bradlaugh and Mrs. Besant were arrested."[31] The tendency to assume that the society was actually the prosecutor in the Bradlaugh-Besant case is probably based on the fact that the group was less circumspect in its insistence that the government also prosecute Mr. Edward Truelove for a similar offense during the same year. Nevertheless, as late as the 1890s, Bradlaugh's daughter, Hypatia Bradlaugh Bonner, still asserted that "the expenses of the prosecution must have been enormous; but to the end the name of the prosecutor was refused."[32]

In April 1877, Bradlaugh and Mrs. Besant had a hearing in the Guildhall Justice Room. Among those appearing as witnesses on behalf of the defendants were "Miss Alice Vickery, Medical Student in Paris" and Dr. C. R. Drysdale, Consulting Physician to the Metropolitan Hospital, the future leaders of the Malthusian League.[33] When Bradlaugh and Besant were formally charged, it was estimated that twenty thousand persons were gathered outside the Guildhall.[34] A number of their friends, including Charles R. Drysdale, stood bail for the two, and they were released to prepare for their forthcoming trial in June. In spite of the split that Bradlaugh's dismissal of Watts had produced in the secularist movement, support for the two was never lacking. The hastily organized Defence Committee provided encouragement and, more importantly, money for the expenses of the trial, a subsequent appeal, and the defense of Edward Truelove in his prosecution. By the end of 1878, the committee had raised at least £1,692 6s. 7 1/2d. to aid in the defense and appeals of Bradlaugh, Besant, and Truelove.[35] Support for the defendants came from individuals in all walks of life, such as, Professor Emile Acollas, a leading French writer on law; Touzeau Parris, a unitarian minister in Bristol; and General Guiseppe Garibaldi, the Italian "champion of the people," or so Mrs. Besant labeled him.[36]

The courtroom was crowded, warm, and quite stuffy on the morning of 18 June when the trial opened promptly at 10:30 A.M. Among those who sat in the jury box was Mr. Arthur Walter, son and heir-apparent of the proprietor of the London *Times*. Lord Chief Justice Cockburn presided.[37] Bradlaugh and Besant chose to defend themselves, and they did so with great skill. Their defense hinged upon the character of the pamphlet in question. Both Bradlaugh and Besant tried to show that what the book advocated was the only logical solution to the ever-pressing problem of poverty. Mrs. Besant presented a detailed analysis of the arguments of Malthus in order to show the importance of the population question and its consequences and went on to plead for acceptance of birth-restricting checks, such as those advocated and described in the Knowlton pamphlet. Their efforts were not in vain. In his summation, the lord chief justice himself admitted that the evils of overpopulation are real and not imaginary, but he was obviously not convinced that the book was harmless.

> No matter what the motives of the defendants may have been, if the work is what the Solicitor-General for the prosecution alleges it,

although we may think we see—and probably we shall be right in saying so—here, in this instance, are two enthusiasts, who have been actuated by the desire to do good in a particular department of society, nevertheless, if in this desire to do good they have done wrong, they must abide by the result. Now, gentlemen, the law is this—that whatever outrages public decency and actually tends to corrupt the public morals is an offence. It is not necessary to load it with all the opprobrious epithets which have been applied to this work. It is enough to say that the work is a corrupt publication, that it tends to corrupt the morals of the population, and that it is, therefore, an offence against morality.[38]

On the fifth and final day of the trial, the jury returned an ambiguous verdict: "We are unanimously of opinion that the book in question is calculated to deprave public morals, but at the same time we entirely exonerate the defendants from any corrupt motives in publishing it."[39] Consequently, the judge interpreted the verdict as guilty on the grounds that the jury's condemnation of the book also condemned the defendants since they acted with deliberation in publishing the book. On 28 June 1877, the defendants were sentenced to six months in prison and a fine of £200 each. In their published transcript of the trial, Bradlaugh and Besant emphasized the manner in which the jury received the judge's interpretation of its verdict since the events would later figure in their appeal. They claimed "the majority neither assented nor dissented," and Mrs. Besant later alluded to a letter she received from a jury member indicating he had not assented to the verdict.[40] Their appeal was upheld, however, not because the verdict was vague but because the statements on which the Knowlton pamphlet was adjudged obscene had not been specifically set forth during the trial. "In an indictment for publishing an obscene book, it is not sufficient to describe the book by its title only, for the words thereof alleged must be set out; and if they are omitted, the defect will not be cured by a verdict of guilty, and the indictment will be bad either upon arrest of judgment or upon error."[41] On 12 February 1878, their sentences were set aside.

Meanwhile, the Society for the Suppression of Vice made no attempt to hide its role in bringing a suit against Edward

Truelove in May 1877, even before the Bradlaugh-Besant trial came up in the High Court of Justice. Truelove, a secularist and a freethought publisher, exhibited Robert Dale Owen's *Moral Physiology* and J. H. Palmer's *Individual, Family and National Poverty* in his shop window at 256, High Holborn, in London. John Green, employed by the Society for the Suppression of Vice and instructed to report any illegal publications he might see, informed Richard Hatt, a clerk for Messrs. Collette and Collette, solicitors of the society, of Truelove's publications.[42] Subsequently, on 15 May, a warrant was issued for a search of Truelove's premises. The investigating police confiscated 219 copies of Owen's book and 1,212 copies of the Palmer publication. On 22 May 1877, Truelove was given a hearing, at which time he was committed for trial before the Queen's Bench in the High Court of Justice. His trial was put off, however, until after the Bradlaugh-Besant litigation was concluded. Bradlaugh, representing the Bradlaugh-Besant Defence Committee, put up fifty pounds bail, and Truelove was released with the promise not to sell any of the works in question in the interim.

Robert Dale Owen's book, like the Knowlton pamphlet, had circulated unobtrusively since it was first published in England in 1832 by James Watson. The book was similar in tone to other nineteenth-century neo-Malthusian works and, in fact, was subtitled "A brief and plain treatise on the population question." It did include, however, like the Knowlton book, not only a detailed discussion of the population dilemma but a frank presentation of known methods of contraception.

The Truelove case came up for trial on 1 February 1878. The prosecution attempted to prove that the pamphlets if circulated would have a deleterious effect on the morals of young people. Mr. J. M. Davidson and Professor W. A. Hunger, president of the English Dialectical Society and later a member of Parliament for Aberdeen, appeared for the defendant. The presiding judge was again Lord Chief Justice Cockburn, who in his summation for the jury once again expressed his agreement with Malthusian doctrine. "That over-population is a fruitful source of evil and misery amongst the poorer classes of society, is undoubtedly true." The point of contention arises out of the author's espousal of early marriage coupled with the use of methods designed to prevent overpopulation. The question is, said Justice Cockburn, "Are the means which the defendant's book advocates, calculated to demoralise and debauch a large, and especially the younger, portion of Her Majesty's subjects?"[43] The prosecution's case was based on the assumption that the information was aimed at young unmarried people as well as at the married. The jury was out only two hours before announcing it could not reach a decision. The jurors disagreed primarily on the degree of punishment that should be levied, a question out of their jurisdiction the judge reminded them; but the jurors still refused to rule on the case, and they were duly dismissed. A second trial was held in May 1878 before Baron Pollock in the Central Criminal Court. The jury deliberated only forty minutes before returning a verdict of guilty. An appeal was denied, and Truelove was sentenced to four months in prison plus a fine of fifty pounds.

Edward Truelove was sixty-eight years old when he was condemned to Coldbath Fields' Prison. Defending the cause of freethought in England was by no means a new thing to this courageous but gentle man. He had been active in the movements for male suffrage, freethought and early nineteenth-century socialism.[44] He took part in the cooperative experiments of Robert Owen in Hampshire and New Harmony. Such experiences had convinced him that cooperation, not competition, was the wave of the future. He served as secretary of the John Street Labour Exchange for nine years, opened a bookshop in 1852, and became a well-known publisher of freethought literature, such as George Drysdale's book in 1854. Having become further convinced, however, that unless the small-family system were adopted no schemes for social improvement could succeed, he remained a valuable member of the Malthusian League from its inception in July 1877 until his death on 25 April 1899 at the age of ninety years.

Efforts to get Truelove released from prison were of no avail. Eleven thousand persons from every part of the country signed petitions asking for his release. A crowd thronged St. James's Hall in London on 6 June 1878 to demand his freedom.[45] But he served the full time in spite of his advanced age. His fine was paid "by a most generous donor to the Malthusian League"; and upon his release, he was met at the prison gate by a large number of enthusiastic and cheering friends.[46]

On 12 September 1878, the Hall of Science was crowded with Truelove's freethought, secularist, and Malthusian comrades all eager to do him honor and present him with a gift and a purse containing £177, raised to over £197 by subsequent donations.[47] The National Secular Society and the Malthusian League combined efforts to honor one of their most faithful associates on this occasion, and Charles Bradlaugh, as president of the NSS, gave Truelove an illuminated address. The wording of the speech made it clear that what Truelove was being celebrated for was not his defense of neo-Malthusianism but his lifelong defense of freedom of the press:

> To EDWARD TRUELOVE, on his release from four months' imprisonment in Coldbath Fields' Prison—suffered in defence of the Liberty of the Press.
>
> The undersigned, on behalf of the National Secular Society, and of the Malthusian League, desire to welcome you on your return to liberty, and to offer you their heartiest thanks for the courage and endurance you have displayed, in defending the right of free publication of opinion.
>
> .   .   .   .
>
> As some slight mark of our gratitude and affectionate esteem, and in recognition of the honor with which you have crowned a long life of unwavering courage, we present you this address, and the accompanying purse of gold, begging you to accept with them our sincerest wishes for your future welfare. Signed on behalf of

THE NATIONAL SECULAR SOCIETY.	THE MALTHUSIAN LEAGUE.
Chas. Bradlaugh, President.	Chas. Drysdale, M.D., President.
Robert Forder, Secretary.	Annie Besant, Hon. Sec.

> Hall of Science, 12th September, 1878.[48]

As in the Bradlaugh-Besant case, the major significance of the prosecution of Truelove to those who supported him was the defense of free speech and a free press. "The great question we are fighting is one of liberty of publication," Annie Besant told the jury in her own defense, "and we ask by your verdict to say that there is a right to sell all honest thought honestly expressed."[49] The effect of both trials, however, was to promote the spread of neo-Malthusian doctrine in a twofold manner: one, by tremendously increasing the sale of books like the Knowlton and Owen publications; and two, by providing the necessary stimulus for the successful initiation of an organization devoted exclusively to promulgating neo-Malthusian principles. "It is scarcely necessary to say," Annie Besant later proclaimed, "that one of the results of the prosecution was a great agitation throughout the country, and a wide popularisation of Malthusian views."[50]

The Knowlton pamphlet had sold in England prior to 1877 at about a rate of a thousand copies annually.[51] During the first three months of the Bradlaugh-Besant trial, Mrs. Besant reported that sales had increased by 125,000 copies.[52] Within three and a half years after the trial, Norman E. Himes calculated that 185,000 copies of the Freethought Publishing Company edition had been sold at sixpence each.[53] Several new editions were issued in the provincial towns of Sheffield, Wakefield, and Newcastle, among others. In the same period, the book was translated into French and Dutch.

Annie Besant and Charles Bradlaugh, however, considered the Knowlton book to be inadequate and proceeded, while awaiting an appeal of their sentence, to publish a pamphlet designed to replace it. They explained their thinking in an issue of the *National Reformer* (18 November 1877):

When we were prosecuted for publishing the Knowlton pamphlet we resolved that some similar pamphlet should be published, written by a woman for women, corrected by scientific discoveries to the present day. At present, although several ladies have spoken of writing such an essay, no lady physician has felt it right to face the possibility of another indictment. Under these circumstances, Mrs. Besant has written a very careful pamphlet entitled "The Law of Population; Its Consequences, and Its Bearing upon Human Conduct and Morals." . . . Part of this has already appeared in these columns, and the medical portion which has not appeared here has been treated with the most thorough desire to place in the hands of

41

the poor a knowledge which it is certain they need, and which it is believed has here been stated so as to be permanently useful.[54]

Besant and Bradlaugh emphasized the outmoded character of Knowlton's medical advice, but undoubtedly just as significant, and probably more so, was the fact that the American doctor had not connected the recommended contraceptive techniques with the pressing social problem of poverty. Knowlton, like the future leaders of the twentieth-century family-planning movement, had stressed primarily the benefits that limitation could bring to the wife, husband, and children of individual families. He was not concerned with solving the Malthusian dilemma of overpopulation as were Besant, Bradlaugh, and the Malthusian League.

Annie Besant's book was unquestionably thoroughly Malthusian in tone and was highly recommended by the Malthusian League well into the twentieth century. It was appropriately titled *The Law of Population: Its Consequences, and Its Bearings upon Human Conduct and Morals* and was dedicated "to the poor in great cities and agricultural districts, dwellers in stifling court or crowded hovel, in the hope that it may point out a path from poverty, and may make easier the life of British mothers." The book first appeared in late 1877.[55] By the time it was withdrawn from circulation in 1890, 175,000 copies had been sold; and the book had been translated into German, Dutch, French, and Italian.[56] The English version was available throughout the British possessions of Hindustan, Australia, and New Zealand. In 1884, Mrs. Besant wrote an introduction to the nineteen-thousandth copy. She said, perhaps correctly and with insight, "A circulation so wide is the sign of the need which this pamphlet has striven to supply."[57]

Mrs. Besant began her small pamphlet, about forty-six pages, with a detailed discussion of Malthus's law of population and its relationship to the problems of nineteenth-century English society. Her message was clear: the working classes must limit the size of their families to their means and thus solve the problem of poverty themselves. Her adherence to nineteenth-century classical economic theory was apparent. She continued with a detailed analysis of the available methods of contraception and comments as to their reliability. She recommended, like Place and Drysdale before her, the sponge as the most effective preventive. It is, she said, "the check which appears to us to be preferable, as at once certain, and in no way grating on any feeling of affection or of delicacy."[58] The douche, "the preventive check advocated by Dr. Knowlton," she admitted, "is an effective one" but she did not recommend it, she said, since "there are many obvious disadvantages connected with it as a matter of taste and feeling." *Coitus interruptus,* the method most often advocated by the early Malthusian League, she declared, "is, of course, absolutely certain as a preventive" and is not harmful, as some claimed, to either husband or wife. In presenting the so-called safe period, she made the same error as George Drysdale: "the avoidance of sexual intercourse during the few days before and after menstruation has been recommended as a preventive check." Not surprisingly, she went on to conclude that "the most serious objection to reliance on this check is that it is not certain. . . . We can scarcely say more than that women are far less likely to conceive midway between the menstrual periods than either immediately before or after them." She went on to dispel an old but enduring belief among peasant women that prolonged nursing prevents conception. This practice, she said, is detrimental to both mother and child and, above all, *"does not prevent conception* [the italics are hers]." Abortion she decried as "distinctly criminal." That she should make a point to comment upon the practice is indicative of its presence in English society. Her opinion of the condom, or baudruche as she called it, is apparent from her description of the device: It is "a covering used by men of loose character as a guard against syphilitic diseases, and occasionally recommended as a preventive check." Her criticism of both the condom and the douche appears to have been based at least in part on her objection to the Contagious Diseases Acts, passed in the 1860s. Both of these techniques were used, she felt, to keep prostitutes (though she did not use the term) "'fit for use' by Her Majesty's soldiers."

The remainder of the *Law of Population* was devoted to defending neo-Malthusian doctrines. She attempted to answer the same kind of objections and arguments that would be addressed to members of the Malthusian League throughout the remainder of the nineteenth century. To those who called the use of preventive methods unnatural, she replied:

> To limit the family is no more a violation of nature's laws, than to preserve the sick by medical skill; the restriction of the birth-rate does not violate nature's laws more than does the restriction of the death rate. . . . Nature flings lightning at our houses; we frustrate her ends by the lightning conductor. Nature divides us by seas and by rivers; we frustrate her ends by sailing over the seas, and by bridging the rivers. Nature sends typhus fever and ague to slay us; we frustrate her ends by purifying the air, and by draining the marshes.

To those who complained that contraception was immoral, she drew upon Bentham's utilitarianism:

> What is morality? It is the greatest good of the greatest number. It is immoral to give life where you cannot support it. It is immoral to bring children into the world when you cannot clothe, feed, and educate them. It is immoral to crowd new life into already overcrowded houses, and to give birth to children wholesale who never have a chance of healthy life.

To those who advocated land reform as the solution to population pressures, she cautioned as to the dangers of revolution:

> Land reform is sorely needed, but, to meet the immediate needs of the present, land revolution would be necessary; it is surely wiser to lessen the population-pressure, and to work steadily at the same time towards Reform of the Land Laws, instead of allowing the population-pressure to increase, until the starving multitudes precipitate us into a revolution.

Adherents of the new Darwinian theory, more particularly, the Social Darwinists, argued that human beings had advanced to their present condition through a struggle for existence consequent upon rapid multiplication. If the human race is to advance further, the Social Darwinists reasoned, the struggle must continue. Hence, the natural rate of increase must not be greatly diminished by any means. Besant, like other members of the Malthusian League, declared that population control would enable human beings to do away with the evils of the "struggle for survival." "Scientific checks to population," she insisted, "would just do for man what the struggle for existence does for the brutes." In other words, human beings could, by using the knowledge and inventions of science, eliminate those aspects of nature that bring suffering and hardship to the human race. Social Darwinists also expressed the fear that if the well-to-do classes of society adopted family limitation while the lower classes did not, the result would be that the "inferior" members of society would supplant the "better" members. By the early decades of the twentieth century, leaders of the Malthusian League, such as Charles Vickery Drysdale, claimed that this fear had been realized in English society. The upper classes had accepted family limitation, he would say, while the "less fit" groups were still breeding just as prolifically as before.

The popularity of Besant's *Law of Population* is evidenced by its wide sale. By 1880, 40,000 copies were in circulation. In addition to Besant's book and the Knowlton pamphlet, Owen's *Moral Physiology,* highly advertised by the Truelove trial, also enjoyed a wider audience. The extent of its circulation is not so easily deduced; however, Himes concluded that "there is no means of estimating the increased circulation of Owen's *Moral Physiology,* but there can be little doubt that the notoriety of the trial increased its circulation."[59] The English press further provided an avenue of publicity for the neo-Malthusian doctrine in its coverage of both the Bradlaugh-Besant trial and the Truelove proceedings. J. A. and Olive Banks described the influence of contemporary journalism in their study of "The Bradlaugh-Besant Trial and the English Newspapers":

> The extensive publicity which the press had unwillingly provided brought the idea of contraception vividly to the minds of thousands unaffected by earlier propaganda. This new publicity, moreover, ought not to be counted in terms of the increased sales of the *Fruits of Philosophy* alone. The newspaper reports reached people who would never have brought a "dubious" pamphlet. Nor is it in the least necessary to assume that this enormous newspaper-reading public was convinced by what it read. The press comments themselves suggest that dismay and disgust were only too frequent reactions. On the other hand the attentive reader was familiarised with the

Bradlaugh-Besant arguments for family limitation, and the way was prepared for the propaganda of the Malthusian League.[60]

It is little wonder that Lord Chief Justice Cockburn muttered during his summation to the jury in the Bradlaugh-Besant trial, "A more ill-advised and more injudicious proceeding in the way of a prosecution was probably never brought into a court of justice. Here is a book which has been published now for more than forty years, which appears never to have got into general circulation to the extent of thousands of copies."[61]

Annie Besant, Bradlaugh's codefendant in the famous obscenity trial of 1877, was also his coeditor of the *National Reformer* and his coproprietor in the operation of the Freethought Publishing Company. Some have suggested she was even more to him, but these have generally been among the many enemies of the two, eager to discredit them with whatever suspicions could be aroused. She was born Annie Wood in London on 1 October 1847 and was married at the age of twenty to Reverend Frank Besant, a minister of the Anglican Church.[62] Her own doubts about Christianity coupled with her baby's serious illness in the winter of 1870–71 brought on a nervous breakdown and caused her to decide to reexamine her Christian faith thoroughly. Her studies, however, only took her further along the path to skepticism. She withdrew from attending Communion and continued to write novels and articles, one of which proved particularly offensive to her husband. It was entitled an *Essay on the Deity of Jesus of Nazareth* and was signed "by the wife of a beneficed clergyman."[63] The marital quarrels grew worse, until finally she was ordered either to resume attendance at Communion or leave. She departed with a legal separation and her young daughter, regretfully leaving a son in the care of his father.

In 1874, Mrs. Besant joined the National Secular Society and met Charles Bradlaugh who offered her a position on the *National Reformer*. She commenced a series entitled "Daybreak" under the pseudonym of "Ajax" and in 1875 began her career as a lecturer in the freethought movement. For many years, she plied the roads of England lecturing several times each week in towns throughout the British Isles while at the same time writing books and pamphlets, editing the *National Reformer,* fighting legal battles, and, after 1877, acting as the first secretary of the Malthusian League. "The minor issues for which she was fighting at this time are," said one of her biographers, "too numerous to be listed."[64] And yet she found time to study and receive with honors from London University in 1882 the first Bachelor of Science degree to be awarded to a woman.

Her hostility to Christianity, resulting from her studies, her personal experience, and the lack of understanding shown by her fundamentalist, clerical husband, increased in 1878 when the English courts deprived her of the custody of her small daughter, Mabel Emily. Her part in the Bradlaugh-Besant trial, her writing of the *Law of Population,* and her activities in behalf of various secularist and freethought groups, such as the Malthusian League, provoked her husband into demanding that the child be removed from her "evil" influence. Besant described the judge in the case, Sir George Jessel, as "a man animated by the old spirit of Hebrew bigotry." He objected to her defending herself and intimated "that her character was tainted and that modest women could not be expected to associate with her."[65] At the time of the trial, the child was ill with scarlet fever, but in spite of his admission that she was receiving the best possible care, the judge decided that Mrs. Besant's refusal to give the child religious instruction was more than sufficient grounds for removing her from her mother. Secular education, he declared, was "not only reprehensible, but detestable, and likely to work utter ruin to the child. . . . I certainly should upon this ground alone decide that this child ought not to remain another day under the care of her mother."[66] Perhaps only a parent who has lost a beloved child through either death or court action could understand the utter despair and agony the event brought to Annie Besant. She collapsed physically, was prostrated by illness, and was unable to do anything for several months. When she did resume her activities, her writings "against Christianity," she later commented in her *Autobiography,* "were marked with considerable bitterness, for it was Christianity that had robbed me of my child, and I struck mercilessly at it in return."[67] When they became of age, both children, however, chose to return to their mother and joined her in the Theosophical Society; but the hypocrisy of nineteenth-century English law continued to haunt her. She later scoffed: "In the days when the law took my child from me, it virtually said to all women: 'Choose which of these two positions, as wife and mother, you will occupy. If you are legally your husband's wife, you can have no legal claim to your children; if legally you are your husband's mistress, your rights as mother are secure'"[68]

Mrs. Besant's relationship with Bradlaugh blossomed in the 1870s. "They were mutually attracted," wrote Bradlaugh's daughter, "and a friendship sprang up between them of so close a nature that had both been free it would undoubtedly have ended in marriage."[69] Bradlaugh, like Besant, had had a most unhappy marriage primarily, according to his daughter, because of Mrs. Bradlaugh's drinking habits. She was, Hypatia Bradlaugh Bonner wrote, "in all points save one . . . the best of mothers. . . . It was this one point, which, overbalancing all the rest, ruined our home, lost her my father's love and her friends' respect, and was the cause of her own sufferings, unhappiness, and early death." She died in May 1877 "from heart disease engendered by alcoholism."[70]

Mrs. Besant remained married, though separated from her husband. Under these conditions, she and Bradlaugh could be only devoted friends. During the 1880s, however, they drifted apart. Annie Besant turned to more radical causes while Bradlaugh became embroiled in the parliamentary fight over his taking the oath of office. In 1887, she resigned as coeditor of the *National Reformer,* and in 1890, their coownership of the Freethought Publishing Company also ceased. In the same year, Annie Besant turned to Theosophy under the influence of Madame Helena Petrovna Blavatsky. She withdrew from all of her previous reform activities and the various secular and socialist organizations with which she had been associated. Henceforth, her career was very different.

Annie Besant's association with the Malthusian League began at the time of its birth in July 1877 and continued until her formal resignation from it in 1890. It was she who suggested that the Defence Committee formed to support her and Bradlaugh in their trial become the nucleus of a Malthusian League. At a meeting of the committee held on 6 July in the Minor Hall at 142, Old Street, City Road, to discuss future activities (the trial was over, sentence had been passed, and an appeal was pending), some in the group expressed dissatisfaction with the verdict. It had left unclear the question of whether or not neo-Malthusian doctrines could legally be discussed in public, primarily because the questionable sections of the Knowlton pamphlet had not been indicated specifically. What was obscene?—the advocacy of preventive checks or the whole doctrine of neo-Malthusianism with its recommendation of early marriage; or was it merely the selling of contraceptive instructions at a cheap price making it available to all, regardless of marital status? Annie Besant described the meeting for the *National Reformer:*

> The verdict of the jury in itself does *not* single out the advocacy of checks as the criminal offense: it condemns equally the assertion of the law of population, the recommendation of early marriage, all instructions on the reproductive functions *cheaply* sold, the information that abuse of the physical powers is injurious, knowledge given at sixpence as to checks to fertility. All these things are equally condemned by the jury, no distinction is drawn between them.... [As it is] the whole of the above points are now by the law tabooed as indecent, and any one discussing them may, if he has any private enemy to prosecute him under cover of a policeman, find himself in Holloway gaol, or in some other of Her Majesty's prisons.[71]

She proposed an organization for the express purpose of preventing further prosecutions of anyone accused of propagating such materials.

> In order that public opinion may be organized against the tyranny which is being attempted, some few of us earnest for freedom, have resolved to start a society with the following objects:—
>
> "To spread among the people—by lectures, cheap books, leaflets, and by all practicable means—a knowledge of the law of population, and of its practical application.

"To agitate for the abolition of all penalties on the public discussion of the Population Question.

"To obtain such a statutory definition as shall render it impossible in the future to bring within the scope of the common law, as a misdemeanor, the publication of works dealing with this question."

She took credit for advancing the idea of the organization but admitted that Bradlaugh had first proposed such a group in 1861. "The idea of this 'Malthusian League' was borrowed by me," she said, "from a League of this name started by Mr. Bradlaugh some seventeen years ago—an effort which was unsuccessful at the time."

At its 6 July meeting, the Defence Committee resolved itself into a temporary committee for the purpose of forming such a league, authorized the printing of the "objects" of the organization as proposed by Mrs. Besant, and provided for the enrollment of members at an entrance fee of sixpence. A ten-member subcommittee plus a secretary, Annie Besant, was appointed to draw up a fuller program to be submitted at the next meeting of the temporary committee set for Tuesday, 17 July. The subcommittee included:

Mrs. Besant, Hon. Secretary	Mrs. Rennick
Mr. Bradlaugh	Mr. Seyler
Mr. Dallow	Mr. Shearer, Hon.
Dr. Drysdale, Hon. Treasurer	Asst. Sec.
Mr. Hember, Hon. Asst. Sec.	Mrs. Swaagman
Miss Vickery	Mr. Truelove

The 6 July meeting fell on a Friday evening; by Monday, Mrs. Besant reported "160 members have enrolled in the League in my own presence and I do not yet know what others may have done." On Sunday, 22 July, she lectured at the Hall of Science on the "Malthusian League." At that time, she said 220 members had been accepted. The temporary committee of the Malthusian League met on 17 July to receive the report of the ten-member subcommittee, approved a code of rules presented by the group for the regulation of the Malthusian League, and arranged for the first general meeting of the organization to be held on

Thursday, 26 July, at 8:30 P.M. in the Hall of Science, 142, Old Street, City Road. The Hall of Science had long served as a meeting place for secularists, neo-Malthusians, and other such freethinkers.

On the indicated evening, the members and friends of the new league assembled in the Minor Hall of the Hall of Science, but finding it too small to hold those in attendance, they adjourned to a larger room in the same building. Mr. Bradlaugh quickly took the initiative and moved that Dr. Charles Robert Drysdale, senior physician to the Metropolitan Free Hospital and brother of the writer of the *Elements of Social Science,* take the chair. It was undoubtedly Bradlaugh's intent that Drysdale should be president of the new organization; and in fact, he publicly expressed the hope that the doctor would be elected to that office by the new council of the league when it met to select officers for the group in keeping with the proposed rules. Annie Besant moved that the meeting ratify the work done by the temporary committee of the Malthusian League. She recounted the events of the origin of the group, read the new rules, and submitted a list of twenty names proposed by the temporary committee as the Malthusian League Council for the first year. The proposed council, she said, "was no fair-weather Council, for those who composed it had come forward in time of danger to defend the principles which were attacked." The list was approved as read:

Miss Vickery	Mr. Hember
Mrs. Rennick	Mr. Shearer
Mrs. Swaagman	Mr. Brown
Miss Mitchell	Mr. Reynolds
Mrs. Parris	Mr. Young
Mrs. Besant	Mr. Dray
Dr. Drysdale	Mr. Page
Mr. Bradlaugh	Mr. Bell
Mr. Seyler	Mr. Rogers
Mr. Truelove	Mr. Standring[72]

By the end of 1877, five council meetings had been held to elect officers, approve branch organizations, and recommend literature to be printed and distributed under the auspices of the league. At least 964 members had been enrolled and the work of the organization was well under way.

1. F. H. Amphlett Micklewright, "The Rise and Decline of English Neo-Malthusianism," *Population Studies, A Journal of Demography* 15, no. 1 (July 1961): 36.

2. C. R. Drysdale, *The Malthusian,* no. 40 (May 1882), p. 319.

3. For a detailed biography of Bradlaugh, see the two-volume work written by his daughter (vol. 1) and his friend (vol. 2) soon after his death in the 1890s. Hypatia Bradlaugh Bonner and John M. Robertson, *Charles Bradlaugh: A Record of His Life and Work* (London: T. Fisher Unwin, 1902). For a detailed study of Bradlaugh's struggle to avoid taking the parliamentary oath, see Walter L. Arnstein, *The Bradlaugh Case* (Oxford: The Oxford University Press, 1965).

4. *The Queen v. Charles Bradlaugh and Annie Besant* (London: Freethought Publishing Company, n.d. [1877]), p. 213.

5. Robertson, *Charles Bradlaugh,* 2:172.

6. Charles Bradlaugh, "Editorial," *The National Reformer* 3, no. 95 (8 March 1862): 5.

7. Charles Bradlaugh, "Proposal For A Malthusian League," *The National Reformer* 2, no. 53 (18 May 1861): 5.

8. Letter to the Editor from John F. Cookson, M.D., Edinburgh, *The National Reformer* 2, no. 55 (1 June 1861): 6.

9. For Bradlaugh's ideas on neo-Malthusianism, see particularly his series of articles entitled *Jesus, Shelley, and Malthus; or, Pious Poverty and Heterodox Happiness,* published in *The National Reformer* during 1861. The series was later reprinted as a pamphlet.

10. Knowlton himself served three months with hard labor in the house of correction at Cambridge, Massachusetts, in 1833 for publishing the book. See Dr. [Charles] Knowlton, *A History of the Recent Excitement in Ashfield,* Part 1. (Ashfield, Mass.: 1834). Part 2 appeared as a letter from Knowlton in the *Boston Investigator* 5, no. 27 (235), 25 September 1835, p. [1], cols. 2–3.

11. Marie Stopes, *Contraception: Its Theory, History, and Practice* (London: John Bale, Sons & Danielsson, Ltd., 1923), p. 337.

12. Annie Besant, *Annie Besant: An Autobiography* (London: T. Fisher Unwin, 1893), p. 206.

13. On his memorandum stationery, Holmes listed himself as a "Bookseller and Dealer in Neo-Malthusian Hygienic Requisites." Letter to Mrs. Edith How-Martyn, 17 November 1929, Palmer Collection.

14. Arthur H. Nethercot, *The First Five Lives of Annie Besant* (Chicago: The University of Chicago Press, 1960), p. 110.

15. "Mr. Watts on His Prosecution," *The National Reformer* 29, no. 3 (21 January 1877): 34.

16. Nethercot, *The First Five Lives,* p. 91.

17. Ibid., p. 113.

18. *The National Reformer* 29, no. 4 (28 January 1877): 57.

19. The whole affair between Watts and Bradlaugh is documented in *The National Reformer,* 14 January 1877–15 December 1878, passim, and in Charles Watts's *A Refutation of Mr. Bradlaugh's Inaccuracies and Misrepresentations* (London, 1877). For a secondhand account, see Nethercot, *The First Five Lives,* pp. 110–15.

20. Bonner, *Charles Bradlaugh,* 1:18–19.

21. Henry Mayers Hyndman, *The Record of an Adventurous Life* (New York: The MacMillan Company, 1911), p. 309.

22. Charles Bradlaugh, "The Prosecution of Mr. Charles Watts," *The National Reformer* 29, no. 3 (21 January 1877): 42.

23. Charles Bradlaugh and Annie Besant, "Publishers' Preface to Dr. Knowlton's 'Fruits of Philosophy,'" *The National Reformer* 29, no. 12 (25 March 1877): 178.

24. Norman E. Himes, "Mr. Hunt Answered," *The New Generation* 7, no. 5 (May 1928): 60.

25. Ibid., p. 59.

26. Besant, *Autobiography,* p. 209.

27. Nethercot, *The First Five Lives,* p. 129.

28. *Queen v. Bradlaugh and Besant,* pp. 52–53.

29. "The Malthusian Prosecutions of 1877 and 1878," *The Malthusian,* no. 5 (June 1879), p. 37. Van Houten may well have been wrong, however. In his study of the *Fathers of the Victorians* (England: Cambridge University Press, 1961), pp. 428–36, Ford K. Brown describes a Society for the Suppression of Vice established in 1802. Brown does not indicate how long the organization existed, however, and recounts only a few incidents related to the group in the first quarter of the nineteenth century.

30. *Queen v. Bradlaugh and Besant,* pp. 255–56. Bradlaugh and Besant published this stenographic report of the trial themselves. In addition, *The National Reformer* carried a running account of the trial as did other journals and newspapers of the day. Bradlaugh and Besant's report, however, is still the best detailed account of the trial.

31. Micklewright, "Rise and Decline of English Neo-Malthusianism," p. 39.

32. Bonner, *Charles Bradlaugh,* 1:27.

33. "Prosecution of Mr. Bradlaugh and Mrs. Annie Besant," *The National Reformer* 29, no. 15 (15 April 1877): 226.

34. *The New Generation* 11, no. 1 (19 January 1927): 1.

35. Besant, *Autobiography,* p. 231. The amount is calculated from collections and disbursements cited by Mrs. Besant.

36. *Queen v. Bradlaugh and Besant,* p. 237, citing Besant in her summation for the jury.

37. Sir Alexander James Edmund Cockburn, Barrister, Lord Chief Justice of England.

38. *Queen v. Bradlaugh and Besant,* pp. 257–58.

39. Ibid., p. 267.

40. Ibid., p. 268.

41. *The Law Reports. Queen's Bench Division,* II, 1876–77, XL, Victoria (London: Printed for the Incorporated Council of Law Reporting for England and Wales by William Clowes and Sons, 1877), p. 607.

42. *The Queen v. Edward Truelove* (London: Edward Truelove, 256, High Holborn, 1878), p. 24.

43. Ibid., pp. 91–93, Lord Chief Justice Cockburn's summation.

44. "In Memory of Mr. Edward Truelove," *The Malthusian* 23, no. 6 (June 1899): 45.

45. Besant, *Autobiography,* p. 228.

46. "Memory of Edward Truelove," p. 45.

47. Besant, *Autobiography,* p. 228.

48. "Edward Truelove," *The Malthusian* 11, no. 7 (July 1887): 54.

49. *Queen v. Bradlaugh and Besant,* p. 150.

50. Besant, *Autobiography,* p. 228.

51. Norman E. Himes made an in-depth study of the circulation of such contraceptive literature in nineteenth-century England. The study was financed in the 1930s by the Rockefeller Research Foundation. *Medical History of Contraception* (Baltimore: The Williams & Wilkins Company, 1936), p. 243.

52. *Queen v. Bradlaugh and Besant,* p. 149.

53. Himes, *Medical History,* p. 243.

54. "Rough Notes," *The National Reformer* 30, no. 23 (18 November 1877): 777. The medical portion of Mrs. Besant's booklet was written by Dr. Palfrey of the London Hospital. "Sixth Annual Report of the Council of the Malthusian League to the Members," *The Malthusian,* no. 53 (July 1883), p. 427.

55. No date of publication was given on the first edition published by Bradlaugh and Besant's Freethought Publishing Company, but the quotation previously cited from *The National Reformer* indicates that the book was already available in November 1877. In addition, Bradlaugh's daughter, Hypatia Bradlaugh Bonner, indicated in her father's biography that the book was first published in November 1877. *Charles Bradlaugh,* 1:28.

56. Himes, *Medical History,* p. 250.

57. Annie Besant, *The Law of Population* (London: Freethought Publishing Company, 1884), p. iii.

58. Ibid., p. 34. In the ensuing discussion of Besant's *Law of Population,* the quotations are from her book.

59. Himes, *Medical History,* p. 250.

60. J. A. Banks and Olive Banks, "The Bradlaugh-Besant Trial and the English Newspapers," *Population Studies, A Journal of Demography* 8, no. 1 (July 1954): 33.

61. *Queen v. Bradlaugh and Besant,* p. 255.

62. Biographies of Annie Besant are fairly numerous. The major one is a two-volume work by Arthur Nethercot, *The First Five Lives of Annie Besant* (1960) and *The Last Four Lives of Annie Besant* (1963), both published by the

University of Chicago Press. A somewhat hostile biography was written by Geoffrey West while Mrs. Besant was still living. *Mrs. Annie Besant* (London: Gerald Howe, Ltd., 1927). An invaluable source, of course, is her own story as told in *Annie Besant: An Autobiography,* but it only covers her life up to her conversion to Theosophy around 1890.

63. J. M. Wheeler, *A Biographical Dictionary of Freethinkers of All Ages and Nations* (London: Progressive Publishing Company, 1889), p. 41.

64. Geoffrey West [Geoffrey Harry Wells], *Mrs. Annie Besant,* p. 40.

65. For Besant's description of the judge, see her *Autobiography,* p. 214. For the judge's description of Besant, see Peter Fryer, *Birth Controllers,* p. 171.

66. Besant, *Autobiography,* p. 217, citing the Master of the Rolls, George Jessel.

67. Ibid., p. 245.

68. Ibid., p. 219.

69. Bonner, *Charles Bradlaugh,* 1:13.

70. Ibid., 50–51.

71. Annie Besant, "The Malthusian League," *The National Reformer* 29, no. 31 (15 July 1877): 490–91. In this short article Mrs. Besant described the activities that led directly to the organization of the Malthusian League. She also listed the objectives that were adopted by the group.

72. "First General Meeting of the Malthusian League," *The National Reformer* 30, no. 8 (5 August 1877): 531.

3: The Anatomy of the League

Charles Robert Drysdale, newly elected president of the Malthusian League, issued a call to action in his first address to the members of the organization:

> Modern Malthusianism, being a *new faith,* requires the individual energies and zeal of every one of its votaries to be enlisted into its cause.
> ....
> When I contemplate this great question, I have no hesitation in saying, and that without any exaggeration, that it is *by far* the most important point that can exercise the attention of a civilized man or woman. . . . Action, then, is needed, and I implore each individual member of the League to do something to aid the cause, and that *at once.*[1]

In many respects, the amazing thing is that the small but devoted band of followers who answered Drysdale's call to action were able to sustain the organization and its activities, to varying degrees, for half a century. The problem of poverty that they attacked was one of great concern in English society, but only a small number were at least publicly receptive to their proposed solution of family limitation clothed as it was in Malthusian doctrine.

The Drysdale family must be accorded the major credit for sustaining the Malthusian League throughout its long existence. George Drysdale never allowed his name to be associated with it publicly but, as already indicated, he provided the major thrust for the organization by incorporating Malthusianism, utilitarianism, nineteenth-century classical economic theory, and a more open view of the sexual functions of the body into a philosophical whole. His brother, Charles Robert Drysdale, provided the major leadership for the group as its president from 1877 until his death in 1907. C. R.'s wife, Alice Vickery-

Drysdale, worked just as diligently alongside her husband and followed him in the presidency from 1907 until 1921. Their son, Charles Vickery Drysdale, began writing articles for the league's journal in the 1890s when he was fresh out of engineering school and newly married. He became president in 1921 when his mother, at age seventy-six, resigned due to ill health. He remained the leader of the organization until his death in 1961 even though the group, for all practical purposes, ceased its activities in 1927. His wife, Bessie Ingham Drysdale, also worked alongside her husband in the various labors of the league, particularly in the second and third decades of the twentieth century. Margaret Sanger paid tribute to the work of the Drysdales in her autobiography:

> From the early "fifties," when George Drysdale first published his epoch-making gospel of birth control, "The Elements of Social Science," throughout the Victorian era, through the tempestuous days of the Great War, down to these chaotic days [the Great Depression of the 1930s] when the whole world has been desperately driven to a realization of the fundamental need for the conscious control of population, it has been those brave self-sacrificing Drysdales who have kept alive the idea. It has been a noble tradition of the Drysdale family—this quiet, unceasing service, this loyalty to an ideal.[2]

Charles Robert Drysdale, the "Malthusian King" as one league member dubbed him, was born in Edinburgh in 1829.[3] Like his brother, George, he was well educated in the schools of Edinburgh; Trinity College, Cambridge; Trinity College, Dublin; and University College, London. He became adept not only in medicine but also in engineering. He took part in the building of the Great Eastern steamship in 1847 while employed by Scott Russell and Company and engaged in railway surveying in Switzerland and Spain.[4] His major profession, however, was medicine. He received his M.D. degree in 1859, studied further in London and Paris, and became a Fellow of the Royal College of Surgeons (F.R.C.S.) and a Member of the Royal College of Physicians (M.R.C.P.) in 1862.

The Drysdales were, on the whole, financially independent. Consequently, they were attracted to the study of medicine not so much for the monetary rewards but because it afforded them the kind of knowledge necessary for delving into social problems that interested them. At the sensitive age of nineteen, C. R. visited Ireland during the height of the potato famine in 1848. The spectacle undoubtedly left its mark on the mind of the young man. In 1898, he recalled the experience for the readers of *The Malthusian:*

> Well do I remember a visit I paid to that distressful country in 1848, when the potato famine had caused such terrible misery and actual starvation. The scenes which I then witnessed of abject misery have remained permanently in my recollection; and, indeed, have caused me never to lose sight of the evils caused by over-population, which so many people are wont to ascribe to mere political or government errors.[5]

As a fledgling doctor, Drysdale gained medical experience among the poor Jewish population of East London and in the Metropolitan Free Hospital. Once established in his practice, he continued to serve as medical officer for a number of London medical charities. He served, for example, as physician to the Rescue Society, a medical service for prostitutes, and to the North London Consumption Hospital in the 1860s. His work for the Rescue Society led him to a study of prostitution and venereal diseases in England.

In 1863, Drysdale published a pamphlet on *The Nature and Treatment of Syphilis and Other So-Called "Contagious Diseases."* In 1866, he presented a paper on "Prostitution Medically Considered With Some of Its Social Aspects."[6] The paper was well received by the Harveian Medical Society of London and was printed as a pamphlet in the same year. As a result of his work, Drysdale became a recognized authority among London physicians on the extent and treatment of venereal diseases. His pamphlet on syphilis was primarily a medical report with little philosophical comment on the problem. He was concerned chiefly with the origin, diagnosis, and treatment of the disease. One can see in his paper on prostitution, however, conclusions that would lead to his acceptance of birth control as the panacea for English social problems; but he made no mention of contraceptive methods in the work even though he noted the seeming sterility of prostitutes and the low incidence of death among them from venereal disease. "One of the most important facts in the picture of prostitution," he pointed out, "is the want of procreative power of prostitutes. . . . The causes of the sterility of prostitutes are far, in my opinion, from having been sufficiently examined and made out."[7] The causes of prostitution are to be found, he said, "in the sex-appetite, in idleness, the love of dress and luxury, in habits of drinking, in the decreasing number of marriages, and the stringency of the marriage laws in most countries; but above all, in the low wages and want of education of the female sex."[8]

Drysdale, like his mentor, John Stuart Mill, believed fervently in "the liberty of women to use their industry and talents to the best advantages for themselves."[9] The solution to prostitution, he proclaimed, lay in providing more job opportunities for women. He joined with a small group of other medical men in the 1860s in opening a small college to teach medicine to women. In 1870, he wrote a pamphlet on *Medicine as a Profession for Women*. One of his students paid tribute to his courage in the undertaking on the occasion of his funeral in 1907:

> This was [that is, teaching medicine to women] at that moment a most unpopular step with the rest of the medical profession. Only the most courageous physicians dared take this work in hand. Dr. Drysdale did more than any others, for he not only lectured to women students, but in the absence of any regular hospital courses then open, he allowed his women students to attend on his practice at several hospitals.[10]

His interest in the social problems of prostitution and venereal diseases led him to join with others in calling for repeal of the Contagious Diseases Acts of 1864, 1866, and 1869. The acts were designed primarily to protect the health of Her Majesty's military troops. They were applicable only in the area of designated naval and military bases and required prostitutes in those areas to submit to medical examination. Women found to be diseased were detained in the hospital for three months, later increased to six months and then nine months. One member of the Malthusian League claimed Drysdale was "*the* leading medical opponent" in the battle to get the hated acts off the books.[11] He and others who shared his views agitated for years for repeal of the acts and were jubilant in 1886 when the decrees were finally revoked.

Drysdale's interest in Malthusianism also became apparent in the 1860s. In 1864, for example, when he read the first paper to be presented before the newly formed London Dialectical Society, his subject was Malthusianism. He served as treasurer for the Dialectical Society for almost thirty years.

His interest in the Malthusian question coupled with his medical specialties led him to offer to testify for the defense in the Bradlaugh-Besant trial. Only three witnesses appeared in the trial on behalf of the defendants: Drysdale; his wife, Alice Vickery-Drysdale; and Henry George Bohn, a London publisher.[12] Drysdale was called upon as a medical authority to give his opinion of the Knowlton pamphlet. Bradlaugh pointed out that Drysdale, "a man known equally in England, in America, and on the Continent as a physician of eminence and as an author of many scientific works . . . considered the work [of Dr. Knowlton] a most excellent work, written by a scientific man, writing with a full knowledge of his subject, and writing with that care and accuracy characteristic of a scientific man."[13]

Mrs. Drysdale was called primarily to testify in connection with her medical studies on midwifery and diseases of women, in modern terminology, gynecology. A good part of her testimony was devoted to the dangers of over-lactation, that is, the tendency of lower-class women to continue nursing babies for as long as two years in the belief that such a practice warded off conception. "Over-lactation is no preventive whatever against pregnancy," she proclaimed, and, in fact, "the result is very great weakness and general debility . . . the fruitful source of other diseases."[14] Both she and her husband testified as to the detrimental effects on the health of women from having too many babies too closely spaced and the health problems faced by large, poor families.

At the time of the Bradlaugh-Besant trial, Alice Vickery had studied medicine for six years and was a fourth-year medical student in the School of Medicine in Paris at a time when women in science as a whole were a rarity. She was born 15 September 1844 in Swinbridge, Devonshire, the daughter of John Vickery and Frances Mary Leah of Brierly Hall, Yorkshire.[15] When the family moved to London, Alice began her medical-related studies and became the first woman to qualify as a chemist of the Pharmaceutical Society of Great Britain.[16] For two years, probably in the early 1870s, she studied midwifery and diseases of women at the London Women's Medical College where C. R. Drysdale lectured. At the same time, she practiced at the City of London Lying-in Hospital and received a certificate for midwifery from the Obstetrical Society of London. It was probably during this time that she met and perhaps married C. R. Drysdale.[17] For several years, she attended medical school in Paris. On 11 June 1880, she became one of only five women in England with a medical degree when she was enrolled as a member of the Royal College of Physicians in Ireland (Dublin) and began a lifelong career of service to the sick and poor in London. Though only her efforts on behalf of the Malthusian League interest us here, she was also a leader in the English feminist movement and a well-known doctor in London with an extensive practice, especially among the poor. She lived to the ripe old age of eighty-four and was one of the few members of the Malthusian League to live during its entire life span (1877–1927). She died 12 January 1929 at Brighton where she had made her home during the preceding five years and was buried in her husband's grave at Brookwood Cemetery, south of London.

Charles Robert and Alice Vickery Drysdale were the undisputed leaders of the Malthusian League until the former's death in 1907, but their efforts would have necessarily come to naught if others had not participated in the organization and work of the league. Its members, however, were never large in number. The group claimed 1,224 on its membership roll in 1879. That proved to be its peak. The number dwindled to under a thousand in the 1890s but rose once again in the early 1920s to 1,213.[18] A few devoted members made up in enthusiasm and perseverance, however, for the numbers the organization lacked.

The rules of the league provided for a president, vice-presidents, a corresponding secretary and a financial secretary, a solicitor, auditors, and a council consisting of twenty members selected annually by the membership and a representative from each branch of the league. Annie Besant served as corresponding secretary until 1880 when she resigned to continue her studies at London University. She was replaced by J. K. Page. William Hammond Reynolds took the office of financial secretary, replacing Robert G. Hember, and continued to serve until shortly before his death in September 1911.

Aside from the Drysdales, no one individual contributed more to the operation of the organization than Reynolds. He was more of a managing director than a secretary, handling most of the league's correspondence, all of its financial transactions, and the distribution of its literature. He was a quiet man who preferred to work in the office rather than on the platform. His interest in secularist circles in the 1870s spurred Annie Besant to invite him to join the council of the newly organized Malthusian League in 1877. In his own quiet manner, he may well have been more effective in spreading the message of neo-Malthusianism than any other member of the organization. "It was, indeed, principally by the circulation of literature," George Standring wrote, "that Mr. Reynolds successfully endeavoured to promote our cause, and he took but little interest in the organization of lectures or public meetings on the subject."[19] Reynolds advertised Malthusian literature in the organs of the press that would allow such advertisements and then responded to those who answered his ads. Being a publisher, he advertised, of course, not only league materials but other Malthusian literature that he had to sell. In 1889, he mentioned at the annual meeting of the league that he received about three thousand letters a month. Most of these came from areas within the British Isles, but his efforts were by no means limited to England. In 1896, he offered to exchange unused foreign stamps for equal value in English stamps from such countries of the British Empire as New Zealand, Australia, Canada, Natal, the Orange Free State, Egypt, Trinidad, Tasmania, and "a few various."[20]

After Reynolds's retirement as secretary of the league, Charles Vickery Drysdale and his wife shared that office until 1921, except for a brief period from 1916 to 1918 when Binnie

Dunlop served while C. V. Drysdale entered government service for the duration of World War I. From 1921 to 1923, Bessie Ingham Drysdale filled the office alone.

The league used the familiar practice of listing a number of individuals as vice-presidents in order to imply widespread and diverse support for the organization. The first tabulation of vice-presidents appeared in the September 1879 issue of *The Malthusian* and contained the names of nine individuals including four foreigners and one labor leader:

Dr. Stille (Hanover)	Mrs. Croly
Touzeau Parris	Samuel Van Houten (Holland)
M. Yves Guyot (Paris)	George Andersen
M. A. Talandier (Paris)	John Bryson, president, North
W. J. Birch	Miners' Association

By December 1880, the list was enlarged to sixteen with the addition of four more foreign vice-presidents: Senor Aldecoa, director of Government Charities, Madrid; Mr. Carl V. Gerritsen, Holland; Mr. Murugesa Mudalier, Madras; and Dr. Giovanni Tari, Naples. Mrs. Annie Besant, Mr. Charles Bradlaugh, M.P., and Dr. Alice Vickery were also added as vice-presidents. Over the years, the list changed from time to time as members died or dropped out and others agreed to be associated with the organization. By July 1889, for example, fourteen of the sixteen names on the list in 1880 were still there. Mrs. Croly and John Bryson had been dropped during the early 1880s. By May 1908, however, out of twenty names only five of those listed in 1880 remained: Aldecoa, Andersen, Van Houten, Mudalier, and Stille.

The vice-presidents list was shortened in 1914 when the league decided to omit the names of foreigners. Sauerkraut was not the only casualty in the anti-German, or antiforeign, hysteria during the second decade of the twentieth century. "Our readers will notice," the editor of *The Malthusian* commented in July 1914, "that the list of Vice-Presidents has been shortened by the omission of a number of distinguished foreign supporters, who formerly figured in it. Although we have been honoured to have these names amongst our supporters, it was felt that their number gave some apparent colour to the charge that our movement was unpatriotic."[21]

The real work of the Malthusian League was done by the devoted members of the council of the organization. This small circle met faithfully every month for over twenty years. The minutes of the meetings were published in *The National Reformer* until the league began publication of its own monthly journal, *The Malthusian*. Rarely was the full council in attendance, however, after the first few meetings. Those present varied from around five to around ten with Annie Besant, Mrs. J. Grout, C. Bradlaugh, J. K. Page, T. Parris, W. H. Reynolds, George Standring, J. Swaagman, E. Truelove, and, of course, C. R. Drysdale among the most faithful in early years. Here again, those among the faithful changed somewhat over the years, though members like Reynolds, Page, Truelove, and later T. O. Bonser were consistently loyal. Others who attended during the 1880s and 1890s included Mrs. Heatherley, Mr. and Mrs. A. P. Busch, Thornton Smith, Angus Macintosh, John Rothwell, G. A. Gaskell, and, on occasion, a visitor or two. For twenty years, the council gathered regularly every month, but by the late 1890s its meetings became more and more sporadic. By the end of 1899, *The Malthusian* no longer reported the minutes of council sessions. The meetings probably continued, at least when needed, but if minutes were kept, they have now vanished. The league was at its lowest point in the late 1890s. Not only was its council less active but also the group failed to hold annual meetings for the years 1897 to 1899, missing only three such meetings, however, in the entire period from 1878, its first, until 1927, its fiftieth.

The league adopted seven *Principles* that served as its philosophical platform. The first four principles sounded like quotations from T. R. Malthus:

1. That population has a constant tendency to increase beyond the means of subsistence.
2. That the checks which counteract this tendency are resolvable into positive or life-destroying, and prudential or birth-restricting.

65

3. That the positive or life-destroying checks comprehend the premature death of children and adults by disease, starvation, war, and infanticide.
4. That the prudential or birth-restricting checks consist in the limitation of offspring by abstention from marriage, or by prudence after marriage.

Numbers five and six revealed the influence of George Drysdale:

5. That prolonged abstention from marriage—as advocated by Malthus—is productive of many diseases, and of much sexual vice; early marriage, on the contrary, tends to ensure sexual purity, domestic comfort, social happiness, and individual health; but it is a grave social offence for men and women to bring into the world more children than they can adequately house, feed, clothe, and educate.
6. That over-population is the most fruitful source of pauperism, ignorance, crime, and disease.

The last was merely a restatement of the objectives of the organization:

7. That the full and open discussion of the Population Question is a matter of vital moment to society, and such discussion should be absolutely unfettered by fear of legal penalties.

Since the prosecutions of Charles Bradlaugh, Annie Besant, and Edward Truelove prompted the organization of the Malthusian League, it is not surprising that the group stressed in its objectives the need (1) "to agitate for abolition of all penalties on the public discussion of the Population Question, and to obtain such a statutory definition as shall render it impossible, in the future, to bring such discussions within the scope of the common law as a misdemeanour," and (2) "to spread among the people, by all practicable means, a knowledge of the law of population, of its consequences, and of its bearing upon human conduct and morals." In keeping with the first objective, the league council sent fifty-three petitions to the House of Commons from July to August 1877, "pressing for such an alteration of the law as to obscene libel, as shall prevent publications dealing with scientific checks to population from coming within the scope of the common law as a misdemeanor."[22] Nothing came of the effort, but league members continued to write to members of Parliament in an attempt to carry out their first objective.

The league employed several techniques in pursuing its second objective, the dissemination of Malthusian information. The annual public meetings plus other such meetings as the council saw fit provided an open forum for the presentation of Malthusian ideas. Over the years, league members gave literally thousands of lectures either under the direct sponsorship of the organization or as guest speakers before other groups. Some of the members wrote letters to medical and scientific societies, to individuals in Parliament, and to periodicals and newspapers. Few journals in the 1880s, however, would include letters advocating birth restriction in their columns. In its Fifth Annual Report, the council sadly commented on the attitude of the press toward the Malthusian question:

> Except in the *"National Reformer,"* which has always consistently advocated the recognition of the population difficulty as a question of pressing importance, in the *"Republican,"* and two or three of the most advanced radical papers, the question continues to be ignored, or only referred to partially and indirectly, as for instance when emigration is recommended to relieve the over-stocked labor market.[23]

Perhaps the most effective technique of propaganda employed by the league was the distribution of Malthusian tracts, leaflets, and pamphlets. On 2 August 1877, the league council designated a subcommittee consisting of C. R. Drysdale, Alice Vickery, Annie Besant, and Messrs. Hember, Shearer, and Seyler to consider what publications the organization should issue and "to report as to the best means of advocating the principles of the League."[24] At the next council meeting (23 August), the Propagandist Sub-Committee, as the small group dubbed itself, recommended distribution of *The Principle of Population* written

67

by C. R. Drysdale and designated it as Malthusian League Tract No. 1. By the end of 1880, the league had published ten tracts ranging in length from four to twelve pages each.[25] In addition, the organization also distributed a number of one-sheet leaflets printed on both sides. Precisely how many leaflets were published by the league during its fifty years of existence is impossible to determine. Between 1877 and 1880, at least six such broadsheets were prepared, but the bulk of them were apparently issued in the first years of the twentieth century prior to World War I. The organization also issued a number of pamphlets from time to time as money allowed and the need arose. There were at least fifteen published in the twentieth century.

Literally millions of tracts, leaflets, and pamphlets were printed for and distributed by the Malthusian League during its fifty years of activity. David V. Glass attempted to make at least a rough estimate of the circulation of league literature and testified "it would be reasonable to conclude that, excluding *The Malthusian,* the League itself issued about three million pamphlets and leaflets between 1879 and the end of 1921."[26] Add to this at least another million leaflets printed and distributed by the organization in 1925 in a campaign to arouse the public to support the giving of birth-control information at government welfare centers. There is, of course, no way to assess with accuracy the effect that this large distribution of neo-Malthusian literature had on English society as a whole, but it would undoubtedly be erroneous to assume it had none.

The Malthusian carried advertisements of not only materials published specifically under the auspices of the league but also other works, written by members or friends of the organization, that furthered its objectives. This Malthusian literature, though not directly connected with the league, constitutes, then, an important part of its propaganda activities. Annie Besant's *Law of Population,* for example, published in 1877, was widely advertised and distributed by the group though it was not an official league publication. When Mrs. Besant withdrew the book from circulation in the early 1890s, George Standring, who printed the league's material after the demise of the Freethought Publishing Company, wrote a pamphlet in cooperation with William Reynolds to replace the Besant publication. The new book, entitled *The Malthusian Handbook, Designed to Induce Married People to Limit Their Families Within Their Means,* first appeared in 1893 and consisted of an introduction and five chapters. It contained a restatement of Malthus's law of population, a description of the work of the Malthusian League, and a section on possible "prudential checks."[27] The checks described were of two kinds. The first were "those in which success depends upon *self*-control" and included the practice of withdrawal, or *coitus interruptus,* and "abstinence from intercourse during a certain period."[28] The second type of check were "those in which *mechanical appliances* were used," including the "sheath, douche, sponge, and pessaries of various kinds." Unlike Mrs. Besant, Standring declared the sheath to be a reliable contraceptive check. *"If sheaths of good quality (not necessarily expensive) be used, and reasonable care taken to avoid accidental breakage, this check is CERTAIN* [the italics are Standring's]." One of the pessaries mentioned by Standring was the diaphragm, unknown when Besant wrote her book in the 1870s. It was invented in the early 1880s by a German doctor and professor of anatomy, Wilhelm Peter Mensinga. It was used in the late nineteenth century in Dr. Aletta Jacob's clinics in Holland and thus earned the misleading nickname, "Dutch pessary." Standring also mentioned a pessary consisting "of a small cone of cacao-butter, charged with quinine. The pessary is inserted a few minutes before connection takes place; the quinine, being liberated by the dissolution of the fatty substance, destroys the vitality of the seminal fluid."[29] A listing of the officers and rules of the Malthusian League filled the last page of the book.

The Malthusian League advertised Standring's *Malthusian Handbook* in the pages of *The Malthusian* for years, but until 1913 the organization itself refused to disseminate practical information on how to avoid conception. It was taken to task many times for this serious omission in its propaganda campaign. As early as May 1881 a correspondent criticized the league for stressing economic theory and ignoring the need for practical information:

> I am well convinced [he wrote] that . . . the vast majority of married people among the lower classes regard a large family as a misfortune which they would gladly avoid if they knew how. It seems to me, therefore, that the efforts of the Malthusian League would meet with far greater success if they were directed to conveying to those concerned the knowledge of a thoroughly reliable "preventive check."[30]

Another reader wrote in 1881: "What is really wanted . . . is plain and practical advice. Cannot this be conveyed to all by means of a leaflet enclosed in the *Malthusian,* or a notice stating where such can be obtained, or a reliable work?"[31] *The Labour Standard,* a newspaper that in its first issue dedicated itself "to defend and advance the interest of Labour," might well have been speaking of the Malthusian League when it commented skeptically:

> There are plenty of philanthropists ready with fine theories for the amelioration of the condition of the working man; but the number of practical men who reduce their theories to practice are few.[32]

In the 1880s, the league referred whose who requested practical information about contraception to Annie Besant's *Law of Population.* For example, the December 1880 issue of *The Malthusian* carried a discreet editorial notice that "Mr. Mason, Leeds, will find the point he seeks information about in Mrs. Besant's pamphlet, 'The Law of Population.'"[33] But at least one reader retorted: "Mrs. Besant's 'Law of population' is practical, but not practical enough to be appreciated to the full by the working classes of this neighborhood."[34] The letter came from Sudbury, Suffolk.

Even in public lectures, league members were beseiged for information. In its annual report to the membership in 1882, the league council remarked:

> It is worth noticing that at some of the lectures at Working Men's Clubs the audience seemed to consider the economic side of the question—the tendency of our high birth rate to keep down wages and profits—as no longer a debatable subject wishing only to know in what way prudence might best be practised.[35]

The criticisms and requests continued:

You may preach for eternity upon the duty of moral restraint, and you will effect—just nothing! Spread the knowledge of the preventive checks to conception, and you will effect—everything! Tell the people they must not love, and they will laugh the bitter laugh of hatred at your teaching! Point out to them, how they may love, without bringing ruin and despair upon themselves, and your work is done![36]

Apparently, however, the league leaders feared that if the organization offered practical information under its own sponsorship, the group might be prosecuted. On several occasions, C. R. Drysdale, as editor of *The Malthusian,* responded to requests for contraceptive advice in a manner similar to the following:

This question has been several times debated by the Council, and in view of the fact that at the present time it is illegal to publish the information referred to, it has been felt that it would not be right to implicate the members of the League conjointly. It has been thought best to leave the imparting of such information to each individual member on his or her own responsibility, and it is well known that every member of the Council is in the habit of giving the required information when suitable opportunities occur.[37]

Nevertheless, letters requesting information continued to beseige *The Malthusian* throughout the nineteenth century. "The 'poorer class'," wrote one reader in 1891, "would only be too glad 'to imitate their thoughtful neighbors in the West' [of London] if they did but know how."[38] Another wrote:

I suggest that the Malthusian League would do well to prepare leaflets in extremely simple language, suitable for distribution (by women) among working-class women. The Malthusian practice spreads among the better-educated, but not among the proletariat, who most need it. They cannot understand the current books and pamphlets. They need something like a primer in style; and, above all, it is the young mothers who need to be advised—by women specially adapted by their tact and discretion.[39]

The pamphlets most generally recommended by the league were Mrs. Besant's *Law of Population* until she withdrew it from publication in the early 1890s; Standring's *Malthusian Handbook;* and Henry Arthur Allbutt's *The Wife's Handbook,* first published in 1886.[40]

It was not until 1913 that the league published its own book of practical information, *Hygienic Methods of Family Limitation.* By that time, however, other individuals and groups were beginning to push for family limitation and many books dealing with sexual topics were readily available. The reticence of the organization in giving practical information instead of, or in addition to, economic theory undoubtedly curtailed its effectiveness in reaching the very groups that it proclaimed should adopt family limitation—the poorer classes. Part of the problem was, of course, merely lack of adequate knowledge about reliable contraceptives, but the group's reticence in making what information was known available could only have compounded the problem. The many letters received by the editor of *The Malthusian* from members of the working class indicate they would have welcomed more information on how to avoid having large families. Nevertheless, various members of the league worked hard in the late nineteenth century to spread the message of the organization either by word of mouth or by distributing Malthusian literature. We have already noted the efforts of William H. Reynolds, financial secretary of the league from 1880 to 1911. Others deserving of recognition include George Standring, T. O. Bonser, and Joseph Williamson.

George Standring was a young man, age twenty-two, when the Malthusian League was organized; but he had already been a rationalist or freethinker since he was eighteen and had served as secretary of the National Secular Society for two years.[41] He was only thirteen when he entered the family printing business and by 1875 was ready to start his own journal in order to espouse his republican views unhampered by editorial censorship. "The perusal of Thomas Paine's 'Rights of Man' had convinced me," he said, "that the monarchical form of government was a mischievous institution, and was doomed to final extinction."[42] His periodical was first called *The Republican Chronicle,* then in 1879 *The Republican,* and finally in 1888 *The Radical.* Standring made his living in a printing business located at 7/8 Finsbury Street, E. C., in London, where he was born and lived his entire life.[43] His leisure time was devoted to numerous secularist, neo-Malthusian, and, after 1884, socialistic activities. He lectured widely for all three movements and printed both *The Malthusian* and the *Fabian News*.[44] He joined the Fabian Society in 1893 and served on its executive committee from 1893 to 1908 and from 1909 to 1911.

Standring was one of those who stood midway between neo-Malthusians and socialists in the late nineteenth century and worked to effect a compromise between the two. To his way of thinking, the two should complement each other. One could not rid the country of poverty without the other. He opposed socialists, such as Henry Hyndman and Herbert Burrows, who maligned neo-Malthusianism relentlessly. He also berated *The Malthusian,* however, for being "more or less distinctly anti-Collectivist in tone" and criticized Bradlaugh for his "strongly Individualistic temperament" and his "anti-Socialist bias."

> I, speaking as a Malthusian and a Socialist, . . . maintain that . . . our *object* is clearly the same. We all—Malthusians and Socialists alike—desire to get rid of poverty, the bane of practically all civilised States, the source from which flow so many dreadful evils. . . . The Socialist endeavors to get rid of poverty by remodelling the moral and economic bases of society. He seeks to substitute co-operation for competition, to reorganise social institutions, so that men may help one another towards a common end—that is to say, the general well being—instead of striving one against the other for personal gain and advantage.[45]

Standring favored such Fabian-proposed reforms as a minimum wage, the feeding of school children, and the provision of proper housing; but none of these could succeed, he maintained, unless a limit were set on the size of families. A minimum wage would have to be based on the size of a family in order to be effective, and the state's ability to feed children or provide adequate housing was not boundless. Socialistic reforms must be accompanied by family limitation in order to be effective. This was Standring's position, but it was shared by only a few in both movements. On the whole, the two groups remained in conflict in spite of efforts by individuals such as Standring to effect a compromise and stimulate cooperation.

Not surprisingly, Standring is one of those who urged the Malthusian League from its earliest years to play down economic theory and stress the benefits of family limitation from the viewpoint of the individual worker. In 1919 he led a quiet revolt against Charles Vickery Drysdale's refusal to follow this recommendation and began publishing a short-lived periodical called simply *Birth Control*. He omitted Malthusian economic doctrine on the whole and stressed the health and financial benefits to be gained by individual families when they practiced family limitation. He never ceased, however, to lend his support to the Malthusian League, whether from a business viewpoint or from a sense of loyalty to the ideals of the group. In 1919, Standring himself described his activities on behalf of the Malthusian League:

> In 1881 I gave my first lecture on the subject [of neo-Malthusianism] in Glasgow; and in the winter of 1914 or 1915 concluded (so far) my oratorical labours by speaking in rain and snow from the tail-board of a van in the New Cut, Lambeth. The intervening period of thirty-five years contained two public debates with Herbert Burrows (one of these at the Hall of Science); innumerable lectures and speeches, all more or less bad; many articles in my *Republican* and other journals, and letters to the press, etc.; besides discreet, but by no means fruitless, propagandist work in the Fabian Society and other bodies.[46]

T. Owen Bonser, an Oxford graduate and a retired fellow of Clare College, Cambridge, served the Malthusian League in both life and death. He supported the league with money and ministry from its earliest years. He served as a walking missionary for the organization throughout England during the 1880s and early 1890s until his health prohibited it. In its 1888 annual report, the league council congratulated Bonser on his "most successful lecturing tour through Manchester, Bolton, Rochdale, Oldham, Hanley (Staffordshire), and other midland towns."[47] In 1889, Bonser made a similar tour through the southwest of England and Wales.[48] "He was accustomed during the summer months," Standring wrote, "to make long walking tours through the country, talking to the peasantry and distributing Malthusian leaflets en route. This was simple humdrum work but how effective it was!"[49] William Reynolds claimed he could always tell where and when Bonser was on one of his walking tours by the number of letters received from various areas. When Bonser died in 1898, Reynolds bemoaned "that subscriptions to the League had been lessened owing to the death of that lamented gentleman."[50]

In his will, Bonser bequeathed eight hundred pounds to the Malthusian League. For several years prior to his death, the league had been running a small annual deficit. There was even talk, as early as 1895, of discontinuing *The Malthusian*. The council decided instead to abandon the annual public meetings and struggle to keep the journal alive "since it formed the means of keeping the party together, and for communicating to the members of the League notices of meetings and information as to the progress of the movement in Great Britain and abroad."[51] Consequently, there were no annual meetings in 1896, 1897, and 1898. With Bonser's legacy, however, the league was able to resume its meetings and reestablish itself on a firm financial basis. In July 1899, the financial secretary, Reynolds, reported "the fund of the League . . . in a very satisfactory condition" as a result of the bequest.[52] But for Bonser's generosity the Malthusian League might well have perished by the end of the 1890s. With his final act of loyalty to the group, he gave it renewed life and energy.

The misadventures of Bonser's fellow Malthusian missionary, Mr. Joseph Williamson of Truro, Cornwall, are somewhat amusing but also perhaps indicative of social reaction to public discussion of family limitation in late nineteenth-century England. Williamson was a strolling minstrel ardently convinced that Malthusian doctrine was correct or that pamphlets advocating family limitation would sell. In August 1886, he appeared in the streets of Gainsborough in Lincolnshire playing his violin and hawking H. A. Allbutt's *Wife's Handbook,* a pamphlet highly touted by the Malthusian League since its publication earlier in the year. He was detained by the local constabulary; convicted by Mr. E. Pearson, the presiding magistrate, for "selling indecent books"; and hauled off to Lincoln gaol to serve fourteen days with hard labor. Upon his release, he immediately wrote to William Reynolds to replenish the stock of materials taken from him.[53] He continued on to Goole where, thinking he had been arrested in Gainsborough for selling literature in the streets, he decided to sell only in his lodgings. He did, however, sell one copy to the proprietor of the local bakery, Samuel Thompson, who promised not to get him in trouble for doing so. He then sold several copies to women who came to his door requesting them. He was arrested immediately after selling a copy of Allbutt's pamphlet to two women "about 40 or 50 years of age" not realizing a policeman, P. E. Dodsworth, was concealed behind a wall nearby observing the purchase. The baker gave evidence against Williamson at the hearing, and he was sentenced to another fourteen days in prison. He sent a detailed report to the Malthusian League Council of the proceedings and concluded, "I was taken and sentenced on September 25th. Please send me another lot of Malthusian tracts and leaflets."[54] Apparently, he managed to avoid any further prosecution until 1888 when he wrote of his encounter with the authorities in King's Lynn. He had distributed only one Malthusian tract, having just gotten to town, when a local officer confronted him, "accused him of drinking, tore up his license to play music," and took him to the mayor. He was ordered to leave town immediately.[55]

In late 1889, W. H. Reynolds, acting for the Malthusian League, employed Williamson to distribute Malthusian literature in Ireland. He was instructed to avoid trouble as far as possible but if taken into custody to engage a solicitor and fight the case. The league promised financial support. Again, he was not long in running afoul of the law. On a Saturday afternoon in early January 1890, he was accosted by "a very tall policeman" in the town of Lurgan and hauled unceremoniously and abusively into the police station where he encountered epithets of "low scamp" and "scoundrel."[56] The clerk on duty, however, was not of the opinion that Williamson's supply of literature was indecent and refused to have anything to do with the case. The local magistrate was also reticent to rule on the matter and favored sending the offender off to Liverpool, but Williamson put up such a fuss that they finally decided just to run him out of town. They put him on a train for Lisburn and washed their hands of the whole affair. Never one to be idle, Williamson

76

distributed leaflets on the train and at the station in Lisburn, but the opposition he encountered there came from the townspeople themselves rather than from the police.[57] He continued on his way undaunted, however, and traversed most of Ireland during the early months of 1890.

In 1897, *The Malthusian* reported that "the General," as Williamson had been dubbed, was still "carrying on a Malthusian tract propaganda."[58] In 1902, he continued his efforts in Canterbury, Chatham, and other towns and villages in Kent, giving away large numbers of old *Malthusians* and other tracts of the league supplied to him by Reynolds.[59] It is perhaps significant that both T. O. Bonser and Joseph Williamson carried on a similar type of Malthusian missionary work for years in the British Isles without the former ever encountering difficulties with the law. "Not once," Bonser commented, "was [I] . . . interrupted or spoken uncivilly to."[60] But, then, as George Standring pointed out in 1909, it was never clear whether Williamson's "terms of imprisonment were due to his propagandist efforts or to his violin-playing."[61] Standring implied that it was perhaps Williamson's antics that got him in trouble, more so than the neo-Malthusian literature he was selling.

We cannot recognize the efforts of every individual who contributed both time and energy to distributing the Malthusian League's message, but some came up with rather ingenious methods of marketing. Gavazzi King suggested placing Malthusian tracts in railway carriages, in newsrooms, and even in prayer books. He confessed to pursuing all these methods in the city of Edinburgh.[62] Perhaps more effective was the door-to-door campaign conducted by G. A. Gaskell and Mr. Little in Bradford, Yorkshire. They covered the poorer districts of Bradford street by street in 1879 distributing Malthusian tracts and leaflets and giving advice when asked. They covered the town in three to four months and encouraged other league members to follow their lead in other communities.[63] Another technique developed by the league was to send Malthusian literature to the parents of newly born children whose names were obtained from listings in the local newspapers. Reynolds even tried to enlist the services of a woman to canvass door to door offering counseling and literature. He ran an ad in *The Malthusian:* "WANTED: A LADY MISSIONARY to work from house to house. Salary and commission. Apply W. H. Reynolds, Secretary of the League."[64] Apparently there were no takers.

The major piece of literature distributed by the league was its own journal, *The Malthusian.* In its first years, the Malthusian League had to depend upon other periodicals to advertise its activities and to publish neo-Malthusian articles. At one of its first meetings, for example, the league council agreed to ask *The National Reformer,* published by Bradlaugh; the *Republican Chronicle;* and the *Labour News and Employment Advertiser,* a small four-page weekly that primarily reported job vacancies, to act as literary organs of the group.[65] Of the three, *The National Reformer* was the most faithful in reporting league activities until the organization got its own journal. In January 1879, C. R. Drysdale proposed at a council meeting that the league issue its own paper, entitled *The Malthusian,* monthly at a price of one pence to begin in February.[66] The first edition of the February issue was soon sold out and a second edition was ordered. The journal was first printed and published by the Freethought Publishing Company at 28, Stonecutter Street, E.C., under the imprint of the Malthusian League. A suggestion from George Standring in late 1879 prompted C. R. Drysdale, the editor, to add the words "A Crusade Against Poverty" as a subtitle for the journal. With the demise of the Freethought Publishing Company in 1891, the printing of the eight-page periodical passed to Standring.

C. R. Drysdale served as editor of *The Malthusian* until his death in 1907. His son, Charles Vickery Drysdale, assumed the editorship aided by his wife, Bessie Ingham Drysdale. They served until 1923 except for two short periods, one during World War I when Binnie Dunlop assumed the position while C. V. Drysdale served in a government position, and the second in the fall of 1922 when Arthur J. S. Preece filled the position for about three months. In 1923, Robert B. Kerr assumed the editorship and retained it until his death in 1951 when C. V. Drysdale once again tried to keep the periodical alive. By the end of 1952, however, no further issues appeared.

The format of *The Malthusian* changed little in its first thirty years of publication. In January 1909, however, the publishers added a cover to the eight pages of printed material in an attempt to make the magazine more attractive and thus interest more readers. The practice was abandoned for a short time during World War I due to the paper shortage but was resumed in 1919. In January 1922, the name of the journal was changed to *The New Generation* in keeping with a change in the name of the organization as a whole. From 1922 to 1925, the Malthusian League was known as the New Generation League. The alteration in title was indicative of an effort on the part of the league leaders to give the organization a new image in an attempt to retain its leadership in the burgeoning birth-control movement. But a name change did not effect a change in the basic position of the organization. Malthusian economic doctrine remained its crumbling foundation. By 1925, the birth-control movement had obviously passed into the hands of new leadership , and the organization reassumed its original name. Its journal, however, remained *The New Generation* until 1949 when the old title, *The Malthusian,* was restored. After 1927, R. B. Kerr disclaimed any connection between the now defunct Malthusian League and *The New Generation.* The January 1928 issue opened with Editor Kerr's manifesto: "This paper, which has hitherto belonged to the Malthusian League, is now an independent organ. It will, however, stand for the same principles as it has always done."[67] Long-time members of the league could thus continue to read the journal and feel no discomfort.

Distribution of *The Malthusian* was always a problem. Repeatedly, George Standring took the initiative in prodding league members to take it upon themselves to increase the circulation of the periodical. Get your newsagent to order a dozen or so copies of *The Malthusian,* he prompted, and guarantee to purchase any copies not sold by the end of the month.[68] The response to his behest could not have been overwhelming. By 1895, he was prompting members to leave two or three copies *gratuitously* with their newsagents and to distribute a dozen copies themselves.[69] Perhaps the amazing thing is that at a time when small, special interest journals were born and died in profusion in late nineteenth-century England, *The Malthusian* survived in spite of low circulation, dwindling interest, and frequently occurring financial crises. That both the league and its journal did survive for at least fifty years can be attributed to the perseverence and financial support of a few devoted members. The primary credit for the durability of the organization, however, must go to the Drysdale family. When the league was officially disbanded in 1927, R. B. Kerr, editor of *The New Generation,* recognized the tenacity and constancy with which the Drysdales had pursued their cause:

> For seventy years the Drysdale family has headed the movement for birth control. When the first Drysdale wrote in 1854, there were about half a dozen people in the world who believed in birth control. Now there are millions. During all that period the family has not only given its time and labour to the movement, but has spent at least £10,000 of its own money, and never got a penny in return. There has been no greater movement in history than the birth control movement, and no greater example of family devotion to a cause than the one we have recorded.[70]

1. C. R. Drysdale, "The Malthusian League," *The National Reformer* 30, no. 12 (2 September 1877): 599.

2. Margaret Sanger, *My Fight For Birth Control* (New York: Farrar and Rinehart, Inc., 1931), p. 278.

3. J. Rothwell called C. R. Drysdale the "Malthusian King" at the Ninth Annual Meeting of the Malthusian League. *The Malthusian* 10, no. 7 (July 1886): 51.

4. "Death of Dr. C. R. Drysdale," *The Malthusian* 32, no. 1 (January 1908): 1.

5. C. R. Drysdale, "Ireland in the Queen's Reign," *The Malthusian* 22, no. 9 (September 1898): 65.

6. Charles Robert Drysdale, M.D., *The Nature and Treatment of Syphilis and the Other So-called "Contagious Diseases."* 4th Ed. (London: Baillière, Tindall, and Cox, 20, King William Street, Strand, 1880). The first edition appeared in 1863. C. R. Drysdale, *Prostitution Medically Considered With Some of Its Social Aspects,* a paper read at the Harveian Medical Society of London, January 1866 (London: Robert Hardwicke, 192, Piccadilly, 1866).

7. Drysdale, *Prostitution Medically Considered,* pp. 13–14. On this point, Drysdale seems to have been somewhat naive. He goes on to suggest that a possible cause of the sterility may be "over-exercise of the female organs." Ibid., p. 14. Never once does he mention the possibility of their having used contraceptives.

8. Ibid., p. 32.

9. Ibid., p. 27.

10. "Memorial Number," *The Malthusian* 32, no. 2 (February 1908): 13. Mrs. Fenwick Miller, the author of the statement, was a long-time member of the Malthusian League.

11. Ibid.

12. Mr. Bohn was called to testify that books on physiology, similar to Knowlton's, had been used in English schools for years. *The Queen v. Charles Bradlaugh and Annie Besant* (London: Freethought Publishing Company, n.d. [1877]), pp. 228–30.

13. Ibid., p. 234.

14. Ibid., p. 218.

15. "Vickery, Alice Drysdale," Record Card. The Royal College of Physicians of Ireland, Dublin, Ireland.

16. "A Pioneer Passes," *The New Generation* 8, no. 2 (February 1929): 17. Also see *The Queen v. Bradlaugh and Besant,* p. 215.

17. A real mystery exists as to the legal relationship of Alice Vickery and Charles Robert Drysdale, who was fifteen years older than she. Their son, Charles Vickery Drysdale, was reputedly born in 1874, but there is no record of the birth in the General Register Office, Somerset House, London. Nor is there a record of the marriage of Alice Vickery and C. R. Drysdale. A young oriental student in London doing research on the feminist activities of C. R. Drysdale suggested to me that Alice Vickery and C. R. had never been married. She had no substantial evidence but had heard a rumor to this effect from Mrs. J. H. Levy, elderly widow of a long-time member of the Malthusian League and friend of the Drysdales. I was understandably skeptical, especially in view of both C. R. Drysdale's and Alice Vickery's persistent defense of monogamous marriage, and dismissed the suggestion as mere hearsay. As my own researches continued, however, and no proof of either a marriage or birth came to light, I became somewhat less incredulous. Victor Robinson, author of *Pioneers of Birth Control in England and America* (1919) and the son of William J. Robinson, a prominent leader in the American birth-control movement and a friend of the Drysdales, described the 1877 Bradlaugh-Besant trial and concluded that "after testifying at the trial, Miss Alice Vickery and Dr. Charles R. Drysdale were married." Victor Robinson. *Pioneers of Birth Control in England and America* (New York: Voluntary Parenthood League, 206 Broadway, 1919), pp. 52–53. Yet their son was allegedly born in 1874. In 1922, C. Killick Millard, M.D., served as chairman of the Medical Section of the Fifth International Neo-Malthusian and Birth Control Conference, spoke of Alice Vickery and the Bradlaugh-Besant trial, and remarked that "it was at that epoch-making trial, I believe, that she made the acquaintance of Dr. C. R. Drysdale" and "in due course" became Mrs. Drysdale. *Report of the Fifth International Neo-Malthusian and Birth Control Conference* (London: William Heinemann, Ltd., 1922), p. 227. Again, this is puzzling if C. V. Drysdale was born in 1874. The fact remains that all during the Bradlaugh-Besant trial, Alice Vickery was addressed as *Miss* Alice Vickery and her residence was given as 333, Albany Road, London. C. R. Drysdale resided during the late 1870s at 17, Woburn Place, W. C., London. During her entire lifetime, Alice Vickery used her maiden name or some contraction of the two names: Vickery-Drysdale or Drysdale-Vickery. If C. V. Drysdale was born in 1874, then he must have

arrived while his mother, Alice Vickery, was attending medical school in Paris. Perhaps this explains the lack of a birth record in London. Perhaps she and C. R. were married in France as well. My own speculation is that the two met when the young woman enrolled in Drysdale's medical classes for women and were married in the early 1870s. Because of Alice Vickery's desire to continue her study of medicine, however, and because of the strong feelings current in English society against single women in the profession, let alone married women, they decided to keep the marriage a secret. Once Alice received her degree in 1880, there was apparently no further need to hide the fact. Herbert Cutner who wrote a memorial to "Dr. Alice Drysdale Vickery" mentioned *two* sons born to the couple, but there is no other evidence to indicate that a second child of the union survived if he was ever born. *The New Generation* 8, no. 3 (March 1929): 30.

18. The Annual Report for 1879 listed 1,224 members; the Annual Report for 1924 listed 1,213.

19. George Standring, "The Late W. H. Reynolds," *The Malthusian* 35, no. 10 (October 1911): 74.

20. W. H. Reynolds. *The Malthusian* 20, no. 5 (May 1896): 43. To give you some idea of the areas of England from which requests for Malthusian literature came, at the 20 October 1885 council meeting, Reynolds submitted, as he often did during the 1880s, a list of places from which communications had been received over the past month: "Liverpool, Croydon (several), Devonport, Alford, Lucknow (India), New Swindon (several), Chatham, Glossop, Wisbeach, Oxford, Bedminster, Birmingham (several), Ramsbotham (two), Salford, Nuneaton, Axminster, New York (U.S.A.), Glatstonbury, Brighton, Orpington, Greenock, Ameno (Italy), Basingstoke (several), Highbridge, Yeovil, Red Hill, Bristol, Exeter, Evershot, Winchester, Chard (several), Henstridge, Chepstow, Stonehouse, Westbury, Aylesford, Portsmouth, Honiton (several), Merstham, Stroud, Dorchester, Bideford, Sherborne, Crewkerne, Ashtead, Winchfield, Bridgwater, Taunton (several), Torrington, Chilver Cotton, Saltley, Sutton, Dulverton, Ilfracombe (several), Snodland, Reigate, Maidstone, Bilston, Wimborne, Burnham, Tewkesbury, Beckenham, Wednesbury, Tunbridge Wells, Ormiston, Hastings, Biggleswade, Worcester, Aston, Aberdeen, Trowbridge (several), Sevenoaks, Almonsbury, Alberton, Dover, Crediton (several), Exeter, Blackheath, Old Hill, Gloucester, Tynemouth, Barming, Ore, Frimington, Faversham, Southsea, Hambridge, Alphington, Chichester, Darlaston, Higham Ferrars, Cambridge, Dudley, Uxbridge, Leamington, Boston, Wellington, Chew Magna, Southampton, Guildford, Hinckley, Hockley, Handsworth, Burbridge, Luton, Highbridge, Hardwick, Maisemore, Sparkbrook, Erdington, Cheltenham, Morsham, Ladywood, Tufnell Park, Brixton, Brouch Hill, Methley-street, S. E., Harrow-road, Gunnersbury, Clapham, Camberwell, St. Luke's, W. Kensington, Dalston, Kennington, and Lambeth." Council Minutes, *The Malthusian,* no. 80 (November 1885), p. 655.

21. "Our Vice-Presidents," *The Malthusian* 38, no. 7 (July 1914).

22. "The First Annual Meeting of the Malthusian League," *The National Reformer* 32, no. 4 (28 July 1878): 60–61.

23. Fifth Annual Report, *The Malthusian,* no. 41 (June 1882), p. 321.

24. *The National Reformer* 30, no. 9 (August 1877).

25. The Malthusian League's many leaflets and pamphlets are listed in the Bibliography.

26. David V. Glass, *Population Policies and Movements in Europe.* 2nd ed. (London: Frank Cass and Company, Ltd., 1967), pp. 42–43.

27. *The Malthusian Handbook, Designed to Induce Married People to Limit Their Families Within Their Means* (London: W. H. Reynolds, New Cross, S. E., 1893), 48 pp.

28. Ibid., pp. 45–46. Standring repeated George Drysdale's and Annie Besant's error when defining the "safe period." "If connection do [*sic*] not take place within five days before, or eight days after, menstruation, the probability of pregnancy is supposed to be diminished."

29. Ibid.

30. "Correspondence," *The Malthusian,* no. 28 (May 1881), pp. 218–19.

31. "Correspondence," *The Malthusian,* no. 32 (September 1881), p. 254.

32. *The Labour Standard,* no. 9 (2 July 1881), p. 5. Actually, the writer was speaking of well-intentioned but inadequate attempts to deal with the housing problems of the poor in England.

33. *The Malthusian,* no. 23 (December 1880), p. 183.

34. "Practical Information. To the Editor," *The Malthusian,* no. 34 (November 1881), p. 267.

35. Fifth Annual Report, *The Malthusian,* no. 41 (June 1882), p. 321.

36. "Correspondence. A Friendly Criticism," *The Malthusian,* no. 48 (January 1883), p. 381.

37. Ibid.

38. *The Malthusian* 15, no. 8 (August 1891): 62.

39. "Correspondence," *The Malthusian* 23, no. 6 (June 1899): 46.

40. At a council meeting in January 1886, Dr. Allbutt announced that his book, *The Wife's Handbook,* would first appear in March 1886. *The Malthusian* 10, no. 2 (February 1886): 15.

41. The biographical information given here is taken primarily from George Standring's own one-page autobiography entitled "Ourself" published in his journal *The Republican* 11, no. 2 (May 1885): 1.

42. Ibid.

43. After Standring's death in 1924, the offices were moved to 17/19, Finsbury Street, but remained in the Standring family. In December 1940, the offices were destroyed in a Nazi bombing raid.

44. *The New Generation* 3, no. 5 (May 1924): 55.

45. "Neo-Malthusianism the Handmaiden of Socialism," *The Malthusian* 30, no. 6 (June 1906): 43. Standring's feelings about both neo-Malthusianism and socialism are fully presented in this article.

46. George Standring, "Memories and Musings of an Old Malthusian," *The Malthusian* 43, no. 9 (September 1919): 69.

47. Tenth Annual Report, *The Malthusian* 12, no. 5 (May 1888): 36.

48. Eleventh Annual Report, *The Malthusian* 13, no. 5 (May 1889): 35.

49. George Standring, "Malthusian Memories," *The Malthusian* 33, no. 8 (15 August 1909): 57.

50. Council Minutes, *The Malthusian* 23, no. 6 (June 1899): 46.

51. Council Minutes, *The Malthusian* 19, no. 11 (November 1895): 84.

52. Council Minutes, *The Malthusian* 23, no. 8 (August 1899): 62.

53. "Notice," *The Malthusian* 10, no. 9 (September 1886): 69.

54. Council Minutes, *The Malthusian* 10, no. 11 (November 1886): 85.

55. Council Minutes, *The Malthusian* 12, no. 9 (September 1888): 70.

56. "Missionary Work in Ireland," *The Malthusian* 14, no. 2 (February 1890): 12.

57. Ibid.

58. *The Malthusian* 21, no. 3 (March 1897): 22.

59. "Annual Meeting of the Malthusian League," *The Malthusian* 26, no. 8 (August 1902): 62.

60. Council Minutes, *The Malthusian* 14, no. 1 (January 1890): 6.

61. Standring, "Malthusian Memories," p. 57.

62. "The Ninth Annual Meeting of the Malthusian League," *The Malthusian* 10, no. 7 (July 1886): 54.

63. "Correspondence: Letter from G. A. Gaskell," *The Malthusian,* no. 6 (July 1879), p. 44.

64. *The Malthusian* 13, no. 10 (October 1889): 75.

65. *The National Reformer* 30, no. 9 (August 1877).

66. "The Malthusian League," *The National Reformer* 33, no. 2 (12 January 1879): 27. The journal sold for one pence all during C. R. Drysdale's presidency.

67. R. B. Kerr, "Passing Comments," *The New Generation* 7, no. 1 (January 1928): 1.

68. A Letter to the Editor from George Standring, "The Official Organ," *The Malthusian,* no. 33 (October 1881), p. 260.

69. Letter to the Editor from George Standring, *The Malthusian 19,* no. 11 (November 1895): 84.

70. R. B. Kerr, "Passing Comments," p. 2.

4: Labor and the Malthusian League

In its first years, the Malthusian League encountered little or no opposition primarily because it had not yet developed an audience outside of its small devoted circle of secularists and freethinkers. Noting the kinds of organizations addressed by members of the league in its early years, it is apparent that they were reaching only those who already shared their views. The Southwark Liberal Club, the Food Reform Association, the Westminster Democratic Club, the Holborn Liberal Association, the Hatcham Liberal Club, the Vegetarian Society, as well as the various branches of the National Secular Society, were typical of the kind of groups that welcomed neo-Malthusian lecturers in the late 1870s. By 1881, the league realized that it was not really reaching the working classes to which it felt its propaganda should be directed. Consequently, the council instructed "that circulars should be sent to the various London working-men's clubs, with offers to lecture on the population question."[1] By December 1882, *The Malthusian* reported "that the working classes are beginning to wish to hear more on the question of the limitation of families. This is shown by the numerous invitations sent to the Council of the League to send Lecturers to the various working-men's clubs in London and the provinces."[2] It soon became apparent, however, that what the members of those clubs wanted was practical information on how to prevent conception, not a rehash of increasingly unpopular economic theories.

The league subscribed to the economic ideas formulated by Adam Smith and his disciples, the classical economists, in the late eighteenth and early nineteenth centuries. According to this group of scholars the amount of wages that workers could hope to receive for their labor was restricted by the amount available to the employer for such expenditures. The amount constituted what was called the wage-fund. Capitalists or employers could not pay more than the amount available for labor without harming other aspects of their businesses. To harm a business meant, of course, endangering the jobs upon which workers depended. Thus, so the reasoning went, workers could only hurt themselves by attempting to force higher wages through such techniques as forming trade unions. "Against these barriers," said J. E. Cairnes, an economist in the 1870s, "trade unions must dash themselves in vain. They [the barriers] are not to be broken through or eluded by any combinations however universal; for they are the barriers set by Nature herself."[3] Or as Sidney and Beatrice Webb wrote in 1897:

> With so complete a demonstration of the impossibility of "artificially" raising wages, it is not surprising that public opinion, from 1825 down to about 1875, condemned impartially all the methods and all the regulations of Trade Unionism. To the ordinary middle-class man it seemed logically indisputable that the way of the Trade Unionists was blocked in all directions. They could not gain any immediate bettering of the condition of the whole wage-earning class, because the amount of the wage-fund at any given time was predetermined.[4]

T. R. Malthus had developed the additional argument that if the number of workers competing for the predetermined wage-fund were increased, the result could only be lower wages for all. Only by decreasing their numbers could laborers hope to increase their salaries. This was the generally accepted economic theory in regard to the setting of wages during much of the 1800s, but by the last quarter of the century, another line of reasoning began to hold sway in the public mind. "Qualification after qualification was introduced" to the old classical economic theory, said the Webbs, "until after the last effort at rehabilitation by Cairnes in 1874, the whole notion of a wage-fund was abandoned. ... But the discoveries of the economists have penetrated only slowly and imperfectly into the public mind, and most of the current opposition to Trade Unionism, is still implicitly based on the old theory."[5] They might well have been speaking in the last statement of the Malthusian League. League leaders clung to the outmoded classical economic theories for over fifty years. It is little wonder that the organization's speakers encountered opposition when lecturing before workers' groups. The opposition was not so much to the idea of voluntary family limitation as it was to the league's Malthusian economic theories. As Margaret Sanger wrote in her autobiography, "It was the name 'Malthus' . . . which kept the idea [of family planning] from spreading to the workers. The very mention of that name brought arguments, usually stereotyped and moth-eaten, from both the radical and the working groups."[6]

Among those who most actively opposed the Malthusian League in its early years were English socialists. Many of these were actually from the English middle class, but in the literature of the league they were all lumped together into the working class. For example, one league lecturer reported in 1882 that "the only working people against Malthusian limitation of families were the Socialists."[7] The same conflict of ideas existed between neo-Malthusians and socialists in the 1870s and 1880s as that which had existed between T. R. Malthus and William Godwin in the 1790s. The neo-Malthusians, like Malthus, insisted that poverty was caused by the actions of the poor themselves, that is, their failure to limit their numbers in the competition for jobs and wages. Socialists, on the other hand, saw the crux of the problem, as Godwin had, in an organization of society that favored the wealthier classes at the expense of the poor.

The league's first encounter with socialism came as early as 1879. C. R. Drysdale reported some antagonism to a lecture he delivered in Edinburgh on the "Population Question and State Remedies for Poverty." There was, he said, "only slight opposition from one gentleman of Socialist (German) opinions, and another who believed all poverty to be caused by alcohol."[8] Socialism, he thus intimated, was a foreign idea to be ranked with such pious and fanatical movements as temperance. Other members of the league were less moderate in their condemnation. One of our obstacles, though "of comparatively small importance," Mrs. Heatherly pointed out to the 1884 annual meeting, is "the savage anti-Malthusian ravings of certain anarchical missionaries who call themselves Socialists."[9]

The arsenal of socialist propaganda was drawn from a number of sources in the nineteenth century. Though not actually a socialist himself, Henry George, for example, played an important role in prompting socialistic groups in English society to call for social and economic change. The debate spurred by the publication of his book, *Progress and Poverty,* in 1879, and his lecture tour in England in the early 1880s went far beyond the issue of a "single tax" on land and contributed significantly to popularizing socialist ideas. "No one who thinks for a moment," wrote Henry M. Hyndman, "can believe that the landlord is the chief enemy of the labourer in our modern society. But Mr. George has roused the people by his moral earnestness and enthusiasm, and to have done this entitles him to our esteem and our sincere thanks, whatever we may think of his theories or his 'remedy.'"[10]

George aligned himself on the side of the socialists and against the Malthusian League by insisting that poverty was the result of a defective organization of society and not of some inexorable economic law. His view of the Western economic system harked back to an age when the possession and control of land provided the way to wealth or, more specifically, afforded a way to live without working. Rents provided "unearned" income in that a landlord expended little or none of his own labor in obtaining revenue from his land. But the industrial revolution had changed the situation. Industrialized nations like England and the United States were rapidly moving in the nineteenth century into an era when unearned income would be the result of the manipulation of capital itself rather than the possession of land. George's proposed tax on land alone would have bypassed these new forms of wealth. The idea of taxing only land was thus outdated almost as soon as George proposed it, but the objection to unearned income is as relevant today as it was in the 1880s.

Particularly odious to the Malthusian League, however, was George's attack on Malthusian doctrine. "It is difficult to reconcile the idea of human immortality," wrote George, "with the idea that nature wastes men by constantly bringing them into being where there is no room for them."[11] What he sought to dispel was the almost messianic faith of Malthusians in the wage-fund theory and in Malthus's law of population as irrevocable laws of nature. Alice Vickery proclaimed, for instance, that to deny the law of population was like opposing "the heliocentric theory, or the law of gravitation, or the circulation of the blood."[12]

It was George's challenge to the eighteenth-century idea that there are incontrovertible and unchanging laws controlling the operation of the economic system which particularly attracted labor reformers in the late nineteenth century. Belief in such laws had served to quash criticism and discourage any efforts to change. The Reverend Stewart D. Headlam, for example, explained that "until he read Mr. George's attack on Malthus, he had found it difficult to see how any reforms could do away with poverty."[13] Reverend Headlam had been a leader for several years in discussions of important social problems of the day. In late 1882, he was compelled to resign his curacy in the East end of London because of his participation in radical movements. He went on to become a leading Christian Socialist in England. He could never agree with the Malthusian League on Malthusian economic theory, but he gave at least some support to the group. Speaking at its 1885 annual meeting, he explained his position saying "that although, being a Christian Socialist, he believed that over-population was not the real cause of poverty, which he attributed to bad distribution and bad land laws, yet he could not help being in favor of early marriage and of small families, and for this reason he was in sympathy with the Neo-Malthusians in their work."[14]

Henry George's work presented no visible threat to the Malthusian League until he lectured personally in England in 1882. As late as September 1881, two years after the publication of *Progress and Poverty* in England, C. R. Drysdale asked in *The Malthusian*: "Can any of our readers tell us something about this Mr. George and his work? As far as we know, it is a work which is antagonistic to the scientific doctrine of political economy as expounded by Malthus, the two Mills, Ricardo, Cairnes, Fawcett, and not quite worthy the serious attention of those who wish to get information upon questions of social reform."[15] From 1882 to 1885, however, many pages of *The Malthusian* were devoted to refuting George's theories. In the early twentieth century, C. V. Drysdale still found it advisable to challenge them. He wrote a series of articles on "The Fallacies of Henry George" for *The Malthusian* in 1917–18 in which he admitted:

> The three books which have probably had the greatest effect in shaping the ideas of democracy are Karl Marx's "Capital," Prince Kropotkin's "Fields, Factories, and Workshops," and Henry George's "Progress and Poverty," and of these the last is probably the most important. It is a painful reflection that the spread of education in a country which was the birthplace of economics should have done nothing to prevent the wage-earners from being deluded by the most extraordinary collection of fallacies that probably were ever included in a single volume. No doubt this is due largely to the attractive style and plausibility of the author, but the main reason for the popularity of the book is its exaltation of the claims of labour as against capital, its supposed overthrow of the "hard-hearted" Malthusian doctrine, and its indictment and proposed suppression of landlordism. At the present time it appears to be more popular than ever, and to be the main source of inspiration of our wage-earners.[16]

A more serious socialistic challenge to the Malthusian League developed when the Democratic Federation was founded in 1881 by Henry Mayers Hyndman, a journalist and former student at Eton and Cambridge. Having read *Das Kapital* and talked with Karl Marx, who lived in London from 1849 till his death in 1883, Hyndman wrote *England for All* in an attempt to explain Marx's ideas to the English people. He was imbued with the Marxist prediction of revolution and believed he should do what he could to help it along. He criticized the trade unions as "mere middle-class and upper-class rate reducing societies" and denied their right to speak for labor.[17] By the late 1890s, however, he was encouraging members of the Democratic Federation to join unions in order to influence them from within.

Under Hyndman's domination the Democratic Federation changed its name to the Social Democratic Federation in 1884 and set out to get some of its own elected to Parliament. The organization was not successful in achieving the latter objective, but it did serve as a training ground for a number of future labor leaders numbering among its members in its early years: for example, Tom Mann, Will Thorne, John Burns, James Ramsay MacDonald, and J. Bruce Glasier, later chairman of the Independent Labour Party. It also attracted such middle-class members as William Morris, the poet and designer; Ernest Belfort Bax; Henry Hyde Champion, an ex-artillery officer; J. L. Joynes; Herbert Burrows; Edward Aveling; and Eleanor Marx. By the fall of 1884, however, Hyndman's disdain for other segments of the labor movement and his dictatorial methods caused a serious rupture in the organization. William Morris and such stalwarts as E. Belfort Bax, Edward Aveling, and Eleanor Marx left the S.D.F. and formed their own Socialist League.

Members of the S.D.F. and the Malthusian League clashed on several occasions during the 1880s in the press and on the debating platform. At the league's annual meeting in 1882, for example, Touzeau Parris, a vice-president of the league, accused the S.D.F. of appointing Herbert Burrows "to oppose them [neo-Malthusians] on behalf of the Socialists."[18] The choice was not a particularly good one; for though Burrows was definitely not in sympathy with Malthusian economic theories, it is apparent from his speeches, lectures, and activities during the 1880s that he was actually in favor of family limitation. As late as 1894, *The Malthusian* cited him as "the chief Socialist who persistently attacks the Malthusian position."[19] But in 1895, Burrows readily admitted in an open forum before the Mansfield House Debating Society in Canning Town that "in individual cases limitation of the family was good."[20]

Burrows, himself a member of the middle class, came to socialism, much as had others in nineteenth-century England, through a realization of the contrast between the wealth of the few and the poverty of the many. He had been for a time an unattached student at Cambridge University and had resided at Norwich, Barnet, and Blackburn. While at the latter, he visited the chair factories and collieries with Henry George and noted the contrast between the workers' lot and that of their aristocratic employer, the Earl of Dudley. From then on his life was devoted to fighting a system that allowed such discrepancies. He joined with Annie Besant in the fall of 1887 to agitate for labor reforms and served as her campaign manager in her successful bid for a seat on the London School Board in 1888. Burrows was at the time, the *Star* tells us, "a tall well-built man of forty with dark brown curly hair, a moustache, and closely shaven chin." He wore the typical garb of the English radical, "a tweed suit, the conventional Socialist flannel shirt, and a crushed strawberry necktie."[21]

In 1883, Burrows and one of his S.D.F. colleagues, J. L. Joynes, attended the annual meeting of the Malthusian League. They were undoubtedly attracted by the publicized subject of C. R. Drysdale's presidential address: "A Few Words on Socialism, Land Nationalisation, and Malthusianism; the most recent proposals for raising wages and making food cheap." Joynes was a clergyman and former housemaster at Eton who had lost his job only a few months before because of his radical views. He had already engaged in a written debate with J. H. Levy and other members of the league in a series of letters in *The Malthusian*. He challenged the basic premise of the Malthusian League that what caused poverty was an oversupply of workers who competed with each other for the limited number of available jobs and thus drove wages down. He contended that even if workers did practice family limitation wages would remain the same or, in fact, fall. His argument was based on David Ricardo's "iron law of wages" whereby the "market price" of labor, that is, the amount actually paid to a worker, tends to follow the "natural price," which is the level at which a worker can sustain himself and his family. If the worker's family were smaller, Joynes contended, the natural price at which he could sustain himself and his brood would fall. In keeping with Ricardo's theory, then, the worker's wages would also fall—exactly the opposite of what the league predicted.[22] The Malthusian remedy "would be of no avail if it were widely practiced, since the low water-mark of the labourer's expenses would fall if no labourers had large families, and with it would also fall the rate of wages. . . . The 'iron law of wages' remains, and the only real remedy is Socialism."[23]

Joynes further argued that even if his interpretation of the "iron law of wages" were incorrect and workers limited their families wages still would not rise because employers would resort to other expedients rather than cut into profits in order to pay a higher price for labor. They would bring in foreign workers who would accept lower pay or take their factories to the source of such labor. Or they would introduce more machinery in order to reduce the number of paid workers. To avoid the first of these, the league advocated a government policy aimed at stopping the immigration of foreign labor. For this, they were accused of abandoning the ideal of free trade so popular in nineteenth-century government circles. J. K. Page defended the league's position in a letter addressed to the editor of *The Malthusian:*

> As to its being illogical for a free-trade nation like England to forbid foreign laborers to come here, I do not see it. We do not advocate free-trade because we consider it an end in itself, or for any sentimental reason, but because it is proved that it is beneficial; beneficial not to the few but to the many. For the very same reason then we should, to be consistent, forbid the entry of foreign competitors. . . . And as I see that many of your Socialist readers are foreigners I may be permitted to inform them that free-trade in this country was gained in spite of the strenuous opposition of the rich and aristocratic classes in order to cheapen the bread of the masses, so that there is no reason to fear any difficulty in carrying out a reform here, when once the majority of the people have declared in its favor. The difficulty is in getting that majority.[24]

Joynes continued his argument. Even if one "vigorously excluded all foreigners," he said, "and reduced the number of the producers in the hope of increasing the proportion of wealth produced . . . [the worker] will still find starvation wages the order of the day. Those who hold the land and the capital will grind the faces of the poor as before, and assuming the theory of the proportion between capital and wages to be correct, English capital will flow to foreign lands sooner than pay higher wages here."[25] The league had no answer for this argument. The scramble among western European nations for at least economic control of vast areas of the world, particularly in Asia and Africa, was well under way by the 1880s.

Malthusian apologists were also at a loss to answer the socialistic contention that even if labor could force wages up by limiting the size of the English working class, the capitalist would counter by encouraging the further development of and buying more machinery. Workers would then have to reduce their numbers even more to compete for the smaller number of jobs and consequently reduce labor's ability as a whole to protect its own position. On this point, the league's only kind of rejoinder came from J. K. Page who in answer to the criticism that the introduction of machinery could be further injurious to the working classes proclaimed:

> If there were any truth in this, to what a state of misery must not the working classes have been reduced by now! Never in the history of the world was so much machinery introduced as during the last fifty or sixty years, yet it is certain that the working classes are not worse off, but much better off than they were.[26]

He adroitly sidestepped the question of what might happen to technological development if workers reduced their numbers in an attempt to raise wages. He simply drew attention to the advances already won by labor. It is true that until the 1870s industrialists had introduced machinery and increased production without laying off workers, except in some areas. As long as the demand for products remained unsatiated and markets continued to expand, this was possible. But when these conditions disappeared, paid labor, not depreciable machinery, was the first to go. This, claimed one socialist, was a major factor in producing the business slump of the late 1870s and the consequent unemployment—not an oversupply of workers due to their own rabbit-like propensities, as the Malthusian League contended.[27]

No wonder J. K. Page lamented in 1883 that "socialistic ideas form the greatest obstacle to our progress among working men."[28] He retreated to the argument that even if socialists were successful in carrying through their social reforms the continued increase in the numbers of the working class would soon cancel out any accrued benefits. His argument was based on the belief that what operated to keep the numbers of the poor down was their poverty and misery. Remove these, no matter how, and their numbers would increase rapidly causing even greater distress. "Numbers are kept down by want," he said. "Remove that want and they would of course start forward."[29] On the contrary, socialists argued, want renders people so mis-

96

erable that they tend to breed indiscriminately. They are, in many respects, without hope. The promise of a better life in such circumstances can not be effective in persuading them to limit their offspring. Give them hope, then the motivation will come. In other words, in order to persuade the working classes to adopt family limitation, one must first develop in them not only a desire for better conditions but the *experience* of such conditions. Even David Ricardo, in the early nineteenth century, had said that "the friends of humanity cannot but wish that in all countries the labouring classes should have a taste for comforts and enjoyments, and that they should be stimulated by all legal means in their exertions to procure them. There cannot be a better security against a superabundant population."[30] The Malthusian League claimed that workers must adopt family limitation before the problem of poverty could be solved. Socialists claimed the problem of poverty must be solved through a redirection of the goals of the economy before the poor could be motivated to limit their offspring.[31] The two positions were in direct conflict.

Several league members accused socialists, particularly those of the S.D.F. brand, of opposing neo-Malthusianism because of a realization that if the working classes adopted family limitation their conditions would improve such that they would be less receptive to radical cries for revolution. In the early 1880s, John Rothwell was especially vituperative on this point. He said "the only argument he had ever heard from such violent persons [as London socialists] against working people contenting themselves with a smaller number of children than was customary was that, if families became small, it would make such persons less anxious, because less miserable, to consummate the Socialistic revolution which was to cure all human evils."[32] Socialists countered by accusing the Malthusian League of using family planning "as a 'red herring' intended to draw the attention of the proletariat away from the real cause of poverty, the monopoly of land and capital by a class."[33]

There is evidence in the pages of *The Malthusian* to suggest that there was some merit in the socialistic contention that the Malthusian League advocated family limitation as a way to placate the lower classes and thus avoid social revolution. "Almost all revolutions," C. R. Drysdale proclaimed, "are caused by starvation."[34] Solve the problem of poverty and you thus stave off revolution. Addressing himself to European statesmen, Drysdale counseled, "you are tormented continually by being urged to pass some law to repress Socialism, or other hunger-created revolution. . . . Why not, as suggested by Mr. J. S. Mill, explain, perchance by some suitable statute, to the uninstructed classes that large families alone are the cause of low wages?"[35] Twelve years later, he wrote, "the Socialistic spectre threatens, because of the terrible destitution of our present States, to overwhelm us, if we do not learn in time to improve society by means of a correct knowledge of the population theory."[36] The message was clear—avoid revolution by pressing the working classes to adopt family limitation. In 1913, Charles Vickery Drysdale addressed the privately initiated National Birth-Rate Commission and observed "that the population difficulty is the principal cause of the labour unrest of the present day."[37] In 1920, after the Bolsheviks had won the civil war in Russia, the Forty-second Annual Report of the League concluded with the following statement:

> Our doctrines are more urgently needed than ever. It is now not only a question of making the present social system satisfactory and thereby of hastening the abolition of poverty, unrest and war, and of improving the race, but also of providing a counter-teaching to Bolshevism. The harassed taxpaying and employing classes, and all who wish to avert revolution, would be well advised to support the Malthusian League to the utmost of their powers and means.[38]

There was no mention of the possible healthful benefits of family planning—only an impassioned plea to the middle class to avoid revolution by pressing the poor to embrace neo-Malthusianism.

Charles Bradlaugh shared the antisocialistic sentiments of the Malthusian League, though his activities on behalf of the group fell off drastically after he was elected to Parliament. He resigned from the league council in 1880 and could not even find the time henceforth to attend the annual gatherings. His regrets were read at the meetings each year; parliamentary business required his full attention. He did, however, take time in April 1884 to accept an S.D.F. challenge to debate Henry M. Hyndman on the topic "Will Socialism Benefit the English People?" The debate was not sponsored directly by the Malthusian League, but its members attended in force to give Bradlaugh their support. Since his election to Parliament, he had toned down his defense of neo-Malthusianism significantly, undoubtedly because of its alleged relationship to such taboo topics as free love, but his stand on economic issues remained basically the same as the league's.

Like Bradlaugh, Annie Besant also drifted away from the Malthusian League in the 1880s but in a different direction. Her activities more and more increased her sympathy with socialistic ideas. As early as 1881, she resigned from the Malthusian League Council in order to devote her time, she said, to her studies at London University. She agreed to be listed as a vice-president and continued to attend and speak at the annual meetings of the group during the 1880s, but her new associations in that busy and eventful decade led her further and further away from both Bradlaugh, her devoted friend and confidant of the 1870s, and the Malthusian League.

According to her own report, Mrs. Besant's conversion to socialism began primarily in 1883. She wrote in her autobiography:

> To me, personally, the year [1883] has a special interest, as being the one in which my attention was called, though only partially, to the Socialist movement. . . . I had realized that the land should be public property, but had not gone into the deeper economic causes of poverty, though the question was pressing with ever-increasing force on heart and brain. Of Socialist teaching I knew nothing, having studied only the older English Economists in my younger days.[39]

Also in 1883, Annie Besant started her own publication, a monthly journal entitled *Our Corner,* which she issued until 1888. The majority of the contributors to her periodical were fellow socialists, such as Edward B. Aveling, G. Bernard Shaw, J. L. Joynes and John Robertson, but also fellow Malthusians, like Charles Bradlaugh, Moncure D. Conway, and J. H. Levy. The year in which her differences with the Malthusian League and sympathy with socialistic ideas and reforms became most pronounced, however, was 1884. "I was more and more turning aside from politics," she said, "and devoting myself to the social condition of the people."[40] In June 1884, she missed the annual meeting of the Malthusian League for the first time. "Unfortunately," President Drysdale reported to the group, "the lady who of all living women has done the most for this noble cause—Mrs. Annie Besant—who was to have been present was unable to do so on account of hoarseness."[41]

Mrs. Besant's first socialist friends were members of the Social Democratic Federation, but she was offended by their crudeness and ferocity. "Their uncurbed violence in discussion, their constant interruptions during the speeches of opponents, their reckless inaccuracy in matters of fact, were all bars standing in the way of the thoughtful," she wrote, but she added:

> When I came to know them better, I found that the bulk of their speakers were very young men, overworked and underpaid, who spent their scanty leisure in efforts to learn, to educate themselves, to train themselves, and I learned to pardon faults which grew out of the bitter sense of injustice, and which were due largely to the terrible pressure of our system on characters not yet strong enough—how few are strong enough!—to bear grinding injustice without loss of balance and of impartiality. None save those who have worked with them know how much of real nobility, of heroic self-sacrifice, of constant self-denial, of brotherly affection, there is among the Social Democrats.[42]

Her own middle-class origins and sensibilities drew her instead to the Fabian Society, especially to those in the group who saw merit in the practice of family limitation. In January 1885, Mrs. Besant met George Bernard Shaw, a member of the Fabian Society, at a meeting of the London Dialectical Society where he gave a speech in praise of socialism. In April, she joined the Fabians. She was henceforth ideologically alienated from the individualistic views of Charles Bradlaugh and the Malthusian League though she remained friends with both. "In truth," she recalled in her autobiography, "I dreaded to make the plunge of publicly allying myself with the advocates of Socialism, because of the attitude of bitter hostility they had adopted towards Mr. Bradlaugh."[43] The plight of the London poor in the recession of the 1880s, however, pulled at her heart and won her to their side.

> The cry of starving children was ever in my ears; the sobs of women poisoned in lead works, exhausted in nail works, driven to prostitution by starvation, made old and haggard by ceaseless work. I saw their misery was the result of an evil system, was inseparable from private ownership of the instruments of wealth production; that while the worker was himself but an instrument, selling his labour under the law of supply and demand, he must remain helpless in the grip of the employing classes, and that trade combinations could only mean increased warfare—necessary, indeed, for the time as weapons of defence—but meaning war, not brotherly co-operation of all for the good of all. . . . With a heavy heart I made up my mind to profess Socialism openly and work for it with all my energy.[44]

Her relationship with Bradlaugh gradually dissolved. In October 1887, she resigned as coeditor of the *National Reformer* explaining her action in a last editorial:

> When I became co-editor of this paper I was not a Socialist; and, although I regard Socialism as the necessary and logical outcome of the Radicalism which for so many years the *National Reformer* has taught, still, as in avowing myself a Socialist I have taken a distinct step, the partial separation of my policy in labour questions from that of my colleague has been of my own making, and not of his, and it is, therefore, for me to go away. . . . I therefore resume my former position as contributor only, thus clearing the *National Reformer* of all responsibility for the views I hold.[45]

The Fabian Society that welcomed Annie Besant in 1885 had been organized in early 1884. It consisted primarily of middle-class intellectuals who advocated a "revision" of the Marxist class struggle from one of violent confrontation into a permeation of the ruling class through prevailing organs of democratic procedure. Once in positions of power, they could then proceed to institute programs of reform in favor of the proletariat. The Fabians took no official stand on the issue of family limitation for the working classes; but during the 1880s, league members appear to have believed Fabian leaders supported population control. Most socialists, Alice Vickery proclaimed at the annual meeting in 1887, "were inclined to deny the Law of Population of Malthus, and to oppose the efforts of the Malthusian League," but, she continued, "I notice that some of the ablest Socialists in London, for instance, Mrs. Annie Besant, Mr. S. Webb, and others, are as much convinced of the truth of the Malthusian doctrine as we are."[46] At the 1888 annual meeting, C. R. Drysdale acknowledged the "Co-operation of Mrs. Sidney Webb, who, although a convinced Socialist, strongly supported the Malthusian theory." The occasion was a lecture given by Drysdale before the Socialist Club on Farrington Road, 20 April 1888. At the same meeting, he had been opposed, he said, by two other socialists, the Reverend Stewart Headlam and Mr. Herbert Burrows.[47] Again in 1891, Drysdale claimed Webb's support of the Malthusian movement, but he was merely grasping at straws.[48]

To suggest that Sidney Webb, or any other member of the Fabian Society, subscribed to the ideas of the early nineteenth-century classical economists or to Malthus's law of population could only have been wishful thinking on Drysdale's part. In their study of *Industrial Democracy*, first published in 1897, Sidney and Beatrice Webb devoted an entire chapter to a refutation of the wage-fund theory and the Malthusian law of population. "What the fanatical Malthusian most relied on," they said, "was [an] . . . increase in births. To him it seemed absolutely demonstrable that, in any given state of the working-class, an increase of wages must inevitably be followed by an increase of births." And yet, they pointed out, incomes had, on the whole, risen in England while the birthrate had fallen. Further, the decline in the birthrate was noticeable not only among the middle and upper class but among the upper ranks of workers as well. "Such facts as are now beginning to be known," they wrote, "point to the conclusion that the fall in the birth-rate is occurring, not in those sections of the community which have barely enough to live on, but in those which command some of the comforts of life—not in the 'sweated trades,' or among the casual laborers, but among the factory operatives and skilled artisans."[49] As evidence of the decrease in the birthrate among the latter groups, the Webbs cited the declining number of "lying-in benefits" paid out by the Hearts of Oak Friendly Society, an organization that claimed over two hundred thousand male members, primarily from the artisan and skilled operative classes. Payments, amounting to thirty shillings for each confinement of a member's wife, fell from 24.72 per 100 in 1880 to between 14 and 15 per 100 in 1896.[50] The Webbs believed that working-class families would and should adopt family limitation given adequate motivation in the form of a higher standard of living. But to assume that the poor could be persuaded or even forced to adopt such a practice before experiencing better living conditions was, they believed, utter nonsense. Here again we see the same basic conflict between socialists and neo-Malthusians.

Drysdale's disillusionment with Sidney Webb was apparant in 1898 when he commented in *The Malthusian*. "As to Mr. Sidney Webb, Mr. Tom Mann, and Mr. Bernard Shaw, they, like Mr. Hyndman, do not seem able to understand the law of Nature, styled the Law of Population. They are like those who deny the Newtonian Law of Gravitation, or any other datum of experience."[51] His final break with the Webbs came in the early twentieth century when the Fabian Society made one of the first attempts at gathering reliable statistics as to the actual extent to which family limitation was practiced. The results of the society's survey were published in 1907 in Fabian Tract no. 131, *The Declining Birth-Rate*. The research showed that birth control had, indeed, become an acceptable practice at least among the middle-class members of the Fabian Society from whom the statistics had been gathered. The tract also served to defend the practice of family limitation from charges of immorality. Prudent regulation of conception, wrote Mr. Webb, does not differ essentially from "deliberate celibacy" practiced on the basis of "prudential motives." Further, he argued:

> . . . If, as we have for generations been taught by the economists, it is one of the primary obligations of the individual to maintain himself and his family in accordance with his social position and, if possible, to improve that position, the deliberate restriction of his responsibilities within the means which he has of fulfilling them can hardly be counted otherwise than as for righteousness.[52]

The Webbs had no personal objection to the practice of family limitation, but they did not see it as a panacea for working-class poverty. One of their long-time associates, F. W. Galton, paid homage to the Webbs on the occasion of Beatrice's death in 1943 and expressed what had been their longstanding perception of the population question:

> Their view was briefly that wars, pestilences and prudential restraint would always keep population within manageable limits, at any rate in the white races. Moreover, they thought there was still much land in the world unoccupied or sparsely populated which could support any increase in numbers likely to occur. The great question to them was the urgent need for a redistribution of wealth so that the masses of the people could enjoy a healthier and happier life than had hitherto fallen to their lot.[53]

The Fabian Society as a whole supported the practice of birth control because of the benefits it could bring to the individual family both in health and economic standing but not as a solution to poverty. Socialists of whatever persuasion in the late nineteenth century appear to have favored family limitation, except for those who feared that such a practice would lull the working class into believing they could by their own individual conduct solve the problem of poverty. "What Socialists objected to," said the secretary of the Letchworth Social Democratic Federation in 1809, "was the assumption that Neo-Malthusianism offered a remedy for poverty without Socialism; but so long as this claim was not made, . . . the correctness and importance of the population doctrine could not be gainsaid, and . . . Socialists ought to give more attention to the subject." One of his colleagues interrupted, however, and maintained that Malthusianism was "simply a trap to lead Socialists away from the true doctrine, that poverty was caused by unequal distribution and the rapacity of capitalists."[54] The debate raged on in the lecture halls of London between members of the Malthusian League, Fabians, Social Democrats, and other varieties of socialists in the 1880s, 1890s, and early twentieth century. As long as the league played down Malthusian economic theories and stressed family limitation as a beneficial practice for the individual working-class family, it drew remarks that suggested possible compromise and cooperation between the two groups: neo-Malthusians and socialists. Any mention of overpopulation as the basic cause of poverty, however, brought cries of "red-herring" and charges of trying to dupe workers out of their rightful share of the economic wealth of the country. For the most part, labor and its leaders remained theoretically at odds with the league as to the reasons for and solutions to poverty in England. Nowhere was this more apparent than in the Malthusian League's reactions to the efforts of the growing labor movement in the late 1880s to force social reforms and win higher wages.

The economic depression of the 1880s brought hard times for England as a whole but particularly to the working classes. In April 1882, a deputation of the unemployed, representing thousands of others, called upon the Lord Mayor of London at the Mansion House. They asked him "to take such steps as he might deem proper to ascertain the extent of the depression among the working classes in London, owing," reported *The Malthusian*, "to the overstocked labour market."[55] The group further requested the government to allow free emigration to Canada and other British colonies. Such a policy would not solve the problem, the league warned. Only government controls on family size could reduce the labor population to a manageable size, an action not likely to be taken, however, in light of English traditions. "The sighs and tears of an ill-fed population, it seems, are of no account, in comparison with the keeping up of the 'tradition of the nursery,' which affects our whole British society from the throne down to the Irish hovel."[56]

As the 1880s continued, the economic situation grew worse. "The year 1886 was a terrible one for labour," Annie Besant wrote, "everywhere reductions of wages, everywhere increase of the numbers of the unemployed; . . . A spirit of sullen discontent was spreading everywhere, discontent that was wholly justified by facts."[57] In September 1887, she wrote: "This one thing is clear—Society must deal with the unemployed, or the unemployed will deal with Society."[58]

In October 1887, the unemployed began street processions in order to spotlight their plight. The police moved to halt the marches and succeeded only in provoking riots. "Sir Charles Warren [commissioner of the Metropolitan Police] thought it his duty to dragoon London meetings after the fashion of continental prefects," Besant commented disgruntledly, "with the inevitable result that an ill-feeling grew up between the people and the police."[59] In November, the demonstrators were forbidden further access to Trafalgar Square, the gathering point of the various labor organizations. The Fabian Society; the Social Democratic Federation; the Socialist League, an offshoot of the S.D.F.; and any others who cared to participate joined for the purpose of challenging the closure. The result was a bloody riot with one man killed and many arrested. Getting nowhere with public demonstrations, which too often became routs, labor reformers turned instead to the burgeoning new trade unions and their newly acquired legal right to strike.

In 1888, Annie Besant led the women who worked at the Bryant and May match works in the first successful strike of female workers. With Herbert Burrow's help, Mrs. Besant organized the employees into a Matchmakers' Union and served as its first secretary. Burrows was appointed treasurer. They won better wages and better working conditions. In September 1888, she joined the S.D.F. She continued to belong to the Fabian Society as well, but help in her activities in the late 1880s came primarily from S.D.F. members, such as Burrows.

With Burrows as her campaign manager, Mrs. Besant was elected to the London School Board in November 1888 as a representative from the Tower Hamlets district in East London. Her neo-Malthusian views were used against her in the election. One of her opponents, the Reverend Edwyn Hoskyns, a thirty-eight-year-old graduate of Jesus College, Cambridge, and the vicar of Stepney, a parish in East London, distributed thirty thousand unsigned handbills containing such passages as, "A Freethinker thus describes the practical outcome of her teaching: 'Chastity is a crime; unbridled sensuality is a virture.' "[60] After winning the election, Besant sued Hoskyns for libel. She argued her own case admirably, but both the defendant's counsel, Sir Edward Clark, and the judge, Baron Huddleston, seemed determined to show that by advocating

106

family limitation she had condemned chastity as a crime.[61] The Reverend Hoskyns stated on the witness stand that he held Mrs. Besant responsible for the whole of the *Elements of Social Science*, that he had great influence among his parishioners, and that he considered it his duty to warn his parishioners against her. He thought it best, however, to issue his warning anonymously. Besant took an hour and a half to sum up pleading "in earnest passionate language . . . for the right, the duty to teach to the poor that doctrine of limitation of the family for the promulgation of which the Malthusian League exists."[62] The jury could reach no decision in the case and was accordingly dismissed. She decided not to pursue a new trial, though she later learned that ten of the twelve-member jury had voted in her favor.

The Malthusian League Council expressed its thanks to Mrs. Besant for her defense of Malthusian tenets during her trial and its congratulations on her election to the School Board. They may well have come to regret her presence on the Board, however, since as a member she proposed a number of educational reforms that proved to be contrary to the doctrines of the league. She advocated free secular education, a system of medical examinations and treatment in elementary schools, and a new procedure of awarding contracts for employees and for the purchase of supplies, the latter designed to break a monopolistic system whereby a few suppliers were granted the contracts consistently. Perhaps her most controversial proposal was her motion for free meals for poor school children. For years, the S.D.F. had advocated "at least one wholesome meal a day in each school." In 1884, *The Malthusian* carried an article taken from the *Congleton and Biddulph Free Press* opposing free meals for school children:

> . . . If children are to have "at least one wholesome meal a day" free in the schools, it simply means that the more improvident, and reckless people are in bringing children into the world, the more freely the prudent and provident will have to be taxed on their behalf. But why stop the claim here? If children are to be fed by the State why are they not to be clothed by the State, say in the regulation charity suits of blue and yellow? Why is not the State to find

bedding for them; and in fact relieve the parents from *every* liability and responsibility; converting every working man's cottage into a sort of human (or inhuman) sty from which each newly born poor little squealer shall be forthwith conveyed to a State piggery?[63]

Even as Mrs. Besant fought the weary battle for poor children in East London after years of fighting similar campaigns for other deprived groups in English society, the quiet life of eastern spiritualism began to attract her. "Since 1886," she admitted in her autobiography, "there had been slowly growing a conviction that my philosophy was not sufficient; that life and mind were other than, more than, I dreamed."[64] She discovered a new philosophy, one that would quiet her tortured spirit for the rest of her life. She became a devoted follower of Madame H. P. Blavatsky and formulated a Western version of oriental mysticism called Theosophy. Her new faith proved to be a demanding taskmaster requiring the repudiation of all her efforts at reform during the 1870s and 1880s. She rejected both neo-Malthusianism and socialism as too materialistically oriented, much to the chagrin of the Malthusian League and her many and varied socialist friends. "The most painful and regrettable incident in the annals of the Neo-Malthusian movement was the announcement by Mrs. Besant, after her conversion to Theosophy, that she had recanted the faith for which she had fought so bravely and suffered so much," lamented *The Malthusian* editor:

> Quite apart from the pain which this recantation gave to those who had been her associates in the fight, the damage done to the cause by it was immense. The mass of humanity is unfortunately swayed by sentiment rather than by reason, and it has an intense aversion to studying questions on their own merits. That a woman of such prominence as Mrs. Besant, who had braved and suffered as she did, should publicly recant of her belief was sufficient for a vast majority of people.[65]

In addition to repudiating neo-Malthusianism, Mrs. Besant also refused to allow any more copies of her booklet, *The Law of Population*, to be printed. This was a real blow to the Malthusian League. In the following years, *The Malthusian* made very little mention of the renegade Annie Besant. In 1908, the editor called attention to the third printing of her *Autobiography* and added, somewhat cynically, "We trust that ere long Mrs. Besant will realize that Neo-Malthusianism is . . . the only way towards true spiritual as well as material improvement, and that we may welcome her back to the true faith."[66]

The labor movement, too, had to continue on its way without the help of Mrs. Besant. In 1889, the dock workers of London went out on strike. The growth of unions mushroomed. Within a year, two hundred thousand unskilled workers were organized. The issue of the eight-hour day became part of the program of organized labor. Strikes continued well into the 1890s; and in 1893, the Independent Labour party was formed under the leadership of men like Keir Hardie. The S.D.F. disdained to cooperate with the new group and subsequently lost its lead to the fresh and more conservative breed of labor leaders. The S.D.F. repeated its mistake in 1900 when the Labour Representation Committee was formed. This group became the British Labour party after the election of 1906.

All of these events were watched with growing horror by the leadership of the Malthusian League. "Whatever . . . may be the advantages of trade unions," C. R. Drysdale wrote, "they have no permanent effect on wages; and it is time that the working classes knew that. The only really useful strike is that against the appearance of a too numerous posterity; and all sensible trade Unionists and able Socialists are dimly beginning to see that truth."[67] In further opposition to strikes, his wife wrote:

> The present craze seems to be to recommend the working classes to try to improve their position by strikes. One would have thought that by this time that remedy would have been thoroughly discredited, and indeed we hear that the older Trades Unions in this country have long ago become acquainted by painful experience with the fact that strikes more frequently lower wages in the end than raise them. The reason of this is self-evident. The loss of production caused in the year by strikes, if these are on a very large scale, must diminish the capital of the country and therefore must tend to lower wages.[68]

As to the notion that an eight-hour day would improve the position of the poorer classes, "that is an entire mistake," Alice Vickery proclaimed. "The classes at the bottom of society are compelled, if they would remain free agents, and not be obliged to enter the workhouse, to work as many hours as will enable them to purchase food for themselves and their dependents; and so long as there is such an enormous supply of the poorest classes, their toil will be incessant."[69]

Part of the Malthusian League's answer to the worker's plight was to urge the laborer to strive to become a capitalist himself. It is the common experience of the human race, said Alice Vickery, "that hard work, sobriety, thrift, and education are the only means by which an individual can attain to independence and comfort."[70] Her husband agreed. "All capital being the result of saving, those who have saved and are willing to employ what they have saved in the production of new wealth are the greatest of all blessings to those who have not saved."[71] Habits of thrift, of course, should include limitation of one's family to fit one's pocketbook. Harry Quelch, a member of the S.D.F., expressed the socialist sentiment on thrift:

> Among the many mischievous doctrines which have been crammed down the throats of the working classes by bourgeois economists, until they have been generally accepted as gospel, none bear a more pleasing aspect or appear so virtuous as thrift, and none perhaps have done more harm [because of the] . . . support it gives to the Malthusian theory, the tendency it has to reduce the standard of life, and . . . the opportunity it affords the capitalist of shirking all the responsibilities which would otherwise fall on his shoulders. . . .[72]

The economic arguments of the Malthusian League were no match for late nineteenth-century socialists. The day of Adam Smith's laissez-faire theories was passing. Even conservatives had begun to concede the need for government to intervene in some areas of the economy in order to protect individuals who encountered economic difficulties through no fault of their own. The trend was clearly in the direction of more, not less, governmental regulation. The Malthusian League was swimming against the tide with its classical economic theories and thus possibly hindering, rather than encouraging, the acceptance of family limitation by the working classes. Opposition to the practice of family limitation died among the working classes just as it did, though sooner, among the middle and upper classes; but opposition to the economic doctrines of the league never ceased. In 1901, C. V. Drysdale spoke on "Malthusianism and Socialism" and contended, as usual, that socialists could effect little social improvement without neo-Malthusianism. In the discussion that followed his presentation, it was apparent that the group, as a whole, considered family limitation as "simply a palliative for individual families and not a remedy for social evils" and that "the hatred of Socialists for Malthusianism arose from its support of the detested capitalistic theory of economics."[73] One would have thought the league would have changed its theoretical approach to the working classes, but it didn't. In 1920, C. V. Drysdale was still using the same old Malthusian shibboleths: "Neo-Malthusians aim at checking the over-supply of labour, and raising wages by the humane process of avoiding the production of too many children to flood the future labour market. . . . We have been frequently taken to task for our strong remarks against trade unions, but we are absolutely unable to see any justification either for their tenets or actions."[74] Such statements were not apt to attract too many admirers from the working classes.

Workers individually gradually came to accept voluntary birth control in the late nineteenth and twentieth centuries. Even the Catholic church had its heretics when it came to family planning, but the British Labour party continued to avoid a direct confrontation with the issue. If the individual worker wished to adopt the practice, the party had no objections. It was just too controversial an issue, however, for a party struggling to achieve a prominent role in the political life of a country still filled with Victorian sentiments about sex. This remained the Labour party's position well into the twentieth century. Even when it gained political power in England for a short time in 1924, the party still refused to consider the issue of birth control.

On 9 May 1924, for example, a deputation initiated by Mrs. Bertrand Russell, a vice-president of the New Generation League, formerly the Malthusian League, presented a petition to the Labour minister of health, J. Wheatley, with over six thousand signatures demanding that birth-control information be given at government welfare centers. The group consisted primarily of female members of the Labour party and the New

111

Generation League. There was a heightened hope among them that a newly elected Labour government would finally approve a reform so directly related to the welfare of a group it allegedly represented. But political reticence remained, and the petitioners were denied. R. B. Kerr, editor of *The New Generation,* formerly *The Malthusian*, commented caustically that "the tendency is for a Cabinet to do nothing which could by any possibility lose votes, and to support nothing new until they see that they are going to lose votes by not supporting it." Labour politicians fear losing the Catholic vote, he maintained. "Politicians are a timid class—almost as timid as hares. It is the business of Labour women to play upon that fear. Labour women have far more votes than Catholics, and can force the hand of a Labour Cabinet whenever they please. . . . So long as the Labour Government thinks it has the Labour women in its pocket, it will do nothing. When it is as much afraid of the women's vote as of the Catholic vote, there will be no bounds to its obsequiousness."[75] First, however, Labour women had to organize themselves in support of family planning.

In May 1924, the largest National Labour Women's Conference ever held met in London and voted overwhelmingly (1,000 to 8) in favor of a resolution proposed by Mrs. Jennie Baker and seconded by Mrs. Bertrand Russell. The resolution read as follows:

> That this conference, while in no way criticising the views of those who for scientific or moral reasons are opposed to the practice of birth control, expresses its opinion that the Ministry of Health should permit public health authorities to provide, for those who desire it, information on the subject of birth control, and that, in cases where local health authorities desire to give such information the Ministry of Health should not, on that account, withhold the usual grants.[76]

As a result of the conference, the Workers' Birth Control Group was formed to promote acceptance of the content of the resolution primarily among labor and socialist groups. The new organization became the third association in England formed to promote public acceptance of voluntary family planning. It was preceded by the Malthusian League (called the New Generation

League from 1922 to 1925) and Marie Stopes's Society for Constructive Birth Control formed in the early 1920s. Miss Dorothy Jewson, a Labour member of Parliament in 1924, served as president of the Workers' Birth Control Group until 1928 when she was succeeded by Mrs. Josiah C. Wedgwood. The secretary for the organization was Mrs. Frida (Harold J.) Laski. During its seven-year existence, the association sponsored innumerable lectures primarily among labor women and trade unionists. At Labour party meetings, the group promoted the resolution in favor of birth-control information being given at welfare centers. In addition, the members helped to initiate and open birth-control clinics and hounded members of Parliament to support the family-limitation movement. In March 1931, the group voted to disband after the minister of health finally issued a memorandum allowing contraceptive information to be given at welfare centers on a limited basis. Most of the members had already joined the new National Birth Control Council that had assumed responsibility for seeing that the memorandum was implemented.

Meanwhile, the fight to win official Labour support for the family-limitation movement continued. In May 1925, the National Labour Women's Conference meeting in Birmingham once again approved the resolution on government welfare centers (876 to 6). In October 1925, however, the executive committee of the British Labour party refused to place any resolutions on birth control before the national party conference on the grounds "that the subject of Birth Control is in its nature not one which should be made a political Party issue, but should remain a matter upon which members of the Party should be free to hold and promote their individual convictions."[77] An attempt to override the executive committee's decision was defeated. "They are afraid of the R. C. [Roman Catholic] bogey," Dorothy Jewson charged.[78] In 1926, the executive committee again used the same argument to keep a birth-control resolution off the party agenda. At the party conference, Mrs. Russell called for a vote to refer the decision back to the executive committee, a move that if approved would mean the issue of birth control would have to be allowed a hearing at the 1927 conference. Standing on a chair amidst a crowd of 1,100 delegates, Mrs. Russell gave a dramatically appealing speech on the plight of poor women who had no access to birth-control information. She berated the 44 Labour members of Parliament who had voted against M. P. Ernest Thurtle's bill that would have authorized local authorities to use government money in providing birth-control information to married women on welfare. She called upon mine workers to support the birth-control resolution just as the women had supported the men in their battle for a seven-hour work day. To counter Mrs. Russell, the executive committee chose their leader, J. Ramsay MacDonald, as their spokesman. He proceeded to haul out the old bugbear of Malthusianism once again to scare the delegates away from family limitation. "Exactly to what do they wish to commit the Party? Is it a question of health? Or is it a question of Neo-Malthusianism?"[79] Since neither the mover, Mrs. Russell, nor the seconder, Dorothy Jewson, had mentioned the economic side of the population question, one member raised a point of order but was overruled. In spite of MacDonald's diatribe and other lamentations that the issue was being used to break the party, the motion carried, and the women looked forward to having the issue aired once again before the October 1927 conference.[80] One more obstacle remained, however, before the national meeting convened.

When the resolution calling for contraceptive information at government welfare centers was placed before the National Labour Women's Conference in May 1927 at Huddersfield, opponents to the motion were even more vocal than they had been in previous years. Miss Quinn, who had led the opposition at the Birmingham Conference in 1925 and who proclaimed proudly that she was an Irish Catholic, rose again to label birth control "a complete capitulation to capitalism," an argument often heard because of its long attachment to Malthusianism.[81] Nevertheless, the resolution carried by 581 votes to 74, a still significant but smaller majority than in previous years. In spite of overwhelming support of the birth-control resolution among Labour women, however, the National Conference of the British Labour party meeting in Blackpool voted 2,885,000 to 275,000 in favor of an executive committee recommendation that birth control should not become a political issue but remain a matter of individual conscience.[82] At their 1928 meeting in Portsmouth, Labour women surrendered to the wishes of party leaders and accepted by a majority of three (257 to 254) the Labour Party Executive Committee's recommendation. Henceforth, the leaders of the birth-control movement would concentrate their efforts on winning the support of individual Labour M.P.s. The movement still had a long road to travel before gaining general public acceptance and the great majority of politicians were not, it was now quite evident, going to be in the vanguard of the action. Perhaps we should mention in all fairness to organized labor that the Independent Labour party which had preceded in origin and finally joined the British Labour party voted in April 1926 to support the issue of family limitation by a huge majority of 501 to 58.[83]

Among the factors that played a role in promoting the acceptance of family limitation by individual workers in the twentieth century were increased educational opportunities enabling the laborer to read and understand the growing amount of contraceptive literature available; acceptance by leaders of the various Marxist, Fabian, and labor organizations of at least the fact that individual workers could improve their lot by limiting the number of their children; and the development of a working-class women's movement, especially following World War I. In addition, improved economic conditions for the upper echelon of artisans in the late nineteenth and early twentieth centuries gave them the motivation to improve their lot still further by accepting and practicing family planning. A further factor was a decline in the monetary value of children as wage earners. No longer could children be exploited by employers or by parents. As compulsory education became more and more common, it left children with fewer hours in which to work for wages, and child labor laws restricted their work activities still further.

In 1913, C. V. Drysdale said, "We have every evidence that the membership of the League would have been very much greater had the doctrines of Malthus not been insisted upon."[84]

In 1928, however, he again blamed the development of socialism in England for the failure of the neo-Malthusian doctrines to reach the poor. Our message, he said, "was enthusiastically welcomed at its outset, but it utterly collapsed after a few years, owing to the opposition of the Socialists with their attractive counter-promises of universal comfort through the social revolution."[85] Forgotten was his own earlier admission that Malthusian views had stood in the way of the league's persuading the lower classes to adopt family limitation.

1. Council Minutes, *The Malthusian*, no. 33 (October 1881), p. 262.

2. "The Propaganda of the Malthusian League," *The Malthusian*, no. 47 (December 1882), p. 370.

3. J. E. Cairnes, *Some Leading Principles of Political Economy Newly Expounded* (London, 1874), p. 338.

4. Sidney Webb and Beatrice Webb, *Industrial Democracy* (London: Longmans, Green and Co., 1902), p. 615.

5. Ibid., pp. 617–18.

6. Margaret Sanger, *My Fight for Birth Control* (New York: Farrar and Rinehart, Inc., 1931), p. 100.

7. "Annual General Meeting of the Malthusian League," *The Malthusian*, no. 41 (June 1882), p. 322.

8. Council Minutes, *The Malthusian*, no. 10 (November 1879), p. 80.

9. Seventh Annual Meeting, *The Malthusian*, no. 64 (June 1884), p. 516.

10. *Justice* 1, no. 9 (15 March 1884): 1. In his autobiography, H. M. Hyndman commented that Henry George "was a boy with a bright farthing dip fooling around within the radius of a man [Marx] using an electric searchlight." *The Record of an Adventurous Life* (New York: Macmillan Company, 1911), p. 259.

11. "The Press and the Malthusian Question," *The Malthusian*, no. 37 (February 1882), p. 294.

12. "Annual Meeting of the Malthusian League," *The Malthusian* 11, no. 6 (June 1887): 45.

13. "Reverend Stewart D. Headlam on Mr. George and Against Malthus," *The Malthusian*, no. 46 (November 1882), p. 366.

14. "The Annual General Meeting of the Malthusian League," *The Malthusian*, no. 75 (June 1885), p. 614.

15. "Current Topics," *The Malthusian*, no. 32 (September 1881), p. 254.

16. C. V. Drysdale, *The Fallacies of Henry George* (London: The Malthusian League, 124, Victoria Street [n.d., probably published after World War I when the league once again increased the number of its publications], p. 3. The pamphlet first appeared as a series of articles in *The Malthusian*, in 1917–18.

17. Philip P. Poirier, *The Advent of the British Labour Party* (New York: Columbia University Press, 1958), p. 24.

18. Fifth Annual Meeting, *The Malthusian*, no. 41 (June 1882), p. 329.

19. Annual Report, *The Malthusian* 18, no. 5 (May 1894): 35.

20. J. K. Page, "Debate on Malthusianism at Canning Town," *The Malthusian* 19, no. 11 (November 1895): 83.

21. "Mainly About People," *The Star,* no. 227 (9 October 1888), p. 1.

22. Ricardo, being a faithful disciple of Adam Smith, had argued, however, that the "natural price" would neither fall nor rise and that as the supply of labor fell below the demand, wages would rise. But what would cause the supply of labor to fall, according to Ricardo, would be the worker's inability to provide adequately for himself and his family and not a conscious attempt on his part to limit his offspring. Ricardo's view thus stipulated a "necessary" and "inevitable" period of suffering for labor while the supply of workers declined to a point below the demand. See, e.g., *The Works and Correspondence of David Ricardo,* vol. 1, *On the Principles of Political Economy and Taxation,* ed. Piero Sraffa (Cambridge, England: Cambridge University Press, 1951), pp. 93–94.

23. "Correspondence: Letter to the Editor from J. L. Joynes," *The Malthusian*, no. 50 [misnumbered] (April 1883), p. 406.

24. "Letter to the Editor from J. K. Page," *The Malthusian*, no. 53 (July 1883), p. 429.

25. "Letter to the Editor from J. L. Joynes," *The Malthusian*, no. 50 (April 1883), p. 406.

26. "Letter to the Editor from J. K. Page," *The Malthusian*, no. 53 (July 1883), p. 429.

27. "Letter to the Editor from C. F. Varenholz," most obviously an ardent socialist in England in the early 1880s. *The Malthusian*, no. 56 (November 1883), p. 462.

28. J. K. Page, "Socialists v. Malthusians," *The Malthusian*, no. 51 (May 1883), p. 409.

29. Ibid., p. 410.

30. Ricardo, *On the Principles of Political Economy,* p. 100.

31. A study by J. A Banks in the 1950s seems to bear out the argument that a group is more likely to accept family limitation if its economic expectations are high. Banks maintains that the English middle class began to accept family limitation in the 1870s when economic recession made it difficult for them to maintain the standard of living to which they had become accustomed during the 1850s and 1860s. *Prosperity and Parenthood: A Study of Family Planning Among the Victorian Middle Classes* (London: Routledge & Kegan Paul Ltd., 1954).

32. Sixth Annual Meeting, *The Malthusian*, no. 52 (June 1883), p. 427.

33. Annie Besant, *An Autobiography* (London: T. Fisher Unwin, 1893), p. 240.

34. "Annual General Meeting of the Malthusian League," *The Malthusian*, no. 41 (June 1882), p. 322.

35. Seventh Annual Meeting, *The Malthusian*, no. 64 (June 1884), p. 516.

36. C. R. Drysdale, *The Malthusian* 20, no. 8 (August 1896): 58.

37. National Birth-Rate Commission, Report on *The Declining Birth-Rate: Its Causes and Effects* (London: Chapman and Hall, Ltd., 1916), p. 98. Testimony of C. V. Drysdale.

38. *The 42nd Annual Report of the Malthusian League,* 1920 [p. 3]. The annual reports of the Malthusian League were sometimes published as separate pamphlets.

39. Besant, *Autobiography,* p. 301.

40. Ibid., p. 303.

41. Seventh Annual Meeting, *The Malthusian*, no. 64 (June 1884), p. 515.

42. Besant, *Autobiography,* pp. 302–3.

43. Ibid., p. 305.

44. Ibid., p. 306.

45. Ibid., pp. 320–21, citing *The National Reformer.*

46. Tenth Annual Meeting, *The Malthusian* 11, no. 6 (June 1887): 45.

47. "Report of the Council of the Malthusian League," *The Malthusian* 12, no. 5 (May 1888): 36.

48. Council Minutes, *The Malthusian* 15, no. 4 (April 1891): 28.

49. S. and B. Webb, *Industrial Democracy,* pp. 635–37. Part 3, Chap. 1, "The Verdict of the Economists," pp. 603–53.

50. Ibid., pp. 637–38.

51. C. R. Drysdale, "Eve and Her Eden," *The Malthusian* 22, no. 3 (March 1898): 19.

52. Sidney Webb, *The Decline in the Birth-Rate,* Fabian Tract no. 131 (London: The Fabian Society, March 1907), p. 16.

53. F. W. Galton, "The Webbs," *The New Generation* 22, n.s., no. 10 (October 1943): 245.

54. "Letchworth (Garden City) Fabian Society," *The Malthusian* 32, no. 1 (January 1908): 5.

55. "The Lord Mayor of London and the Unemployed," *The Malthusian*, no. 39 (April 1882), p. 305.

56. Ibid., pp. 305–6.

57. Besant, *Autobiography,* pp. 316–17.

58. Ibid., p. 319, citing her own journal, *Our Corner*, which she published from 1883 until 1888.

59. Ibid., p. 323.

60. Thornton Smith, "Besant *v.* Hoskyns," *The Malthusian* 14, no. 1 (January 1890): 3.

61. Besant, *Autobiography,* p. 359.

62. Smith, "Besant *v.* Hoskyns," p. 3.

63. "The Socialists and Modern Malthusians," *The Malthusian*, no. 65 (August 1884), p. 531.

64. Besant, *Autobiography,* p. 339.

65. C. V. Drysdale, "Theosophy and the Law of Population," *The Malthusian* 37, no. 9 (September 1913):67.

66. "Notes," *The Malthusian* 32, no. 8 (August 1908): 61.

67. "Anti-Malthusian Socialists," *The Malthusian* 22, no. 3 (March 1898): 19.

68. Alice Vickery, "Over-Population and Its Remedies," *The Malthusian* 14, no. 3 (March 1890): 18.

69. Ibid.

70. Alice Vickery, "Over-Population and Its Remedies," *The Malthusian* 14, no. 4 (April 1890): 27.

71. C. R. Drysdale, "A Millionaire [Andrew Carnegie] on Poverty," *The Malthusian* 15, no. 4 (April 1891): 29.

72. Harry Quelch, "Thrift: From a Worker's Point of View," *Justice* 1, no. 36 (20 September 1884): 4.

73. "Reports of Meetings," *The Malthusian* 33, no. 1 (January 1909): 8.

74. C. V. Drysdale, "Trade Unions," *The Malthusian* 44, no. 5 (May 1920): 38.

75. R. B. Kerr, "Mr. Wheatley's Refusal—Labour Women Demand Birth Control—What Next?" *The New Generation* 3, no. 6 (June 1924): 61.

76. F. W. Stella Browne, "Women Vote for Birth Control," *The New Generation* 3, no. 6 (June 1924): 65.

77. Dorothy Jewson, "The Labour Party Conference and Birth Control," *The New Generation* 4, no. 11 (November 1925): 127.

78. Ibid.

79. F. W. Stella Browne, "Labour Demands Birth Control," *The New Generation* 5, no. 11 (November 1926): 111.

80. The vote was 1,656,000 for reference back and 1,620,000 against. Ibid.

81. F. W. Stella Browne, "Liberal and Labour Women's Conferences," *The New Generation* 6, no. 6 (June 1927): 67. The women of the Liberal party held their National Council on May 4 at Blackpool and passed a resolution, with only three dissenting votes, in favor of contraceptive information being given at welfare centers. F. W. Stella Browne, a member of the Communist party in England until 1923, was critical because the resolution specified that the information should be available only to those who asked for it and "where the doctors are in possession of the medical history of the mothers, and know *to whom such information should be given.*" Ibid., p. 66.

82. F. W. Stella Browne, "Labour Sandbags Birth Control," *The New Generation* 6, no. 11 (November 1927): 123.

83. R. B. Kerr, "Passing Comments," *The New Generation* 5, no. 5 (May 1926): 49.

84. C. V. Drysdale, *The Declining Birth-Rate: Its Causes and Effects* (London: Chapman and Hall, Ltd., 1916), p. 88.

85. C. V. Drysdale, "The Birth Control Movement: Its Scientific and Ethical Bases," *The Eugenics Review* 20, no. 3 (October 1928): 175.

5: The Doctors, Clergymen, and Politicians

Most of the English medical profession preferred to ignore the topic of voluntary family planning in the late nineteenth century. The Malthusian League's most active members, however, were doctors, such as the Drysdales, who insisted upon pursuing the subject whenever the opportunity arose. Consequently, the profession was compelled to deal with the issue. Churchmen, too, would have preferred to leave the whole matter closeted in obscurity. Here again, though, a few clergymen thought they saw in the league's doctrines a solution to the crushing impoverishment of their parishioners, especially in East London. Politicians were more successful in ignoring the league and its suggested cure for the burdensome problem of poverty. Whether they were members of the Conservative party, the Liberal party, or in the early twentieth century the Labour party, political leaders had their own panaceas for poverty to propose. They avoided risking their political careers with mention of such an opprobrious topic as family prudence. Even Bradlaugh soft-pedaled his association with the Malthusian League once he was elected to office. In other words, professional groups in England tended either to ignore the issue of voluntary family planning or to disapprove of it, except for the few who saw in it a possible cure for poverty.

THE MEDICAL PROFESSION

As a doctor and as president of the Malthusian League, Charles Robert Drysdale was dedicated to alleviating physical suffering wherever he encountered it. He hoped, of course, to persuade his fellow medical practitioners that one way to reduce misery was to convey available contraceptive information to their patients or, at least, to give encouragement to a movement dedicated to checking disease and death among the poor. Optimistically, he also hoped the medical profession would lead the way in the search for a safe, reliable, and inexpensive contraceptive that could be made available to the indigent and illiterate. He was therefore dismayed by the attitude with which his proposals were received at medical meetings, which he addressed throughout England and Continental Europe year after year. For example, Dr. Charles Henry Felix Routh, fellow of University College, senior physician to the Samaritan Hospital for Women and Children, and consulting physician for diseases of women to the North London Consumption Hospital, ended his speech before the obstetrical section of the British Medical Association in August 1878 with a ringing denunciation of the "evil practices" advocated by the newly organized Malthusian League.

> As medical men we are often the guardians of female virtue. We are admitted into the closest confidence of our patients. We know the secrets of many a household. We are trusted, respected, nay loved, for our considerate kindness to the sorrowful and the sick. Shall we now remain silent when attempts are made to introduce into our happy homes, habits of immorality, which are so vile in their character, so dishonourable in their development, so degrading in their practice! Let us protest as medical men, as moral men, as Christian men, against recommendations, by whomsoever made, so filthy, so base, and so abominable.[1]

The enthusiasm with which the audience responded to Routh's oration would seem to indicate that he expressed their sentiments. They applauded when he called upon the medical profession as a whole to "drive this many-headed monster from the realm, and bring down a blessing from Him who overruleth all things for our good."[2] Medical journals of the time bear out the contention that Routh was expressing official medical opinion of the late nineteenth century. In 1896, for example, the well-known medical publication, *The Lancet*, included a letter from one of its readers commenting upon the "horrible trade" of selling "various preventatives of pregnancy." This evil "which the law does not notice," said the reader, "is as distasteful as it would be to the most fastidious divine."[3] In the same year, *The Lancet* severely criticized a religious newspaper for carrying

122

"immoral advertisement" of a publication "which treats . . . of large families with a check."[4] In his 1964 article on "Contraception and the Medical Profession," John Peel contended that *The Lancet* reflected the anti-birth control viewpoint of the profession well into the twentieth century."[5]

Dr. Routh's primary criticism of contraceptive techniques was that using such means to prevent conception was unsafe. This constituted probably the most rational argument put forth by the medical profession against such practices in the late nineteenth century. Routh, however, exaggerated somewhat. "The effect on the health of both men and women," he maintained, "is very injurious." Using such "sexual frauds," he claimed, can cause acute metritis, chronic metritis, leucorrhoea, menorrhagia, haematocele, hysteralgia, hyperaesthesia, galloping cancer, ovarian dropsy and ovaritis, sterility, mania leading to suicide, nymphomania, as well as general nervous prostration, mental decay, loss of memory, intense cardiac palpitations, and mania in men, any of which could also lead to suicide.[6] According to Routh's prognosis, a patient with any of the above ailments or symptoms could be suspected of "trafficking with the devil." His diagnoses were, of course, extravagant, and the Malthusian League had no difficulty finding physicians as fully qualified as Routh and his major source of information, L. F. G. Bergeret, to refute the charges. Doctors Leblond and Lutaud, both physicians to the St. Lazare Hospital in Paris, testified at a Malthusian meeting held in conjunction with the International Medical Congress in Amsterdam, 1879, that conjugal prudence "was not productive either of cancer, or of hysteria, or any other disease worth mentioning."[7]

Nevertheless, the debate over the safety of contraceptive methods raged on throughout the nineteenth and into the twentieth century. *The Lancet* contended that "when the sexual appetite is habitually stimulated in an incomplete and unnatural manner one or other of the misguided participants in the act, if not both, must inevitably suffer."[8] The statement was modest though unmistakably hostile to the practice. There were undoubtedly doctors, such as Routh, who made exaggerated claims about the dangers of using artificial devices to prevent

123

conception primarily because of their own personal convictions that the practice was immoral. It is also undoubtedly true, however, that there were physicians sincerely concerned about the possible harmful effects of the various practices and appliances devised for the purpose. At the end of the century, for example, two brothers were sentenced to jail for selling harmless drugs under the pretense that they were abortifacients. Some 12,000 women in the course of two years had been bilked into buying the drugs through a series of advertisements distributed by the brothers.[9] The case pointed up public ignorance of contraceptive techniques, the need for some kind of control of their distribution, and the enormity of the prevailing demand for such products. In this instance, the drugs were found to be harmless, but they might well have been otherwise. Even the safety of the method most often advocated by the Malthusian League in the first decades of its existence, that is, *coitus interruptus*, was seriously questioned. Prominent individuals such as Havelock Ellis and Richard von Krafft-Ebing indicated that the practice of withdrawal was perhaps dangerous to the nervous systems of both men and women. In 1890, *The Malthusian* reported on a new pamphlet in German "from the pen of Dr. Krafft-Ebing" which dealt with the "injury alleged to be done to the male by this check." "If the check be injurious," Drysdale professed, "it is the male sex that it will injure, not the female," as if to say that made it all right.[10]

Dr. Routh further claimed that the practice of family limitation would "lead to a diminution of population." Echoing Adam Smith's concern, he said, "The prosperity of a nation depends on plenty of population and plenty of work for that population." Routh also claimed the use of contraceptive methods would "produce a deterioration of the physique of a race."[11] At this point, he appealed to history for his evidence and reminded his audience that the French birthrate had been declining for decades. The once great French nation, he intimated, would never again enjoy the kind of influence and prestige it had held in the world when its birthrate was climbing. Using techniques of birth prevention, Frenchmen had squandered their energy in sexual debauchery and were subsequently doomed to fall prey to the vigorous race of Germans to the North.

The French armies conquered the world under the first Napoleon. The very Prussians were overcome. Under the third Napoleon how was the position changed! If the general proved less competent, the men, accustomed to waste their strength in unholy debauches, were, like the luxurious nations of old, less able to cope with the sturdy sons of the North, and in their turn they were conquered: and the Commune [of 1871] proved that brutality had taken the place of courage, and Socialism of manliness.

And lastly, Routh avowed that such habits tended to demoralize a nation.

A man who is accustomed to gratify without restraint his lustful desires, is not likely to improve in moral tone. It is a passion, and like drunkenness will know no bounds. His conversation, his habits, his business, will become tainted by the moral perversion, and he will seek in baser debauches for new channels wherewith to gratify his baser desires.

Routh maintained that if a married couple found it necessary for reasons of health to avoid having children and were unable to practice abstinence then they should "methodise" their conjugal relations. They could by restricting their connections to the interim from the twelfth day following the woman's period to the onset of the next prevent impregnation. He thus repeated the physiological error so prevalent in the nineteenth century. Routh's protestations also reflected the nineteenth-century view that women were private property that must be guarded from theft and defilement. "If you teach them vicious habits, and a way to sin without detection," he warned, "how can you assure yourself of their fidelity when assailed by a fascinating seducer? And why may not even the unmarried woman [future private property] taste of forbidden pleasures also, so that your future wife shall have been defiled ere you know her?"

On the whole, members of the English medical profession shared the economic views of the Malthusian League, but they were slow to lend their public support to the practice of family limitation. In 1887, *The Lancet* carried a notice of a meeting of the Edinburgh Health Society at which time the gentleman chairing the session "expressed an opinion that the views of Malthus had better be impressed on those who are responsible for the existence of children." *The Lancet* editor agreed that "without doubt this is a practical view of the matter, and it is one that goes to the very root of the difficulty as to the management of children—'Don't have so many of them.' "[12] The journal carried no comment, however, on how one could avoid having them. Further, medical authorities agreed with the league that the death rate was higher among the poor than among the rich. Here again, in an editorial on "Class Mortality Statistics," *The Lancet* concluded "that the proportion of children in the several social classes is constantly in inverse ratio to the capacity of the several classes to support their children in a manner to favour their becoming, physically and morally, healthy members of society."[13] The way to reduce the mortality rate, *The Lancet* editor argued, was to improve the sanitary conditions in which the poor were obliged to live. "If landlords were held more distinctly responsible for the sanitary condition of their . . . tenements, such a pressure would be put upon the tenants as would teach them the necessity for decent living."[14] Dr. Drysdale disagreed with this point of view. "I submit that we must no longer content ourselves with drainage schemes, or charitable schemes for building modern lodging-houses."[15] His solution, of course, was to promote family limitation among the poor.

At a meeting of the Medical Society of London in 1879, Drysdale presented the league's view as to the cause of poverty, that is, overly large families. In the discussion that followed, it was apparent the doctors thought otherwise. "It was not the number of a family that was the difficulty," suggested Dr. Paramore. "Drinking was the chief cause of social misery." Another, Dr. Heywood Smith, advanced the theory that "the poor often succumbed because they preferred to take their chance of an operation, which, if richer, they would not undergo. Any infirmity to the poor [such as pregnancy] interferred so much with their trade that they preferred to risk such operations rather than remain incapacitated for work."[16] Such a casual reference to abortion as being *preferred* by the poor would seem to indicate that the middle class held a somewhat callous it's-just-as-well attitude toward abortion among the lower classes. One would have thought birth prevention would have been deemed much more humane, but the same Dr. Smith was of the opinion "that the idea of limiting, by volition, the number of children, was contrary to ethics." He suggested, however, that perhaps emigration might solve the problem. A colleague corrected him pointing out that emigration "withdrew only the most able-bodied and ablest, and left the weaker at home." Once again, perhaps no one expressed the attitude of many of the medical profession toward the poor more succinctly or more directly than Dr. C. H. F. Routh. Indigence was not the main cause of early death among the poor, he proclaimed:

> It was the habits of the poorer classes which caused their greater death-rate. There was, he said, no country where the working classes were more despicable than in this. In his whole professional life, for instance, he had never received a farthing from any member of that class. They habitually ate up and drank all their gains. Many workmen who made thirty shillings a week only brought back a part of it to their families and consumed a great part in the public-house. Then the man would join a union, and henceforward would work as little as he possibly could. The accursed principles inculcated in their trades' unions were the bane of industry.[17]

The Malthusian League realized what a boon medical approval of family limitation would be to the movement. A public statement by a medical organization in support of conjugal prudence would provide a powerful weapon against the arsenal of the church, which thundered from almost every pulpit in opposition to the practice. As a member of the medical profession, C. R. Drysdale was in a position to at least attempt to sway the group to his way of thinking. At every conceivable opportunity he addressed medical organizations, local, national, and international, on the dangers of overly large families, especially among the poor. Disease and death are rampant in areas with high birthrates, he proclaimed. If medical men want to reduce the death rate, he continued, they must first reduce the birthrate in areas of inevitable, unmitigated poverty. Drysdale himself attended countless medical meetings over the years in defense of the league's position, and when he couldn't attend, he sent a paper to be read or a representative to take his place.

127

In 1878, Drysdale served as vice-president of the International Congress of Hygiene in Paris. At the International Medical Congress in Amsterdam, 7–14 September 1879, he read a paper in French before the section of public health. Taking advantage of the large gathering of medical personnel, the Malthusian League arranged to hold a public meeting during the congress, at a time when there were no sessions, in order to air their Malthusian views. Carl Gerritsen, a Dutch vice-president of the league, made the necessary arrangements. Dr. Drysdale addressed the large gathering in German explaining the position taken by the Malthusians of England on the question of poverty. The cause of poverty whether in Holland, England, Germany, and "even in some parts of France, was the production of large families by the masses," he proclaimed.[18] Among those accompanying Drysdale to the meeting from England was Dr. Henry A. Allbutt, a member of the council of the league, and one of the few doctors in the 1870s and 1880s to lend his support to the cause of family limitation.

In October, Drysdale was back in England for a meeting of the Social Science Association in Manchester where he and J. K. Page gave papers on "Emigration" and "The Present Depression of Trade." In early November he addressed the Medical Society of London, where he met, he said, "with a very kind and friendly reception . . . which made him think that the medical profession were beginning to reflect on this important point in hygiene," that is, the necessity to attack the birthrate as well as the living conditions of the poor.[19] In 1880, he sent papers to be read before the British Medical Association meeting at Cambridge and before the annual International Congress on Hygiene at Turin. The latter paper was entitled "Over-Population as a Cause of Disease."[20]

In 1880, the members of the Malthusian League who were also members of the medical profession decided to organize a medical branch of the league. C. R. Drysdale was to serve as president of the branch as well as of the parent organization. Henry Arthur Allbutt, who had particularly urged the formation of the medical group, was selected as secretary. The objectives of the branch were:

1. To aid the Malthusian League in its crusade against poverty and the accompanying evils by obtaining the co-operation of qualified medical practitioners, both British and foreign.

2. To obtain a body of scientific opinion on points of sexual physiology and pathology involved in the "Population Question," and which can only be discussed by those possessed of scientific knowledge.

3. To agitate for a free and open discussion of the "Population Question" in all its aspects in the medical press, and thus to obtain a recognition of the scientific basis and the absolute necessity of neo-Malthusianism.[21]

Several vice-presidents were selected for the medical branch from as far afield as India, and the members included physicians from Holland, Spain, France, Greece, and Italy. The medical branch held meetings from time to time during the 1880s and early 1890s, but nothing of any substance seems to have come from the activities of the group. The members of the branch did, however, continue to agitate for recognition of the dangers of overpopulation in terms of the health of indigent peoples and to encourage research into more reliable methods of birth control than those known at the time. In 1881, for example, the medical branch arranged to hold a meeting at the same time that the International Medical Congress was meeting in London. This, of course, allowed their international members to attend both conferences and also afforded the league a route of communication with and possible influence upon other members of the medical profession.

Meanwhile, Drysdale continued his individual efforts to reach and persuade the medical profession to join the neo-Malthusian cause. In August 1881, he read a paper before the British Medical Association meeting on the Isle of Wight and in 1882 addressed the public health section of the British Medical Jubilee meeting at Worcester. He never missed the international medical congresses, which were held from time to time in either a European or an American city. In 1884, the congress met in Copenhagen; in 1887, it was held in Washington, D.C.; in 1890, Berlin. Drysdale gave one or more papers at all of these. He, of course, continued his efforts within England itself and welcomed every occasion to address either local or national meetings of the British Medical Association. He encountered resistance, however, wherever he went. His plans for presenting a paper before the British Medical Association meeting in Newcastle in 1893, for example, went awry. He submitted a paper, "The Influence of High Birth-Rates on the Production of Premature Mortality," to the local secretary of the organization and then proceeded to Newcastle to read it. Meanwhile, however, the council of the association met and decided to disallow the subject. Drysdale's denunciation of the group in *The Malthusian* was bitter and uncompromising. "There is no doubt in my mind," he wrote, "that some of these anti-Malthusian bigots prevented the reading and discussion of my paper."

> I presume that they consider they know all that can be said about the question, and have made up their minds that other people shall only hear about it as much as they choose to tell them. This conduct of the Council of the Association shows that all bodies of men unconsciously act according to their own supposed interests. Being practitioners of medicine, they seem to think that it is necessary that there should be a fair quantity of disease for themselves to cure or alleviate.[22]

To suggest that a doctor would purposely desire to avoid measures that would prevent illness was, one might think, stepping beyond the bounds of professional and ethical considerations; but Drysdale was not the first to suggest that at least some doctors might bemoan a diminution of disease because of the possible remunerative consequences. In 1892, a writer in the *National Reformer* condemned doctors who were brought face to face with the problems of large families among the poor on a daily basis but who refused to use their influence to alleviate the situation.

> . . . Many of the medical profession are to be found with sound private judgment on the matter. Can it be that the fear of losing caste among the conservative unprogressive practitioners restrains them? Or are they apprehensive that the inculcation of Neo-Malthusian doctrine will lessen the number of remunerative and disastrous accouchements, and accelerate the production of stronger children, with native resistance to the infantile diseases that kill off the ill-begotten?[23]

His suggestion that a doctor might be afraid to speak in favor of neo-Malthusian doctrines for fear of losing the support of his fellow practitioners merited consideration. One speaker at the annual meeting of the Malthusian League in 1890 seemed to feel this was a strong motivation for the failure of doctors to advance the idea of family limitation. "Competition was keen among its members," he said, "and, if any doctor weighted himself by avowing unpopular opinions, he could only expect to lessen his chances of obtaining wealth and the first places in his profession."[24]

Doctors in the early 1890s already had before them proof of what could happen to a member who dared to advocate heretical doctrines within the hallowed confines of the medical profession. Dr. Henry Arthur Allbutt was tried, convicted, and officially ousted from the group in 1887. The Allbutt case served as a glaring example of what might well happen to an errant physician in the late nineteenth century and almost undoubtedly had the intended result of keeping doctors in line with accepted medical dogma. Marie Stopes, a prominent leader of the English family-planning movement in the 1920s, evaluated the Allbutt incident and called it "important because of the far-reaching repressive reactions involved and because the *medical* opinion of this country has undoubtedly been swayed by this event to a much greater degree than its inherent significance should warrant."[25] Dr. Allbutt's defense was essentially a defense of neo-Malthusianism, thus the Malthusian League took an active part in his case. In addition, of course, Allbutt had been a valued member of the organization for a number of years. His case, therefore, deserves a place in a history of the league.

Henry Arthur Allbutt (1846–1904) was a member of the Royal College of Physicians of Edinburgh and of the London Society of Apothecaries. He specialized in dermatology and practiced in Leeds. He had been active in the neo-Malthusian movement since at least 1879 when he sent a letter of congratulations to C. R. Drysdale on the founding of *The Malthusian*. "I wish it every success," he wrote. "May it be circulated by thousands! It is just what was wanted. Kindly send me a number of the first issue."[26] Allbutt was not only an ardent supporter of neo-Malthusianism but also a secularist and a republican. The combination made him part of a minority in English society who were pushing the claims of science against the centuries-old authority of the Christian church. What really got him in trouble, however, was a six-penny booklet that was first published in March 1886 under the lengthy title *The Wife's Handbook: How a Woman Should Order Herself During Pregnancy, In The Lying-In Room, And After Delivery. With Hints On The Management Of The Baby, And On Other Matters Of Importance Necessary To Be Known By Married Women.* The book contained advice on how to prevent pregnancy and was sold at such a price that it was readily available to anyone, young or old, married or unmarried. Allbutt had been prompted to write the pamphlet by J. K. Page, the corresponding secretary of the Malthusian League. His objective was to fill an obvious need for an inexpensive, simply written book at a price that would make it available to the poorest household. "It was to render the lot of the poor happier, better, more comfortable, and more moral, that I wrote *The Wife's Handbook,*" Allbutt stated in his own defense. "I wanted to do something to remove from our civilization the foul blot of poverty."[27]

The first six chapters of Allbutt's "handbook" were designed to help the young wife recognize when she was pregnant, keep her health during pregnancy, and understand the signs, stages, and treatment of labor in the birth process. It also included information on what to do after delivery and how to care for the baby during its first few months of life. These were all topics with which any young woman newly married should be familiar, but unfortunately few went into marriage in the nineteenth century with this kind of knowledge. In chapter six, Allbutt made it a point to warn the young woman of the dangers and penalties connected with "the crime of procuring miscarriage."[28] He expressed the general opinion of the members of the Malthusian League when he pronounced abortion "far too common" and "a crime which deserves the heaviest punishment. It is a sin against the life unborn—in fact, it is murder of the child in the womb, which has a right to live."

The seventh chapter was the one that drew the major criticism of physicians because it gave a short description and evaluation of the known methods of contraception. Allbutt specifically stated in the title of the chapter, however, that it was intended to convey information only on "How To Prevent Conception When Advised By the Doctor." Among the birth control methods described were "sitting up in bed directly after connection, and coughing" though he admitted "I do not, however, see how all the semen can be expelled, because the vagina has ridges in it, and the semen lodges in the ridges; and coughing—however violent—could not entirely dislodge it." He repeated the common nineteenth-century physiological error of recommending that "connection should be avoided from three days before the monthly flow till eight days after it. I am bound, however, to point out," he admitted, "that this method fails in about five cases in every hundred." His proclaimed measurement of reliability here is highly suspect in light of more recent knowledge of the so-called safe period.

The method of birth control most often recommended by the Malthusian League in its first years was withdrawal, or *coitus interruptus,* in spite of criticism that the method might well be injurious to the parties involved. Allbutt, interestingly enough, agreed with those who argued that "the practice of withdrawal is hurtful to the nervous system in many persons"; therefore, he said, "I cannot strongly recommend this means of preventing conception. This method is, however, advocated by many eminent physicians," a statement added perhaps to temper league objections. The douche he judged to be too cumbersome and expensive ever to become a widely used method though he admitted "that if a quinine solution was used in place of an alum one, conception would be impossible." He passed no judgment on the reliability of using a piece of sponge but implied that the method might be satisfactory so long as the sponge was soaked in a quinine solution and not just in water.[29] The "French Letter," as he preferred to call the condom, was perfectly safe if "warranted not to break, and not to become unfit for service." He recommended a brand obtainable "at 5s. per dozen by M. Constantine, bookseller, Waterloo Retreat, Clapham, London, S. W., sole agent for them in Europe."

Allbutt is believed to have been the first to introduce in a birth-control tract in English a mention of the diaphragm, known more commonly in the late nineteenth century as the Dutch cap.[30] The diaphragm was invented in the 1870s by Wilhelm Peter Johannes Mensinga, who often used the pseudonym Karl Hasse or C. Hasse. Originally from Flensburg, Mensinga became a professor of anatomy at Breslau. When Allbutt wrote his pamphlet in the mid 1880s, the diaphragm was still in the experimental stage, but it became the most popular contraceptive recommended by doctors prior to the discovery of the birth-control pill in the second half of the twentieth century. In Allbutt's opinion, quinine pessaries that dissolve were also "only on trial" in the 1880s and "time will show," he cautioned, "whether they can be relied upon to prevent conception. My opinion," he added, "is that they will do all that their inventor [W. J. Rendell, Chemist, London] claims for them."

Allbutt's last chapter dealt with menstruation, the "change of life," and a few hints on how to maintain a happy marriage. At the end of the book, either Allbutt or his publisher added a series of advertisements of companies which supplied the kinds of devices described in the pamphlet. A picture of a pessary was included in one of the ads. The companies included were reputable and longstanding manufacturers and suppliers of surgical instruments, medical supplies of every sort, and chemical compounds of every description. Among the companies, for example, were E. Lambert and Son located in Kingsland, London, and Mayer & Co. in Leeds. Nevertheless, the advertisements did seem somewhat out of place in a book designed for young married women who would assumedly seek the advice of a doctor on how to prevent conception. The content of the ads seemed more appropriate for a publication directed to the attention of medical doctors. Later, apparently Allbutt realized the incongruity of the added material, discharged his publisher, W. J. Ramsey of London, and removed the offending notices. They may well have been included in the first place, however, as a way in which to finance the publication of the book without having to charge a higher price for it. As Allbutt's lawyer later maintained, "the sum received from the advertisements was only sufficient to cover the cost of printing."[31] But Allbutt's action came too late to spare him the expense, despair, and agony which the late 1880s held in store for him.

The first edition of *The Wife's Handbook* appeared in March 1886. It attracted little notice until it came to the attention of Mr. Joseph Latchmore, secretary of the Leeds Vigilance Society for enforcing the Criminal Law Amendment Act and the Protection of Girls.[32] Latchmore, as secretary of the Leeds Vigilance Society, wrote to Sir Henry Acland, president of the General Medical Council of Great Britain and Ireland, on 13 January 1887: "The enclosed book, published by a Leeds Medical Practitioner, appears to have matter of a decidedly immoral tendency, and your Council would be doing a good public service if you suppressed it."[33] The General Medical Council forwarded the pamphlet to the Royal College of Physicians of Edinburgh, since Allbutt was a member of that organization. G. A. Gibson, secretary of the R.C.P.E. answered the council's communication on 19 January 1887: "The pamphlet which you have sent . . . has engaged the very serious attention of the Council of the College."[34] He promised to inform the council when the college decided on a course of action. Subsequently, on 15 February, Gibson informed the council that at a meeting of the R.C.P.E. held on that date a motion was proposed, seconded, and entertained:

> That HENRY ARTHUR ALLBUTT, of Leeds, a Licentiate and Member of the Royal College of Physicians of Edinburgh, be deprived of the Licence and Membership of the College, and of all rights and privileges pertaining thereunto, for having published and exposed for sale an indecent publication, title *The Wife's Handbook,* and for having published as attached thereto advertisements of an unprofessional character, titled *Malthusian Appliances.*[35]

According to the rules of the college, the motion had to stand for three months at the end of which it would be voted upon by the group as a whole.

The General Medical Council also informed the Society of Apothecaries of London of the offending pamphlet. It received a reply on 25 January 1887 indicating that the society could remove Allbutt's name from its list of Licentiates only "after due inquiry had been made, *and* the person shall be judged by the GENERAL COUNCIL to have been guilty of infamous conduct in any professional respect."[36] The specific wording required to remove Allbutt's name henceforth became part of the charge levied against him by the General Medical Council.

The council proceeded to refer the case to its own English branch council which, in turn, set up a committee of inquiry to investigate the charges. On 27 May, the three-man committee met to discuss its findings and consider further action. The chairman of the group, Dr. Matthews Duncan, reported the results of its meeting to the English Branch Council, which included the report in its own statement to the General Medical Council as a whole. The committee of inquiry pointed out "the objectionable popular character of . . . [Allbutt's] book, its accessibility to unmarried women, and its tendency to 'demoralise the world.'" Further, the committee claimed to have found the pamphlet "extensively sold."[37] This conflicted with the testimony of a bookseller in Leeds who had testified in writing that he had sold only about thirty copies before the case opened. But the book had enjoyed wide publicity as an "indecent" publication by the time the committee got around to investigating the matter, and sales had undoubtedly increased significantly in the interim. The committee declined to take any further action at that point:

> On the supposition that the Royal College of Physicians of Edinburgh is taking steps for the removal of Mr. Allbutt's name from the list of their members, and as it is very probable that Mr. Allbutt will resist this proceeding by appeal to the Court of Session, the Committee decided not to proceed to take further advice till the result of these proceedings should be announced.[38]

In June, the Royal College of Physicians of Edinburgh also declined to take any action in the matter on the grounds that even if they removed Allbutt's name from their *Register,* the General Medical Council would still have to act in order to have his name removed from the *Register* of the Society of Apothecaries as well.

Supposing the GENERAL MEDICAL COUNCIL should come to the conclusion (which is quite possible) that Allbutt's name should not be removed from the *Register,* this College would be placed in a very unpleasant position, had it in the meantime struck the name off its roll; and therefore it is the opinion of the Council that the ends of justice will be best met by leaving the case where it is.[39]

The college's action almost undoubtedly was a consequence of the barrage of appeals and criticisms that it had endured ever since news of the attack on Allbutt had first been made public.

On 17 February 1887, Dr. Allbutt was informed by the R.C.P.E. of the action pending against him as set forth above. He was notified that the college would reach a decision on the action after the required interval of three months. In that three-month interval the Malthusian League took it upon itself to defend Allbutt through every channel open to it. The columns of *The Malthusian* were filled with news of the case, appeals for funds, and copies of letters sent to the college protesting its proposed action. The league strongly urged all interested parties to write similar letters of protest. The league itself printed five hundred copies of a lengthy petition addressed "To the Honorable Council of the Royal College of Physicians, of Edinburgh" and mailed it to members of the group.[40] A similar letter of protest was sent to the fellows of the college by the Dutch Neo-Malthusian League. The Dutch organization was an outgrowth of C. R. Drysdale's efforts among his Dutch friends and was, in some respects at least, a stronger group than the English Malthusian League. "It is beyond our comprehension," the Dutch leaders wrote, "that, in your country, a College of Physicians—even when it is a Royal College—takes upon itself the right to judge about moral and social questions, and to condemn a member with the result that he should be unable to practise any longer, which may amount to condemning him to beggary."[41] They went on to indicate the openness with which contraceptive information could be distributed in the Netherlands.

The Madras Secular Society sent a petition of support for Allbutt with six hundred signatures. Several branches of the National Secular Society registered their protests, and Dr. Allbutt himself received nearly 150 letters in a month "from doctors in almost every part of the kingdom, and many from Ireland; mostly sympathetic."[42] Even socialists like Herbert Burrows declared himself "ready to speak against the unfair way in which Dr. Allbutt had been treated."[43] But Drysdale's surreptitious attempt to get a message of protest printed in the *British Medical Journal* failed. Knowing that the addresses delivered before meetings of the British Medical Association were always printed in their *Journal,* Drysdale included a commentary on the Allbutt case in a paper prepared for the public health section of the association. The remarks were duly placed in typeset and a proof sent to Drysdale for editing; but when the *Journal* appeared, the remarks regarding Allbutt's case had been deleted.[44] Perhaps most poignant of all was a letter from Lawrence Allbutt, the accused's brother and a minister of the Gospel, who wrote to the college pressing upon them the philanthropic motivations that led his brother to publish the book in question. He himself did not approve "of the modes recommended in the work," he said, but "when the benefit of mankind is the ultimate purpose," one should treat the matter with leniency.[45] When the R.C.P.E. declined to take any further action in the case and left the matter squarely on the backs of the General Medical Council, the league promptly sent each member of the council "a copy of the petition formerly sent to the Royal College of Physicians of Edinburgh, together with an admirable petition of the Dutch League, and some letters from among the many formerly addressed to the Edinburgh College."[46]

On 9 November 1887, in accordance with its powers as set forth in the Medical Act of 1858, the General Medical Council notified Dr. Allbutt that a hearing would be held on 23 November at which time he could defend himself against the charge "That you, being the author of a certain pamphlet or book entitled 'The Wife's Handbook,' did print, publish, and publicly sell, or cause or procure to be printed, published and publicly sold, copies thereof in London and elsewhere, at so low a price as to bring such work within the reach of the youth of both sexes, to the detriment of public morals."[47] No mention was made of the advertisements objected to in the R.C.P.E.'s indictment earlier in the year. The major complaint of the council appears to have been the price at which the work was sold, a price so low as to make it available to anyone no matter how poor, how young, or, more importantly to the council, married or not. The indictment was not intended as a condemnation of Allbutt's qualifications as a doctor; it was purely and simply a morals charge. He had attempted to corrupt the youth of England by placing knowledge at their disposal that could only lead to their degradation.

Thirty of the 32-member Council met on Wednesday afternoon, 23 November, to hear Dr. Allbutt's defense presented by his solicitor, Robert Lamb Wallace. Mr. C. G. Wheelhouse, a member of the council, rose at the outset of the trial to indicate he would record no vote in the case "for certain reasons of his own." Dr. Allbutt alleged "that the reason for this reticence was that this gentleman had himself published a sixpenny pamphlet addressed to young men."[48] Meeting from two to four o'clock each afternoon, the council took three days to hear the testimony in the Allbutt case and make its final decision. The major question to be decided, Mr. Muir Mackenzie as legal adviser of the council pointed out, was: "(1) whether the practices described and inculcated in chapter vii. of the book were calculated to promote immorality and vice; and (2) whether consequently, Mr. Allbutt, in publishing this book, was guilty of infamous conduct in a professional respect."[49] The council decided against Allbutt and subsequently removed his name from the *Medical Register*.

The Royal College of Physicians of Edinburgh also removed Allbutt's name from its roster but neglected to notify him until February 1895, almost eight years later. Allbutt later declared that he was never notified by the Society of Apothecaries that his name had been removed from their rolls. Meanwhile, Allbutt appealed the Medical Council's decision to the English courts. Once again he asked the Malthusian League, which had raised £80 to help defray the costs of his defense before the council in November, to help him raise funds for a court appeal. They were only able to provide £20, whereas the expenses totaled over £300. Allbutt lost both his appeal of the council's decision, which came up in the Court of Queen's Bench on 24 January 1889, before Baron Pollock, and the appeal of that judgment in the Court of Appeals on 28 May 1889.

Nevertheless, Allbutt continued to practice medicine in Leeds and prospered. When he was ordered to pay the Medical Council's cost incurred in defending their decision in his case before the Court of Queen's Bench, he readily wrote out a check for £253. The amount was set on 8 May 1889; the plaintiff was presented with an order to pay on the very next day. The procedure usually followed was to notify the plaintiff's solicitor with a demand for payment within so many days. "I have no doubt," Allbutt charged, "the Council thought I should not be prepared for a sudden call for a large amount, and that they would have the pleasure of selling my goods, and knocking me up, and destroying my credit. If so, they have received a lesson, and are perhaps bitterly disappointed that I was not so poor as they anticipated."[50] Allbutt's accusation was perhaps the act of an individual suffering from paranoia, but he was a much maligned man. "Can it be possible," he wrote, "that through local professional interest and underhand work an attempt has been made to drive me from the town, on account of my name and reputation."[51] Indeed, his cousin, Dr. Clifford Allbutt, a vice-president of the Leeds Vigilance Society and a respected physician, moved from Leeds in the late 1880s, whether from embarrassment over his cousin's position or from harassment.

"I am not crushed," Allbutt proclaimed, "I am in a better pecuniary position, have a better practice, better fees, and more reputation than ever, and I can afford to snap my fingers at the Council."[52] In 1895, charges were brought against him for using the titles L.R.C.P. and L.S.A. In spite of Allbutt's insistence that he had never been officially notified by the R.C.P.E. until February 1895 that his name had been dropped from the college and not at all by the Society of Apothecaries, he was fined £5 and £2 2s. costs. Henceforth he included the words "non-registered" on his professional cards.

If it was the purpose of the General Medical Council to discourage the sale of Allbutt's book by discrediting him as a doctor, then they failed miserably. His book sold in ever increasing numbers after 1887 and was in its fifteenth edition in 1927 having sold in the amount of 500,000 copies. Unfortunately, by then, it was very much out of date and probably did as much harm as good in conveying contraceptive information. F. H. A. Micklewright concluded in 1961 that "Allbutt's case seems to have had little general effect upon the neo-Malthusian movement, save possibly to frighten off some more timid members of the medical profession."[53] If by "neo-Malthusian movement," he meant the drive for acceptance of family limitation as a whole, then he was probably correct. But certainly the Allbutt case did nothing to reduce the animosity of the medical profession toward contraceptive practices. Further, it could only have convinced those who felt that to allow such knowledge to become widespread would be detrimental to the moral fiber of the nation that they were right.

The fight for medical recognition of the right of the individual to practice birth control went on well into the twentieth century. In 1913, an obstetrician testifying before a privately initiated birthrate commission declared, "I have no doubt that prevention of maternity by *artificial* methods invariably produces physical, mental, and I think moral, harm to those who resort to it—to one, or probably to both."[54] Further, that overweening tendency on the part of nineteenth-century medical men to feel that they were in some way personally responsible for the moral as well as the physical well being of their patients was hard to overcome. In 1923, even a female doctor lamented, "It would not be easy to convey this knowledge rightly to the individual it is hoped to benefit, without doing harm to others."[55] The moral objections of physicians to the practice of voluntary family limitation were, of course, based on the dogmas of Christianity. It might well be true, a longtime member of the Malthusian League wrote in the 1890s, that "among the upper and middle classes there is a great amount of disbelief in the current religion," but the fact remains, he contended, that publicly these classes, including doctors, still let the Church be their guide. To do otherwise was to court financial ruination. He continued:

141

... The open avowal of "unbelief" in Great Britain has always meant, and will long mean, for one thing, a certainty of pecuniary loss, and a certain measure of ostracism to professional men and men of business. Let a merchant, or doctor, or shopkeeper, declare himself an active Atheist, and he will find it appreciably harder to get customers or clients. A man of established position and personal popularity may fairly hold his own while avowing scepticism in general intercourse; but even he will incur calumny and loss if he takes trouble to spread his opinions.[56]

THE CHURCH

In the early 1920s, Marie Stopes emerged as a prominent leader in the family-planning movement. She ignored economic theories and emphasized the individual benefits to be derived from voluntary birth control. She was contemptuous of the Malthusian League and, in fact, accused the organization of having impeded acceptance of family planning in England by associating it with anti-Christian and nonspiritual movements. Because of the great amount of publicity afforded the Bradlaugh-Besant trial in 1877 and the Allbutt case in 1887, she charged, the whole topic had become associated with ideas repulsive to the sensibilities of Victorian England. The two incidents "in conjunction with the general unpopularity of the Malthusian League, [she contended] all together resulted in a severe set-back in this country to public expression in favour of the subject of contraception." Further, she maintained, "The clergy became active in opposing an 'atheistical and materialist doctrine,' and the doctors kept silence, so the closing years of the nineteenth century were not times of progress or inspiration [for the family-planning movement]."[57] She may well have been correct since Christian churches in the nineteenth century, whether Catholic or Protestant, taught that eternal damnation awaited those who interferred with the natural process of procreation. The objective of matrimony was purported to be the propagation of the human race, and any attempt to frustrate that end was presumed to be sinful.

The devout Christian was admonished from pulpit and Scripture to "Be fruitful and multiply. Replenish the earth and subdue it." But the Malthusian League challenged literal interpretation of that injunction claiming that a new time and new circumstances demanded a reevaluation. The command was given twice, C. V. Drysdale acknowledged, first to Adam and Eve, who were allegedly the only representatives of the human race on earth, and secondly to Noah after the flood, when he was already 600 years old and when assumedly all but eight persons had been destroyed. "Such an injunction may have been perfectly reasonable in these circumstances," Drysdale admitted, "but there is not the slightest justification for claiming it to be of universal application, especially when the population of the world has grown to 2,000 millions."[58] In 1897, the league circulated a pamphlet, entitled *A New Commandment,* designed to counter the biblical injunction. Propagation was sorely needed in the early centuries of human existence, the anonymous leaflet proclaimed, but by the time of Christ the world was fairly well replenished and so He said: "'A new commandment I give unto you, that ye love one another.'" The pamphlet continued, "We realise but imperfectly what love is, but we know that 'love worketh no evil.'"[59] The church remained unconvinced.

The major clerical attack on the use of contraceptives was based on a scriptural passage in Genesis chapter 38. In the passage Jacob's son, Judah, sired three sons. The first born, Er, married Tamar. Upon the youthful death of Er, Judah ordered the second son, Onan, to "Go in to your brother's wife, and perform the duty of a brother-in-law to her, and raise up offspring for your brother." But when he did so, Onan "spilled the semen on the ground, lest he should give offspring to his brother." The act "was displeasing in the sight of the Lord, and he slew him." A brother's obligation to marry and beget children by his brother's widow was a Mosaic law.[60] Early church leaders interpreted the passage as indicative of God's prohibition of contraceptive techniques. By thwarting the purpose of sexual intercourse, Onan was adjudged by God to have sinned and was accordingly slain for his transgression. The Malthusian League argued that what had angered the Judaic God was not the act of birth prevention but rather the breaking of the law given to Moses. "It is supposed by the Catholic writers on this subject," wrote C. R. Drysdale in 1891, "that Jehovah destroyed Onan because of this act, whereas it seems clear that the punishment was directed against the Biblical character because he would not raise up children to his deceased brother."[61] Nevertheless, onanism, as the use of contraceptives became known in the church, remained a serious offense.

Thomas Aquinas wrote that to thwart the procreation of offspring within marriage was "a vice against nature which happens in every carnal act from which generation cannot follow."[62] Christian sects, both Catholic and Protestant, accepted this pronouncement well into the twentieth century. A shift began in the 1930s when some of the Protestant groups gradually began to concede that companionship as well as the procreation of children could constitute a valid objective of both matrimony and sexual union. During the fifty years of the Malthusian League's official existence, however, no such compromise was forthcoming.

Nevertheless, in May 1885, the league claimed a breakthrough when the Honorable A. Lyttelton, master of Selwyn College, Cambridge, gave a paper on "Marriage and Neo-Malthusianism" before the Junior Clergy Society of London. Mr. Lyttelton expressed belief in the Malthusian proposition "that much of the misery of human life arose from overpopulation caused by large families."[63] He further agreed with the Malthusian League that "the evils of celibacy were quite as great as those of prostitution" and that early marriage and small families were both desirable, but he could not accept the use of physical checks. He retreated to T. R. Malthus's solution of continence within marriage, a practice considered by the league to be near to impossible and, at any length, detrimental to health. Drysdale contended that "both conjoints would be an unceasing temptation to each other, and that would, in most cases, be most injurious to body and mind."[64] At least, Lyttelton had recognized the possibility that overly large families cause problems, a point "the older clergy have not even yet abandoned," Drysdale lamented.[65]

In 1888, Drysdale hailed three young members of the clergy for speaking out from their pulpits and for writing in favor of neo-Malthusianism. The first, Mr. Frederick Lawton, a Unitarian cleric, condemned late marriage as a means of bringing greater comfort into the home life of the working classes and advocated early marriage coupled with some kind of family restriction. "Science teaches us how this may be done," he said.[66] The other two clergymen, Mr. Arthur E. Whatham and Mr. Leonard Dawson, were Anglicans. Mr. Dawson, curate of St. Michael's Church, Alnwick, lectured on the population dilemma; labeled late marriage, emigration, and celibacy unsatisfactory solutions; and also recommended preventive checks. Mr. Whatham wrote a pamphlet intended as a reply to Mr. Lyttelton's speech before the London Junior Clergy Society. He dedicated it to C. R. Drysdale. In it, he unabashedly advocated "artificial prevention of child-birth" as "the only means of preventing the alarming increase of pauperism, sickness, crime, and immorality."[67] Whatham was one of the rare clergymen in the nineteenth century to admit publicly that gratification of sexual desire might alone be an acceptable objective of sexual intercourse.

> We have . . . heard it stated that artificial prevention of childbirth assumes that intercourse is sought for mere gratification, and this is anti-Christian. Is intercourse ever sought for any other motive? What married couple are we to suppose ever had their entire thoughts bent upon the delight of parentage? I do not mean to say that this thought is never present, but I maintain that it is never the sole reason for intercourse between the most respectable and virtuous of married couples, and if never the sole reason, then all intercourse, according to anti-preventionists, is degrading to the Christian ideal of marriage, an assumption too absurd to contest. But to the root of the matter,—Is moderate intercourse, when gratification is the sole idea, degrading? No, no more than the moderate gratification of any other sensuous desire, such as the unnecessary but pleasant and lawful indulgence of the palate, or other harmless luxuries.[68]

Few clerics of any Christian sect shared Whatham's view, at least publicly, until well into the twentieth century. The bishop of London allowed Whatham to distribute his pamphlet only among the medical profession and by early 1889 asked him to withdraw it from publication entirely.

In 1891, *The Malthusian* reported a "fourth clergyman who had taken up the Neo-Malthusian views" and had written "a pamphlet giving advice as to the limitation of the family." "This showed," *The Malthusian* proclaimed, "that, ere long, clerical prejudices against the doctrines [of neo-Malthusianism] would die out."[69] At the rate of four clerical converts over a period of fourteen years, the league's optimism seems somewhat exaggerated. Not included in the list of converts, however, were individuals like Moncure D. Conway who had given up the clerical life as a Unitarian to become minister of South Place Chapel, hardly a conventional Christian church. He was active in the league for many years. A few dedicated clergymen like Stewart Headlam, who had lost his curacy in Bethnal Green because of his support of unorthodox movements, such as, secularism, neo-Malthusianism, and socialism, as well as his support of Bradlaugh in the parliamentary struggle, could perhaps be included among the clerical converts.

To the Christian clergy as a whole the practice of voluntary family limitation remained unacceptable, at least publicly, in spite of the Malthusian League's efforts. The Church of England reaffirmed its opposition to neo-Malthusianism in the Lambeth Conference of 1908 and again in 1920. The conferences have been held once every decade since 1867 at the Lambeth Palace, the London residence of the archbishop of Canterbury. The purpose of the meetings has been to bring together Anglican bishops from every part of the world to discuss their mutual problems and to lay out guidelines in the form of resolutions for future action. The resolutions have never been regarded as synodical decrees, but their weight in terms of influence in the Anglican church has increased with each gathering. At the 1908 meeting the bishops summarized their general view of neo-Malthusianism with a resolution expressing alarm at "the growing practice of the artificial restriction of the family, and earnestly . . . [calling] upon all Christian people to discourage the use of all artificial means of restriction as demoralising to character, and hostile to the national welfare."[70] They further called for "the prosecution of all who publicly and professionally assist preventive methods."[71] In 1920, the bishops reiterated their position and issued "an emphatic warning against the use of unnatural means for the avoidance of conception, together with the grave dangers—physical, moral and religious—

thereby incurred, and against the evils with which the extension of such use threatens the race." They continued to oppose "the open or secret sale of contraceptives."[72] Not until after the Malthusian League's official demise in 1927 did the Anglican bishops issue a limited but significant resolution in support of family planning. In 1930, the conference recognized that in cases where there was clearly a "moral obligation to limit or avoid parenthood" and abstinence was not feasible, then "other methods may be used provided this is done in the light of the same Christian principles."[73]

Even though the official position of Christian churches on neo-Malthusianism remained unchanged, individual clergymen apparently adopted the practice in their own private lives by the early decades of the twentieth century. In the late nineteenth century, the Malthusian League berated the clergy time and again for their tendency to breed overly large families. At the annual meeting in 1889, C. R. Drysdale cited the case of seven clerics who among them had fifty children and a combined annual income of £920, an average of £131 for each family of nine if divided equally. My conclusion, said Drysdale, "is that the study of the relations between population and means of subsistence should be enforced in all theological colleges, and the result rigorously tested in an examination of all candidates for holy orders."[74] By 1911, however, the national census indicated "that Church of England clergymen, whose fertility forty years earlier had been above average, were now almost 30 percent less fertile than the population as a whole."[75] They might harangue against family limitation from the pulpit; but in private life, at least, some of them apparently approved.

The position of the churches in regard to neo-Malthusianism was further clarified in 1913 when the National Council of Public Morals appointed the National Birth-Rate Commission to study the problem of the declining English birthrate. The National Council of Public Morals had been founded in 1910. It numbered around sixty-eight members and included in its ranks at least thirty-eight clergymen, a number of doctors, and even a few members of Parliament, such as J. Ramsay MacDonald. The group took as its motto an utterance of George

V: "The findings of National Glory are in the homes of the people. They will only remain unshaken while the family life of our race and nation is strong, simple and pure."[76] Concerned with the declining birthrate and aware that the middle and upper classes were practicing family limitation while the poor continued to breed indiscriminately, they were fearful of the possibility of race degeneration if the trend continued. The exigencies of the situation appeared to be forcing them into acceptance of the Malthusian League's long-advocated proposals. In 1913, the council appointed a 42-member birthrate commission to study the problem. The commission spent two and a half years interviewing witnesses and finally published their condensed findings in 1916.

Among the witnesses appearing before the National Birth-Rate Commission were representatives from the major religious sects in England. Testifying, for example, were the Reverend W. F. Lofthouse, secretary of the Wesleyan Methodist Union for Social Service; the Right Reverend Monsignor W. F. Brown, a Roman Catholic and a member of the commission; the Very Reverend Chief Rabbi Dr. J. H. Hertz; and the Very Reverend William Ralph Inge, Dean of St. Paul's. After hearing extensive testimony from each, the commission concluded:

> It was found that our clerical witnesses were almost without exception opposed, on moral and religious grounds, not only to the practice of abortion, which has had no defender among those who have given evidence before the Commission, but to the use of mechanical and chemical means to prevent conception. There was not the same unanimity as to the morality of restricting the family in other ways.[77]

The Malthusian League praised the work of the National Birth-Rate Commission for spotlighting the problem of overpopulation in England even though it was not at all pleased with some of the commission's findings. The commission tended to uphold the prevailing view of the major religious sects in England and recognized only the safe period as an acceptable way of limiting one's progeny. The latter in itself, of course, constituted an admission that family limitation per se was not evil— only the means whereby it was accomplished. In many respects

148

the commission and the religious leaders were only making public confession of a situation already known to exist by 1913. The upper and middle classes, and even the upper ranks of the working class, were practicing family limitation.[78] But the churches lagged behind in publicly accepting the practice of family limitation, once again allowing social forces other than religion to lead in the formation of public opinion and following only when the reality of the situation forced them to accept a fait accompli.

POLITICS AND THE LAW

As with the clergy, English politicians preferred to remain silent, at least publicly, on the issue of neo-Malthusianism. Any subject tinged with sex in Victorian England could bring a political aspirant only trouble.[79] The political fate suffered by Lord Amberley in 1868 when his comments in favor of neo-Malthusianism before the London Dialectical Society were used against him to secure his defeat as a Liberal candidate from South Devon lingered as a reminder to the politician of the penalty for speaking out on socially taboo subjects.[80] Memory of this incident coupled with the continuing belief that a large population is indicative of national prosperity and imperative for national defense augured ill for the acceptance of an idea like family limitation among candidates for political office. It would take the popularization of eugenics with its emphasis on quality instead of on quantity and further additions in military technology to dispel, at least to some extent, the longstanding belief that large numbers of people were evidence of a nation's wealth and strength. On this point, as well as on others, the Malthusian League was fighting an uphill battle.

Until the electoral reforms of 1867 and 1884, political leaders were under little compulsion to concern themselves with the problem of poverty other than to quiet humanitarian pleas for alleviation of the plight of the poor. But once the male members of the working class were added to the electorate, winning their support became important. The problems of low wages, unemployment, bad working conditions, and poverty in general became issues with which every politician must grapple, at least

149

verbally, if he wished to win or maintain his political office. Liberal vied with Conservative in proposing solutions to these pressing problems in the 1880s and 1890s. Political leaders, as a whole, though, agreed with the economic theories of the Malthusian League. There was no need for league members to argue with them that an over-supply of labor was the main cause of poverty. They had been brought up, like Drysdale and other league leaders, on the writings of T. R. Malthus, Ricardo, the Mills, and other nineteenth-century classical economists, and agreed that England faced a population problem, at least among the poorer classes. A quotation from the speeches of Lord Derby, the fourteenth earl of Derby and Conservative prime minister of England in 1852, 1858, and 1866, adorned the heading of *The Malthusian* along with statements from Malthus and John Stuart Mill. "Surely it is better," said Lord Derby, "to have thirty-five millions of human beings leading useful and intelligent lives rather than forty millions struggling painfully for a bare subsistence."[81] What government leaders did not accept, at least publicly, were the methods of family limitation advocated by the Malthusian League.

Further, C. R. Drysdale's proposal that the government enforce a restriction on the size of families was not only repugnant to politicians but to most league members as well. "Nothing could teach the poor so quickly and so clearly," said Drysdale, "as a statute law imposing some slight penalty for the producing of an over-numerous offspring."[82] One of his major lecture topics from 1877 until his death in 1907 involved, in some form, the need for state regulation of population size. He believed a small fine, perhaps only ten shillings, should be imposed on all, whether rich or poor, who produced over a maximum of four children.[83] His wife, Alice Vickery, and his son, Charles Vickery Drysdale, agreed with him on the necessity for state action. But only a handful of the remaining league members went along with the idea of fining a couple, no matter how small the amount, on the birth of a fifth child. "This advocacy of State coercion," George Standring pointed out, "is not generally approved by the Malthusian party. Nevertheless, they agree to differ amicably on this minor point."[84] Such a plan of penalty would be both impracticable and inexpedient, Standring argued.

To many around him, Drysdale seemed inconsistent. On the one hand, he opposed in true nineteenth-century liberal fashion, any government legislation that interfered with the liberty of the individual, especially in the economic sphere, and on the other, advocated direct intervention in the private activities of families. In the early twentieth century, the Drysdales asked John M. Robertson, a newly elected member of Parliament, to propose a bill providing for a government-imposed fine on families with over four children. Robertson had long supported the doctrines of neo-Malthusianism and the league itself, but this was too much. "Practically considered," he said, "any fine upon producers of large families was at this stage of social evolution impossible. Not a single member of Parliament . . . would vote for it [apparently including himself]." He went on to suggest that such a proposal seemed to him "to involve a socialistic premise—that the State ought so far to secure for all couples the opportunity to have families of four or less, as was involved in enacting that no couple should have more."[85] Undaunted by Robertson's remarks, C. V. Drysdale merely pointed out that any other form of socialistic legislation enacted before some kind of population control was imposed would only increase misery by encouraging the poor to have even larger families at state expense. The Drysdales never gave up their belief in the need for government legislation to control family size, but on this point they found little support within the Malthusian League itself and none among the nation's politicians.

During the late 1870s, the Conservative ministry of Benjamin Disraeli was more prone to recommend emigration as the solution to the seeming oversupply of labor in England. The measure became even more popular in the 1880s when W. E. Gladstone became the head of a Liberal government and faced growing problems of unemployment and labor unrest. Representative of the governmental position was Lord Derby, the fifteenth earl of Derby. He was often praised by the Malthusian League during the 1880s for adhering to the belief that labor problems were primarily a result of overpopulation, but he was criticized by league members for touting emigration as the solution. He particularly recommended South Africa, Australia, Canada, and the United States as areas of settlement for emigrants. "We are, and we must be," he exclaimed, "an emigrating country. With our small area and growing population we have no choice in the matter. We cannot employ or feed 400,000 more human beings every year."[86] He recognized that emigration was only a stopgap measure, but he could see no other solution at the time.

The Malthusian League waged an unrelenting campaign against emigration as a solution to poverty in the 1880s and early 1890s but to no avail. Until the 1930s, England continued to disgorge a large number of emigrants each year. It was, however, no cure for poverty in the homeland, as C. R. Drysdale was so fond of reiterating: "Emigration could never go nearly as fast as reproduction and, hence, . . . no European emigration could raise wages among the persons who remained in the old countries, although, of course, it was a cure for the poverty of those who emigrated."[87]

As long as the doors of English colonies, and of other areas as well, were open to immigrants, emigration seemed the best answer to unemployment in the mother country. Acting as an escape valve, it also tended to discredit Malthusian claims of overpopulation. "Perhaps no other single cause has done more to prevent ordinary people from recognising the necessity for a lower birth-rate," Drysdale lamented, "than the fact of our colonial possessions."[88] As long as colonial areas remained open, statesmen could urge the unemployed to seek opportunities elsewhere and could thereby avoid a direct confrontation with the attendant problems of alleged overpopulation. League members could argue all they liked that emigration was only a temporary expedient that drained the country of its ablest workers leaving the most undesirable portions of the impoverished classes of the population still in England and creating other problems as well. Alice Vickery, for example, repeatedly called attention to the fact that emigration deprived England of her male population leaving "a surplus of women over men of nearly a million."[89] But the government continued to encourage emigration, "girls especially, if they will fit themselves for domestic service, which is one of the most crying wants of an undeveloped country."[90]

Another favorite political solution for poverty in the late nineteenth century was land reform. Just what that reform should be, however, was open for debate. The proposals ranged from higher taxes on land to the nationalization of all lands in the British Isles. The problem of land tenure was centuries old in England. It was heightened by the enclosure acts, the industrial revolution, and the concomitant growth of cities. The problem involved primarily the extent to which ownership of the lands of England had become concentrated in the hands of a few large landholders. As Annie Besant pointed out, "five persons own estates exceeding two millions of acres" and "less than 2,200 individuals own more than one-third of the United Kingdom."[91]

Practically all the members of the Malthusian League readily conceded that land reform was needed; but what kind of reform? *The Malthusian* was full of articles on the issue during the 1880s when the problem waxed hot in English society as a whole. Particularly at fault, most of the league members claimed, were the laws of primogeniture and entail that fixed the inheritance of land for generations and prevented the division of vast estates. In a time of burgeoning cities, had the large tracts of land been used efficiently for agricultural production, the problem would have been less acute. But in too many cases productive land had been allowed to lie fallow year after year simply because the owner preferred to avoid the problems involved in bringing it under the plow. Consequently, Annie Besant called for the cultivation or sale of cultivable land, a simplification of land-transfer procedures, a graduated tax upon large estates, and the establishment of a class of peasant proprietors. On the whole, Charles Bradlaugh agreed with her and introduced a bill in Parliament requiring that all agricultural land not being cultivated be sold.[92] Such a reform would be effective, he was quick to point out, only if a limited number of new persons were born to participate in the yield of the land thus to be utilized.

Bradlaugh was less active in the Malthusian League after his election to Parliament, but he never forsook his belief in the Malthusian law of population.

C. R. Drysdale repeatedly cited France as an example of the way in which land should be utilized for the benefit of the population as a whole. During the French Revolution, he maintained, the huge estates of the nobility had been confiscated and used to create a large class of small landholders. Wishing to retain a position so dearly won through revolution, peasants adopted the practice of limiting the number of their children in order to avoid division of their land among many offspring, as stipulated by the *Code Napoléon*. The result, claimed Drysdale, was a prosperous and happy French peasantry. His wife agreed:

> ... The possession of land by the cultivator has been found in France, together with equal division, to tend greatly towards the keeping of population within limits; because the peasant proprietors, fearing lest their holdings should be too greatly subdivided if their families are large, are prudent enough to restrain the number of their children to an average of three to a family, or even fewer in some districts of France, such as Normandy.[93]

Alice Vickery proceeded to argue that the drive for land reform in England should be directed toward creating a similar class of small landowners, "who would, by being raised out of the uncertain position of hired labourers, become as prudent in the direction of the birth-rate as the richer classes are at this moment."[94] "What France has, we need," Bradlaugh agreed. "But we want it without revolution."[95] Any such reform, of course, would have to be accompanied by either voluntary or enforced family limitation, according to the Malthusian League. In fact, the league as a whole agreed with J. K. Page, a longstanding and faithful member, who concluded that "land-tenure reform would be useless without a limitation of families; while with . . . [limitation] it would be unnecessary."[96]

The Malthusian League remained adamantly opposed to proposals from politicians to alleviate the suffering of the poor through plans for better housing, sanitation campaigns, or school lunch programs. Such proposals smacked too much of socialism for the league and would ultimately come to rest in the pocketbooks of the middle-class taxpayer. "What is there that a certain section of the Progressive Liberal does not demand?" Alice Vickery asked.[97] Just whom she meant was not clear. Apparently, her definition of Progressive Liberal included any who proposed such schemes. All such programs are useless, she proclaimed, without an accompanying law enforcing family limitation.

The league also objected to government proposals to help the working classes. In the 1890s, members of Parliament, such as Keir Hardie and John Burns, advocated the establishment of old-age pensions, a minimum wage, the eight-hour day, and a public works program. It is the duty of the state, Hardie maintained, "to furnish an opportunity to persons to earn their living."[98] The trend was toward more governmental programs. By 1898, even C. R. Drysdale admitted that the government had, on occasion, intervened in the economic system with humane results:

> The State . . . has most usefully interfered in the case of the Factory Acts, in the matter of unwholesome employments and in the prevention of contagion, and, if the State could raise the standard of comfort of the poorest classes by establishing a minimum wage in the various trades, it would certainly accomplish more for the health and happiness of the masses than any legislation has ever accomplished.[99]

But without some well-devised scheme for checking the production of large families, he continued to maintain, the condition of the poorest classes is hopeless.

Throughout the years the Malthusian League tried to influence government leaders by writing to them, sending them Malthusian literature, and, when possible, questioning them in person on their knowledge of the population dilemma. In 1879, for example, the league council voted to petition Parliament for a clear definition of "obscene libel."[100] They were concerned that no further persecutions, such as those suffered by Besant, Bradlaugh, and Edward Truelove, would ever again occur. Bradlaugh, however, gave them little hope that such a bill, even if proposed, could get through. He proved to be right.

In 1927, when the Malthusian League ended its official existence, the Campbell Act of 1857, under which Bradlaugh and Besant had been prosecuted, was still on the books. It was no longer used, however, as a basis for the prosecution of individuals printing birth-control literature. Throughout the years, though, the league had been called to the defense of a number of persons brought to court for publishing or distributing materials on neo-Malthusianism. Some of the cases were settled to the satisfaction of league members; others were not. In December 1888, for example, the league claimed a resounding victory for the neo-Malthusian movement when a favorable decision was won in a case in Sydney, Australia. Mr. W. W. Collins was convicted by a local police magistrate of selling the "obscene" pamphlet, *The Law of Population,* written by Annie Besant. When the case was appealed to the Supreme Court, Sir William Windeyer, the presiding Senior Puisne Judge, ruled in favor of the defendant and declared the book to be a proper work for private perusal.[101] The league assumed that if such information were deemed legal in a British colony, surely it should be acceptable at home as well. But in 1891, the home secretary, Mr. Matthews, brought a suit against Mr. Henry S. Young of Pimlico for sending through the mail circulars advocating the use of preventive checks to limit births.[102] The league held a crowded public meeting on his behalf in October 1891 and collected funds for his defense. Nevertheless, he was convicted and fined £10 plus £20 12s. in costs on the grounds that the materials were obscene.[103]

An even more serious case occurred in early 1892 when Henry Loader, a 67-year-old phrenologist in Newcastle-on-Tyne, was tried for unwittingly selling a copy of H. A. Allbutt's *Wife's Handbook* to a policeman. The first trial ended in a hung jury, but he was convicted in a second one and ordered to pay a surety of £50 and a recognisance of £100 pledging himself never again to sell such literature. He was given overnight to arrange for the amounts, but the next day he refused to pay and was sentenced to a month in prison "with such hard labor as you can do."[104] Henry Loader and his wife, Caroline, were devout Christians who believed in family limitation as a way to relieve the suffering of the poor. Mrs. Loader had distributed contraceptive materials to women for years, but she and her husband had been in Newcastle only three months when their activities as neo-

Malthusian missionaries came to the attention of the Watch Committee, a group composed of local businessmen entrusted with controlling the actions of the police. The harsh charges subsequently brought against the Loaders and the months of harassment they endured between the two trials ruined their meager livelihood and so distressed Mrs. Loader that she fell ill in 1893 and died shortly thereafter. Mr. Loader left Newcastle-on-Tyne but remained, he said, "as much as ever in favor of the humane teachings of the [Malthusian] League."[105]

The prosecution of George Bedborough in 1898 is fairly well known since it involved the sale of a book written by Dr. Havelock Ellis on *Sexual Inversion.* The work was part of a series, *Studies in the Phychology of Sex,* which Ellis was preparing. Because of the conviction of his publisher, Bedborough, Ellis decided that it would be better to have the rest of the series published outside of England. He did not wish to become involved in the struggle to maintain a free press; he only wanted to be left alone to do his work. Nevertheless, the case and subsequent conviction of Bedborough stands as another episode in the fight to get the courts to distinguish between materials that were blatantly obscene, a still undefined term, and those of a scientific nature that dealt with the long taboo subject of sex.

Even the manufacturers and distributors of contraceptive appliances on occasion ran afoul of the law. E. Lambert and Son, Dalston, London, makers of surgical appliances and long-time supporters of the Malthusian League, were summoned to court in December 1898 on a charge of engaging in illicit traffic. A policeman had obtained from the company through the mail a copy of *The Wife's Medical Adviser* and later a preventive device together with an illustrated price list. The company had, the prosecutor maintained, violated (1) the Post Office Protection Act of 1884 and (2) the Indecent Advertisements Act of 1889. The defense argued that many people advocated the use of preventive checks by married people for the limitation of families and that several works on the subject were sold openly. If the use of such checks were advocated without challenge, then someone had to supply the necessary means. There was, therefore, nothing illegal in the manufacture and sale of the articles, and they should not be called indecent. The presiding magistrate agreed and dropped the case. A precedent was thus established, and yet J. R. Holmes was prosecuted and convicted on a similar charge in May 1912 when he sent an illustrated price list of his products through the mail. He was summoned under a new Post Office Act of 1908 that provided for the prosecution of anyone mailing indecent or obscene materials. Holmes made the mistake of sending his advertising booklet unsolicited to a gentleman in Ireland, who was himself a magistrate and who complained to the director of public prosecutions. Holmes's indiscretion cost him £41 in fines and fees.

Holmes's little booklet, entitled *True Morality, or the Theory and Practice of Neo-Malthusianism,* also brought the wrath of the law down upon another neo-Malthusian, James White. White distributed the booklet and was duly charged. Holmes came to his defense with financial aid but to no avail. They lost both the trial and the subsequent appeal, and White was ordered to pay around £30 in fines and costs. The events served to enhance the position of those within the Malthusian League who argued that distributing practical information and devices could only bring trouble for the group. The league gave aid and encouragement to Mr. White but implied that he might have been less than discreet in his actions:

> In our opinion the result of this trial is another justification of the attitude taken towards practical instruction in family limitation by our League. Had we undertaken this work, we should have been kept in such continual embroilment as to utterly ruin all possibility of temperate consideration of the population question. . . . Our business is to continually explain and urge the need for such instruction, and to come to the aid of any who may be attacked for giving it, provided that they have not done so in a needlessly offensive or reckless manner.[106]

White was unable to pay the amount stipulated and was sentenced to three months in Durham Prison. The league helped by asking for donations to a fund for the convicted man and by paying five shillings a week to Mrs. White while her husband was in prison. In addition, the International Bureau of Correspondence and Defense voted White the sum of £4. The league council wrote to the home secretary asking for White's release from prison, but they labored in vain. The home secretary wrote to C. V. Drysdale on 6 May 1911 that "the prisoner is in good health mentally and physically," but on 20 May, Mr. White, aged 54, died in prison with a ruptured blood vessel.[107]

The fate of both White and Holmes served as a warning to the league to be cautious when it finally did open a campaign to distribute practical literature in 1913. The group encountered no legal difficulties, however, from the distribution of their practical leaflet. Others were not as fortunate. In 1920, Mr. Edmund Howarth, the treasurer of a society called the Liberator League, was fined £20 for selling a pamphlet, *Large or Small Families? Legitimate Methods of Birth Control,* at the close of an open-air lecture on the subject. The section on preventive methods had, on the whole, been copied from the Malthusian League's own practical leaflet. It was that section which was ruled obscene. In view of such prosecutions, the league's caution in its own methods of distribution is understandable.

The indictments continued in the twenties. Mr. and Mrs. Guy Aldred were arraigned in December 1922 on the charge of selling an obscene publication, Margaret Sanger's pamphlet, *Family Limitation: A Handbook For Working Mothers.* They were convicted in January and lost an appeal in February 1923. Support poured in; Mrs. Bertrand Russell and J. Maynard Keynes offered to assume liabilities of £50 each as sureties for the costs. The Malthusian League held a large rally to raise funds for the Aldreds, and Bertrand Russell offered to be the main speaker. Sir William Arbuthnot Lane, a well-known physician, testified that the pamphlet in question was not obscene and was, in fact, a most valuable book for the married or about to be married. Mr. J. S. Loe Strachery, editor of *The Spectator,* Harold Cox, H. G. Wells, and other well-known individuals, offered to testify but their offers were declined on the grounds that they were not experts in the area concerned. The appeal was lost, and Gramma Grundy thrived in the twentieth century.

In many respects, the various neo-Malthusian prosecutions over the years undoubtedly served to publicize the family limitation movement and to disseminate its propaganda. As James A. Field wrote in the 1930s, "Attempts to suppress . . . [the movement for birth control] have again and again given it fresh notoriety, and have aroused its partisans to new enthusiasm."[108] But the debate over what is obscene and what is not still rages in the churches, the homes, and the courts. Since the latter are entrusted with the decision as to whether an individual is guilty and therefore punishable of publishing or distributing obscene materials, it becomes the most important of the three. As the Honorable Bertrand Russell once proclaimed, "It is clear that the definition of 'obscenity' is difficult; in practice, it is whatever shocks the Court."[109] Fortunately, few, if any, judges view contraceptive information as obscene today. The case load would surely break the court system asunder if they did.

The Malthusian League continued to try to influence changes in the law throughout its years of existence. In 1880, the group voted to ask Bradlaugh, their member-in-residence as they called him when he was first elected to Parliament, to present a petition calling for freedom of the press, especially for neo-Malthusian literature.[110] He declined to do so. In 1883, copies of *The Malthusian* were mailed to the cabinet and to select members of the House of Commons in order to publicize the league's objectives.[111] Their appeals, however, seem to have had little effect. Alas, said George Standring, "the Neo-Malthusian movement suffers perhaps more than any other from that detestable 'conspiracy of silence' which is the first and last resort of cowardly weakness." As far as government officials are concerned, he continued, "they live in dread of Mrs. Grundy; they are overawed by the stupendous aggregation of prejudice and ignorance which is pompously styled 'public opinion.'"[112]

Family limitation, conjugal prudence—call it what you will—to Conservative and Liberal politicians it was a subject to be avoided in polite company and particularly on the political platform. They might practice it themselves, but to advocate it publicly could turn out to be political suicide. For Labour politicians, the issue could mean not only political and social ostracism but also the possibility of being accused of caving in to

Malthusian economic theories and to the capitalists. They, too, might employ devices whereby to limit their own families, but they dared not publicly advocate it as a general practice for the working classes.

Statistics indicate that by the early part of the twentieth century political leaders, doctors, and even clergymen were practicing family limitation in their own homes, but few of them would allow their names to be associated with the movement publicly. By the 1920s, however, the situation began to change. In 1921, the king's physician, Lord Dawson of Penn, spoke in favor of artificial birth control before a Church congress meeting in Birmingham. The Church, he maintained, should reconsider its stand on the subject. The dike had been broken; henceforth, acceptance of voluntary family limitation would flood the land. The Malthusian League itself, however, may well have slowed acceptance of the idea among medical, religious, and government leaders by attaching it to such doctrines as secularism and among the working classes by associating it with the classical economic theories of A. Smith, T. Malthus, and their disciples.

1. Charles Henry Felix Routh, M.D., M.R.C.P., *The Moral and Physical Evils Likely To Follow If Practices Intended To Act As Checks To Population, Be Not Strongly Discouraged and Condemned* (London: Baillière, Tindall, and Co., 1879), p. 21.

2. Ibid., p. iv.

3. "A Horrible Trade," *The Lancet,* 1 February 1896, pp. 336–37.

4. "The Religious Newspaper and Immoral Advertisements," *The Lancet,* 18 January 1896, p. 183.

5. John Peel, "Contraception and the Medical Profession," *Population Studies, A Journal of Demography* 18, no. 2 (November 1964): 133–43. Also see J. A. Banks, *Prosperity and Parenthood: A Study of Family Planning Among the Victorian Middle Classes* (London: Routledge & Kegan Paul Ltd., 1954), pp. 155–59.

6. Routh, *Moral and Physical Evils,* pp. 13–14. Routh cited as his references "several French authors," such as L. F. G. Bergeret, Médècin-en-Chef de L'-Hôpital d'Ardois Imas, *Des Fraudes dans l'Accomplissement des Fonctions Génétrices,* 5th ed. (Paris: Baillière & Fils, 1877); Dr. Bourgeois, *On the Passions,* and others; and Dr. Meyer, *Conjugal Relations Considered in Relation to Population, Health, and Morality.* "All confirm these views," said Routh.

7. "The Population Question in Amsterdam," *The Malthusian,* no. 9 (October 1879), p. 69.

8. "The Wail of a French Philanthropist," *The Lancet,* 29 February 1896, pp. 564–65.

9. C. R. Drysdale, "The Malthusian Question at Home and Abroad," *The Malthusian* 23, no. 4 (April 1899): 26.

10. "Literature," *The Malthusian* 14, no. 12 (December 1890): 94.

11. Routh, *Moral and Physical Evils.* The quotations from Routh's book are taken from pp. 15–21, passim.

12. "About Children," *The Lancet,* 8 January 1887, p. 88.

13. "Class Mortality Statistics," *The Lancet,* 30 April 1887, p. 889.

14. Ibid., p. 888.

15. C. R. Drysdale, *Medical Opinions On the Population Question* (London: George Standring, 1901), p. 9.

16. Meeting of the Medical Society of London, *The Malthusian,* no. 11 (December 1879), p. 84.

17. Drysdale, *Medical Opinions,* p. 12, citing Dr. Routh.

18. "Population Question in Amsterdam," p. 67.

19. Council Minutes, *The Malthusian,* nos. 9 and 11 (October and December 1879), pp. 71–72 and p. 86, respectively.

20. *The Malthusian,* no. 20 (September 1880), p. 160.

21. *The Malthusian,* no. 22 (November 1880), p. 176.

22. C. R. Drysdale, "The Population Question and the Newcastle Meeting of the British Medical Association," *The Malthusian* 17, no. 9 (September 1893): 65.

23. M. Secundus, "The Poor and the Population Question," *The National Reformer,* cited in *The Malthusian* 16, no. 9 (September 1892): 70.

24. Thirteenth Annual Meeting, *The Malthusian* 14, no. 6 (June 1890): 44. The speaker was Mr. Allen D. Graham.

25. Marie Stopes, *Contraception: Its Theory, History, and Practice* (London: John Bale, Sons & Danielsson, Ltd., 1923), p. 299.

26. "Current Topics," *The Malthusian,* no. 1 (February 1879), p. 7.

27. H. Arthur Allbutt, *Artificial Checks To Population: Is the Popular Teaching of Them Infamous?* An address delivered at Leeds, Bradford, Pudsey, and Morley in February, March, and April 1888. (London: R. Forder, 1889), p. 30.

28. H. Arthur Allbutt, *The Wife's Handbook: How a Woman Should Order Herself During Pregnancy, in the Lying-In Room, and After Delivery. With Hints on the Management of the Baby, and on Other Matters of Importance Necessary to be Known by Married Women* (2nd ed. London: W. J. Ramsey, August 1886), pp. 45–46. English law in the 1880s listed abortion as a felony and provided "a punishment of penal servitude for life, on any woman who is guilty of using means of procuring abortion on herself, and, further, a punishment of penal servitude for five years on anyone who unlawfully supplies or procures any poison or other noxious thing, or any instrument or thing what-

soever, knowing that the same is intended to be unlawfully used, or employed with intent to procure the miscarriage of any woman, whether she be or be not with child, and whether she be or be not aware of such an intention." Ibid., p. 46. Further quotations from *The Wife's Handbook* are taken from pp. 46–50, passim.

29. Allbutt recommended that "properly prepared sponges" could be obtained from "Davies, chemist, Park Lane, Leeds." His testimonials smack somewhat of commercialism and leave one wondering if he received any kind of remuneration for his advertisements.

30. John Peel suggests that Allbutt's *Handbook* contained "mention, for the first time in an English publication of the Mensinga diaphragm." "Contraception and the Medical Profession," *Population Studies,* p. 135.

31. "The Case of Dr. Allbutt," *The Malthusian* 12, no. 1 (January 1888): 3. The entire transcript of Allbutt's hearing before the General Medical Council, 23–25 November 1887, was published in *The Malthusian;* whereas, the minutes of the General Medical Council itself contain only a brief resumé of the proceedings. *The Lancet* also included the General Medical Council's detailed minutes depicting the hearing of the Allbutt case. *The Lancet,* 26 November 1887, pp. 1085–86, and 3 December 1887, pp. 1119–20.

32. For example, a shopkeeper in Holywell Street, Leeds, signed a declaration that "he had not sold more than thirty copies" of the book "and these only to adults, and, as he supposed, married people." "The Case of Dr, Allbutt," p. 4. His sales undoubtedly increased after the book was called "obscene." The Leeds Vigilance Society appears to have been one of several such local groups set up in England after William T. Stead's disastrous attempt in 1885 to spotlight the extent to which young English girls were deviously and unwittingly drawn into the practice of prostitution. The Criminal Law Amendment Act was designed to stop such activities. Stead devised a scheme whereby he hired two underage girls to pose as young unattached females in London where they could be enticed into the practice of prostitution. He ended up in jail on a charge of contributing to the delinquency of minors.

33. "Dr. A. Vickery on the Prosecution of Dr. Henry Arthur Allbutt By the General Medical Council," *The Malthusian* 12, no. 2 (February 1888): 12. The minutes of the General Medical Council confirm that the letter was written in the name of the Vigilance Society. See the Report by the English Branch Council on the Case of Henry Arthur Allbutt, Minutes of the General Medical Council for Wednesday, 23 November 1887. *Minutes of the General Medical Council, Of Its Executive and Dental Committees, and of Its Three Branch Councils, For the Year 1887* 24 (London: Spottiswoode & Co., 1888), pp. 310–11.

34. Letter to the registrar of the General Medical Council from the Royal College of Physicians of Edinburgh, cited in the minutes of the General Medical Council for 17 February 1887. *Minutes of the General Medical Council,* p. 122.

35. Ibid.

36. Ibid., p. 123. The Society of Apothecaries could not by itself remove Allbutt's name from its list. Such an action required a decision by the General Medical Council in keeping with the society's own *Amendment Act* of 1874 which provided that:

It shall be lawful for the Master, Wardens, and Assistants for the time being of the said Society of Apothecaries to strike off from the list of Licentiates of the said Society the name of any person who shall be convicted in England or Ireland of any felony or misdemeanor; or in Scotland of any crime or offense; or who shall, after due inquiry, be judged by the GENERAL COUNCIL to have been guilty of infamous conduct in any professional respect, and the said Society shall forthwith signify to the GENERAL COUNCIL the name of the Licentiate so struck off.

The latter part of the statement applied to Allbutt's case.

37. Ibid., p. 309

38. Ibid., pp. 309–10.

39. Ibid., p. 308.

40. The petition is cited in full in *The Malthusian* 11, no. 4 (April 1887): 28–29.

41. The Dutch League's protest was published in full in *The Malthusian* 11, no. 4 (April 1887): 29–30.

42. Letter to the Editor from Allbutt, *The Malthusian* 11, no. 5 (May 1887): 36. Of course, when one considers that there were around six thousand fellows, members, and licentiates in the R.C.P.E., the number of letters received by Allbutt seems anything but overwhelming.

43. Tenth Annual Meeting, *The Malthusian* 11, no. 6 (June 1887): 45.

44. Council Minutes, *The Malthusian* 11, no. 9 (September 1887): 71.

45. Letter to the R.C.P.E. from Lawrence Allbutt, *The Malthusian* 11, no. 7 (July 1887): 52.

46. "The Persecution of Dr. Henry Arthur Allbutt," *The Malthusian* 11, no. 12 (December 1887): 89.

47. Ibid. Until the nineteenth century, almost anyone could call himself a doctor and set up an office for the treatment of ailments or an apothecary shop. The Medical Act of 1815 restricted the activities of apothecaries, but doctors remained unlicensed until the Medical Act of 1858. Henceforth, anyone wishing to be licensed to practice medicine in England was expected to have passed examinations in the various branches of medical knowledge. For a sum of five pounds his name was thence recorded on the *Medical Register* of the British Isles. The General Council of Medical Education and Registration was organized to implement the legislative act and was to be aided by three branch councils. Under section 29 of the Act of 1858, the General Council was further empowered "to erase the name of such medical practitioner from the Register" who "after due inquiry, be judged by the General Council to have been guilty of infamous conduct in a professional respect." Section 29 of the Medical Act of 1858 was cited in *The Malthusian* 11, no. 12 (December 1877): 90.

48. "Dr. A. Vickery on the Prosecution of Dr. Henry Arthur Allbutt," *The Malthusian* 12, no. 3 (March 1888): 18.

49. "The General Medical Council. Attack on the Liberty of the Press," *The Malthusian* 12, no. 2 (February 1888): 10.

50. Allbutt, *Artificial Checks to Population*, p. 44.

51. Ibid.

52. Ibid., p. 35.

53. F. H. Amphlett Micklewright, "The Rise and Decline of English Neo-Malthusianism," *Population Studies, A Journal of Demography* 15, no. 1 (July 1961): 45.

54. Dr. Amand Routh, *The Declining Birth-Rate: Its Causes and Effects*, Report of the National Birth-Rate Commission, instituted by the National Council of Public Morals (London: Chapman and Hall, Ltd., 1916), p. 247.

55. Norman Haire, "What Lady Barrett Admits—And Omits," *The New Generation* 2, no. 1 (January 1923): 10.

56. Hypatia Bradlaugh Bonner and John M. Robertson, *Charles Bradlaugh: A Record of His Life and Work by His Daughter Hypatia Bradlaugh Bonner With an Account of His Parliamentary Struggle, Politics and Teachings, By John M. Robertson* (London: T. Fisher Unwin, 1902), p. 143.

57. Stopes, *Contraception*, p. 302.

58. C. V. Drysdale, review of *The Problem of Population* by Harold Cox, *The New Generation* 2, no. 3. (March 1923): 33.

59. "A New Malthusian Leaflet," *The Malthusian* 21, no. 4 (April 1897): 29–30.

60. According to Mosiac (or Judaic) law, under such circumstances, the first son born of the widow impregnated by the brother would be given the name of the deceased brother. Deut. 25: 5–6.

61. C. R. Drysdale, "M. Paul Bert on the Morality of the Jesuits," *The Malthusian* 15, no. 9 (August 1891): 60.

62. Thomas Aquinas, *Summa Theologica*, Secundae 2 ae, Ques. 154, Article I.

63. [C. R. Drysdale], "The Neo-Malthusian Question in the Junior Clergy Society of London," *The Malthusian*, no. 75 (June 1885), p. 609.

64. Ibid., p. 610.

65. C. R. Drysdale, "The Thaw!" *The Malthusian* 12, no. 4 (April 1888): 23.

66. Ibid.

67. "Report of the Council of the Malthusian League," *The Malthusian* 12, no. 5 (May 1888): 35.

68. "Rev. A. E. Whatham's Reply to Mr. Lyttelton," *The Malthusian* 13, no. 1 (January 1889): 3. The article features extensive excerpts from Whatham's pamphlet, *Neo-Malthusianism, A Defence*, except the final seven pages, which were written by Dr. George Henry Napheys and designed as "Advice to husbands." A tenth edition of the pamphlet was issued in 1907 by J. King & Co., Walthamstow. Excerpts of Whatham's pamphlet appeared in *The Malthusian* in both December 1888 and in January 1889.

69. Council Minutes, *The Malthusian* 15, no. 12 (December 1891): 94.

70. C. V. Drysdale, *The Small Family System: Is It Injurious or Immoral?* (London: A. C. Fifield, 1913), p. 34.

71. David V. Glass, "Western Europe," in *Family Planning and Population Programs*, Proceedings of the International Conference on Family Planning Programs, Geneva, August 1965 (Chicago: University of Chicago Press, 1966), p. 184.

72. Binnie Dunlop, "Bishops Vote for Poverty, Wars and Bolshevism," *The Malthusian* 44, no. 9 (September 1920): 66, citing the Lambeth Conference Report of 1920.

73. Reverend Charles Fiske, "The Church and Birth Control," *The Atlantic Monthly* 146, (November 1930): 601. In 1958, the Lambeth Conference gave unanimous approval to the use of contraceptives:

> The Conference believes that the responsibility for deciding upon the number and frequency of children has been laid by God upon the conscience of parents everywhere: that this planning, in such ways as are mutually acceptable to husband and wife in Christian conscience, is a right and important factor in Christian family life and should be the result of positive choice before God. Norman St. John-Stevas, *Life, Death and the Law* (Bloomington: Indiana University Press, 1961), p. 73.

74. C. R. Drysdale, Presidential Address Before the Twenty-third Annual Meeting, *The Malthusian* 14, no. 6 (June 1890): 43.

75. Peter Fryer, *The Birth Controllers* (London: Transworld Publishers, Ltd., 1965), p. 182.

76. Drysdale, *Small Family System*, p. 40.

77. *The Declining Birth-Rate: Its Causes and Effects*. Report of the National Birth-Rate Commission, instituted by the National Council of Public Morals (London: Chapman and Hall, Ltd., 1916), p. 63. Anyone wishing to determine official church policy toward family limitation in the early twentieth century would find the report of the National Birth-Rate Commission most helpful.

78. Banks, *Prosperity and Parenthood*.

79. This is not to say that interest in sex was lacking in Victorian England. Such publications as Steven Marcus's *The Other Victorians: A Study of Sexuality and Pornography in Mid-Nineteenth-Century England* (New York: Basic Books, Inc., 1964, 1965, 1966) indicate a lively trade in pornographic literature and an avid interest in sexual activity of all kinds in nineteenth-century England. Also see: Ronald Pearsall, *The Worm in the Bud, The World of Victorian Sexuality* (London: Weidenfeld & Nicolson, 1969 [Also available in Penguin Books, 1974]).

80. For accounts of the Amberley affair, see Bertrand Russell and Patricia Russell, eds., *The Amberley Papers: The Letters and Diaries of Lord and Lady Amberley*, 2 vols. (London 1937), and Peter Fryer, *The Birth Controllers,* pp. 137–46.

81. Added as a motto to the heading of the second issue of *The Malthusian* in March 1879.

82. Twenty-third Annual Meeting, *The Malthusian* 24, no. 3 (March 1900): 22.

83. In 1890, he suggested that such a fine should not exceed forty shillings and might even be as low as one shilling. Further, it "can only be levied on the father, until women are enfranchised, since the present law of marriage places the wife under the control of the husband." *The Malthusian* 14, no. 4 (April 1890): 28.

84. George Standring, "Dr. C. R. Drysdale," *The Republican* 12, no. 4 (July 1886): 26.

85. "Monthly Lectures at Caxton Hall," *The Malthusian* 31, no. 1 (January 1907): 5.

86. Lord Derby on the Population Question," *The Malthusian* 15, no. 3 (March 1891): 18.

87. C. R. Drysdale, "The Population Question at the Social Science Congress," *The Malthusian*, no. 10 (November 1879), p. 72.

88. "Emigration a Failure," *The Malthusian* 18, no. 9 (September 1894): 68.

89. Third Annual Meeting, *The Malthusian*, no. 20 (September 1880), p. 155. The actual number in 1881 was 733,000 women over men.

90. "Lord Derby on the Population Question," p. 19.

91. "The Land Question," *The Malthusian*, no. 13 (February 1880), p. 97.

92. Ninth Annual Meeting, *The Malthusian* 10, no. 7 (July 1886): 52.

93. Eighth Annual Meeting, *The Malthusian*, no. 75 (June 1885), p. 618.

94. Ibid.

95. *The Malthusian*, no. 2 (March 1879), p. 11.

96. J. K. Page, "Land Reform No Remedy for Over-Population," *The Malthusian* 16, no. 1 (January 1892): 1.

97. "Report of the [Twenty-third] Annual Meeting," *The Malthusian* 24, no. 1 (January 1900): 11.

98. C. R. Drysdale, "The Committee on the Unemployed," *The Malthusian* 19, no. 4 (April 1895): 26.

99. C. R. Drysdale, "The Rationale of the Minimum Wage and the Eight Hours Day," *The Malthusian* 22, no. 9 (September 1898): 69.

100. Council Minutes, *The Malthusian*, no. 5 (June 1879), p. 36.

101. Twelfth Annual Meeting, *The Malthusian* 13, no. 6 (June 1889): 50.

102. The incriminating pamphlet was entitled *Some Reasons for Advocating the Prudential Limitation of Families* and was printed in full in *The Malthusian* 15, no. 11 (November 1891): 82–83.

103. *The Malthusian* 15, no. 11 (November 1891): 84–85, citing an account of the trial in the *Weekly Times and Echo*, "Important Prosecution For Obscenity." The case was tried under the Post Office Protection Act of 1884, which provided for a maximum fine of £10.

104. "The Loader Case: Defendant Goes to Gaol," *The Malthusian* 16, no. 5 (May 1892): 36.

105. Council Minutes, *The Malthusian* 17, no. 11 (November 1893): 86.

106. "The James White Trial," *The Malthusian* 35, no. 2 (February 1911): 10.

107. Letter to C. V. Drysdale from W. P. Byrne, Home Secretary, "The James White Case," *The Malthusian* 35, no. 5 (May 1911): 39 [misnumbered 93].

108. James Alfred Field, "The Early Propagandist Movement in English Population Theory," *Essays on Population and Other Papers,* comp. and ed. Helen Hohman Fisher (Chicago: University of Chicago Press, 1931), p. 213.

109. "Opinions of the Month," *The New Generation* 2, no. 5 (May 1923): 60, citing Bertrand Russell.

110. Council Minutes, *The Malthusian*, no. 17 (June 1880), p. 135.

111. Council Minutes, *The Malthusian*, no 51 (May 1883), p. 415.

112. George Standring, "Why Don't They Speak Out?" *The Malthusian* 14, no. 8 (August 1890): 60.

6: Neo-Malthusians Abroad

The great British "workshop of the world" faced difficulties as the nineteenth century waned. Industries in other countries were growing by leaps and bounds and were beginning to challenge the smug complacency of an England long without serious competitors in industrial production. She found herself more and more at a disadvantage in economic relations not only with her European neighbors but also with the rapidly growing United States. Those in power were hard pressed to deal with the growing economic problems of maintaining a competitive world position while at the same time placating their own labor force. By the turn of the century, Conservatives were calling for fair trade instead of free trade; but it would take the events of a devastating world war and a depression to return England to a protectionist policy. Liberals tended more in the direction of governmental social reforms, deviating somewhat from the longstanding Liberal doctrine of "the less government, the better."

The Malthusian League took part in debating proposals for government action but always concluded that any such attempt to alleviate England's economic problems would fail unless it included legislation to implement family limitation, especially among the poor. During the 1890s, however, the league suffered a period of eclipse. For almost twenty years, the Drysdales and their band of faithful supporters had battered the walls of Victorian England with their neo-Malthusian doctrines, but what influence they had had was not reflected in support for the organization itself. The situation calls for "Courage and Perseverance!" George Standring proclaimed in 1894. "We must never hope to stand bowing before a hurricane of popular applause," he continued. "The roll of membership is necessarily a very misleading measure of our success," necessarily, that is, because of the socially taboo nature of the cause. "But when we come to examine the results of our work by the only true standard, the birth-rate, the testimony to our success is absolutely overwhelming."[1] Statistics do indicate that the birthrate in England began to fall just about the time that the Bradlaugh-Besant trial occurred and the Malthusian League was formed. The trend was not immediately recognized, of course; and even when it was, it appeared to prevail primarily among the upper and middle classes. Just how much credit for the decline should go to the Malthusian League is indeed a moot point; but the fact remains that the league readily assumed a major share of the credit for it, whether to bolster the sagging morale of their own supporters or out of a sincere conviction that they had played a primary role in causing the birthrate to fall. Nevertheless, the last decade of the century was a low point for the league in England.

The late 1890s were slow times for English reform activities as a whole. Even the labor movement at the end of the century "appeared to be standing still," says Philip Poirier in his history of the origins of the Labour party. Though, with hindsight, he says, we know it was on the verge of a new resurgence.[2] G. B. Shaw commented that the period was characterized by "an utter slump in Socialism and everything else intellectual."[3] The league went through the same doldrums. Its leader was sixty-eight years old in 1897 and had served the group faithfully for twenty years, but his health was declining and his patience growing thin. The movement to which he had devoted so many years of his life seemed about to flounder. As early as 1895, it became more and more difficult to bring enough members together even for a council meeting. In the same year, the secretary-treasurer, still the loyal William H. Reynolds, announced "we are now not only without funds, but much in debt; and unless we can get some assistance, the Council at their next meeting will have to consider the question of continuing the Journal."[4] These were ominous words, but the small remaining group managed to hang on and keep *The Malthusian* going. They cut down on the publication of other materials and decided to forego the expense of annual meetings. In 1898, however, T.

170

O. Bonser died and left the league an inheritance of eight hundred pounds. The amount was sufficient to give new life to the ailing organization.

Meanwhile, the aging Drysdale occupied himself with maintaining *The Malthusian* and with encouraging the foreign branches of the league. His disenchantment with the English scene drove him to turn his attention more and more to the sister organizations of the Malthusian League that had cropped up in various parts of the world, especially in Europe, since the birth of the parent English organization. He began including in the league's journal articles in French, German and even Russian. Just what his objective was is not clear. This was certainly no way to increase circulation of *The Malthusian* in England. Did he imagine that the journal circulated enough in Europe to warrant the inclusion of such articles or was he aiming at the poor alien worker in English society? Unfortunately, we have no statistics as to the circulation of *The Malthusian* in Europe. The probable explanation for Drysdale's aberration is that, having become discouraged with the progress of family limitation in England, he began to devote his energy to pursuing a longstanding interest in internationalism. He believed family limitation to be the solution not only to the problems of the British Isles but of all the world. "Our views alone," he explained, "can secure lasting peace to the nations."[5]

Both C. R. Drysdale and his brother, George, had been interested in European affairs from their youth. They had worked and played on the Continent as young men and knew the languages fluently. They abhorred the European wars and continual squabbles between nations and dreamed of a day when Europe, including England, would form "a federation, similar to that of the United States."[6] Federal unification is nothing new, Drysdale wrote. We have the recent examples of Germany, Italy, Canada, and Australia before us. These instances indicate, he urged, that the only hope of preventing war is to federate. "The real cause of war evidently lies in the absence of federation in Europe: for it would be impossible for our European States to indulge in the luxury of patriotism if only they were cemented together in a bond similar to that which unites the States of the American Union."[7] What caused the nations to fight, in the view of the Drysdales, was overpopulation that prompted each nation to desire the conquest of the other for its land and resources. Unite the Continent into a "United States of Europe" and carry out the program outlined by the Malthusian League. The result would be an end to war, pestilence, and famine, they maintained.[8]

Perhaps with the ultimate goal of federation in mind, C. R. Drysdale encouraged the development of neo-Malthusian movements in every country in which he could establish a contact. In 1896, the league proclaimed the existence of four strong neo-Malthusian organizations in Europe: one in Holland, one in France, and two in Germany. By 1911, C. V. Drysdale claimed leagues in "Holland, Germany, France, Austria, Spain, Brazil, Belgium, Switzerland, Cuba, and Portugal" and "affiliations in America and Algeria."[9] His claims were perhaps somewhat exaggerated, but the fact remains that the English organization did play a major role in promoting family-planning organizations abroad, especially in Europe. David V. Glass, who has written extensively on population policies and practices, concluded that "the English neo-Malthusian movement really inspired the continental birth-control movements in the late nineteenth century, though some of the continental movements were considerably more militant than the English original."[10]

One of the most successful of the Malthusian League's offsprings was the group organized in Holland. C. R. Drysdale visited Amsterdam in September 1879 to attend an International Medical Congress. Arrangements were made in advance for him to address a neo-Malthusian meeting to be held apart from the Medical Congress itself. One of the more important consequences of the meeting was the establishment of a long-existing link between the English Malthusian League and those in Holland who were interested in the neo-Malthusian movement. At least two Dutch scholars, however, had already spoken out in favor of the movement several years before. H. B. Greven, professor of law at the University of Leyden, submitted a thesis for the degree of Doctor of Laws in 1876.[11] His dissertation was entitled the *Study of Population* and revealed the author to be an exponent of neo-Malthusianism. Samuel Van Houten, at the time a member of the Second Chamber of the Dutch Parliament (1869–94), was the second scholar to endorse neo-Malthusianism publicly. He published an article entitled "The Theory of Population in Relation to Sexual Morality" in the *Vragen des Tyds* [*Questions of the Day*]. Their activities marked them as "the intellectual fathers of Neo-Malthusianism in Holland."[12] It was, however, C. R. Drysdale who gave the first public lecture on the subject in the Dutch provinces in 1879.

Following Drydale's advice and example, Carl Victor Gerritsen, a merchant in Amersfoort and the man who had arranged for Drydale's talk in Amsterdam, decided to work toward the establishment of a league in Holland. In his first efforts, he found only two other individuals willing to help: Mr. H. B. Heldt, president of the General Confederation of Dutch Workmen and later a member of Parliament, and Professor J. M. Smit, a teacher in one of the Dutch intermediate schools in Apeldoorn who lost his position because of his outspoken opinions on such subjects as universal suffrage.[13] The three worked as a committee to bring a Dutch neo-Malthusian organization into being. Gerritsen tried to persuade someone knowledgeable in the social sciences to serve as president, but finding none, he took the responsibility himself.

The three-man committee met on 12 November 1881 to draw up the statutes of the Dutch Nieuw-Malthusiaansche Bond. Realizing the emotional response that their subject matter often engendered, the three worked cautiously to build a membership. Their first advertising circular was mailed to 500 persons believed to be in sympathy with neo-Malthusian principles. It netted 120 to 125 members. Another mailing of 1,200 letters, this time to the members of societies with principles not in conflict with neo-Malthusianism, brought another 100 recruits. The committee wisely divided the members at the outset into two groups, active and passive, later designated as public and private. The names of the latter remained anonymous other than to the leaders of the organization. Over half the original members were inscribed as passive thus giving them anonymity while at the same time lending the organization the support

173

that it so badly needed. Out of seventeen doctors enrolled in the first year, for example, only one was willing to be named publicly.[14]

In 1882, when the first meeting of the new Dutch Neo-Malthusian League was held in Amsterdam, 233 members attended, representing almost every area of the small country. A few at the meeting questioned the choice of "Neo-Malthusian" as part of the name of the organization. It holds no meaning for the great masses of people, they claimed; but their objections were overruled and Malthus prevailed. At least the founders of the Dutch group avoided the English organization's dilemma by selecting "Neo-Malthusian" instead of just "Malthusian." New officers and eighteen additional members were selected at the meeting to form a council to conduct the business of the group for the coming year. C. V. Gerritsen remained as president, somewhat against his wishes; L. J. Hansen, vice-president; N. A. Calisch and B. H. Heldt, secretaries; and Dr. J. M. Smit and C. Dekker, treasurers. Having no journal of its own, the league had to depend upon publications like Heldt's *Werkmansbode*, the literary organ of the General Confederation of Dutch Workmen, and *De Dageraad* to publish news of their activities.

The Dutch league first tried to spread its neo-Malthusian message through a series of pamphlets. The most important of these was first published in 1884 without an indicated author and was entitled *The Origin and Development of the Moral Sense*. It was written "by several persons, among whom were physicians, who , however, did not wish to be known."[15] The last pages contained a description and diagrams of known preventives but were left uncut "in order not to shock those persons who were too easily alarmed." Apparently the Dutch populace was not too offended; 2,000 copies were sold in three weeks. The last sixteen pages were republished as *The Means of Preventing Large Families* and immediately became the league's best seller. Unfortunately, the organization neglected to obtain a copyright and less scrupulous publishers began issuing the pamphlet under more provocative titles. The league did all it could to prevent such abuse of the book but rationalized that though it had undoubtedly fallen "into the hands of young

174

people, and even of young women, . . . the most wicked act often causes some good to follow."[16] In other words, at least the neo-Malthusian message had been circulated. By 1900, the league itself had distributed over 200,000 copies. A number of other pamphlets were issued as the years passed but none as important as the one that gave direct and explicit instructions on how to go about limiting one's family.[17] This was an action neglected by the English Malthusian League until well into the twentieth century because it feared government censorship.

Year after year, in the pages of *The Malthusian*, Drysdale perhaps somewhat jealously commended the Dutch Neo-Malthusian League on its freedom and progress. "In Holland alone do we find real freedom of the press; and a Malthusian League which has no prosecution to fear."[18] The situation, though better than in England, was not quite as ideal for the Dutch organization, however, as Drysdale would have his readers believe. The same groups that attacked the Malthusian League in England had their counterparts in Holland. In its early years, the Dutch league like its English parent stressed neo-Malthusian economic doctrines. Consequently, it conflicted directly with unseasoned nineteenth-century socialism that was as dogmatic in its approach to the problem of poverty as were the early neo-Malthusians. Socialists insisted that the only solution lay in an immediate reorganization of the economic system. "The Socialist workingman's party in Holland . . . has no sympathy for this League, partly because they prefer revolution to evolution," one Dutch member wrote in 1883.[19] But the league's willingness to distribute practical information in pamphlet form and later to give clinical assistance to those requesting it won over large sections of the working class and at least the revisionist socialists. The crucial year for the league was 1899, according to Dr. Jan Rutgers, an important member of the Dutch league in the 1890s and early twentieth century and himself a socialist. Until that year, he later wrote, the league as a whole was averse to socialism. But the latter movement had become so popular in Holland that the league leaders decided they would have greater success if they worked with socialists. Subsequently, Mme. Rutgers-Hoitsema, Dr. Rutgers's wife and newly elected president of the Dutch Neo-Malthusian League, undertook a lecture tour, which was advertised in the socialist papers. She was, her husband proudly wrote to C. V. Drysdale, immensely successful in dealing with socialists and even anarchists. [20]

In 1895, the Dutch government extended legal recognition to the Dutch Neo-Malthusian League. The organization capitalized on the action by implying that such recognition constituted an avowal of the neo-Malthusian principles by the government itself. Not so, wrote H. Pierson, a clergyman and a member of the government. A league or institution has only to formulate its rules and send them to the state. If nothing is found in them contrary to the national laws, then the organization is granted a "legal personality" for thirty years. "The Dutch Government therefore has no title at all to your eulogies; it has done nothing at all to either recommend or dissuade Malthusianism."[21] What the governmental action did do, however, was to stir up a clerical-led movement in the Dutch Parliament to have official sanction of the league rescinded. The old shibboleths of Christianity were called into action. Catholics and Calvinists joined hands to get Parliament to withdraw recognition from the Neo-Malthusian League. A Catholic member of Parliament, named Bahlman, introduced a bill to that effect, but it was thrown out after speeches by Liberals, such as Samuel Van Houten, minister of the interior. In 1899, two doctors in Amsterdam, aided by theological groups, assembled an Anti-Malthusian League. Within a year the organization had 363 members. It, too, was recognized by the government. By 1900, however, control of the Dutch Neo-Malthusian League had passed to new leadership and was on the verge of an even more vigorous program of activities.

The Dutch league was always more practical in its approach to the problem of family limitation than the English organization. Though it, too, in its early years suffered from an overemphasis on Malthusian doctrine, it had practical literature in circulation by 1884. In addition, the league claimed at least some responsibility for the activities of Dr. Aletta Jacobs, the first Dutch woman to be awarded a degree in medicine.

Aletta Henriette Jacobs was born in the Dutch village of Sappermeer in 1854.[22] She was the daughter of a physician who believed in equal educational opportunities for all eleven of his children whether male or female. In addition to an education, he conveyed to Aletta his concern for others, and she decided that only through a medical career like her father's could she work to improve the lives of Dutch women and children. At the age of seventeen, she applied for admission to the State University of Groningen. After a valiant struggle against rules barring women, she was admitted for a one-year probationary period and allowed to attend lectures. As the year neared its end, she appealed to the prime minister of Holland for help and got permission to continue her studies. Henceforth, Dutch universities were open to women. The young Aletta completed her medical studies at the Universities of Groningen and Amsterdam and received her degree in 1879 at the age of twenty-five. She then visited London where she met the leaders of the English Malthusian League, C. R. Drysdale, Charles Bradlaugh, and Annie Besant, as well as other free thinkers of the time.

In 1880, Dr. Jacobs began a series of lectures on the care and feeding of infants. She lectured twice a week at the headquarters of the Trades Unions Council in Amsterdam. In addition, she administered free medical advice and treatment two mornings a week. From her work, she came to a realization that what poor women needed was a way to avoid frequent pregnancies. She was not interested in the effect of family limitation on the economy as a whole; she was concerned for the individual health and well being of those in her care. But she knew of no reliable method of contraception. In 1882, she read an article by Dr. Mensinga, a gynecologist in Flensburg, who recommended a pessary he had invented in 1880. The article so impressed her than she wrote to Mensinga and, through a long correspondence, learned how to use the method that she subsequently popularized. It was the only contraceptive method she recommended in almost fifty years of conducting consultations. This probably explains why it became known in England as the "Dutch cap," though in the United States it has been more commonly known as the diaphragm. The major drawback to the method was that each pessary had to be fitted for the individual and required some instruction for proper use. For this purpose, Dr. Jacobs began giving contraceptive information to the poor women who came to her semiweekly free clinic and to those who consulted her in her private practice as well.

In the early 1890s, the Dutch League expanded its practical activities not only by continuing to distribute its pamphlet on contraceptive methods but also by adding to its ranks three doctors who were willing to give gratuitous advice to working women and to others among the poor on how to limit the number of their offspring. In 1891, Dr. Jan Rutgers was engaged to give advice in Rotterdam and Dr. R. de Waard in Groningen. In 1892, Dr. Th. de Groot agreed to work in Drachten (Friesland).

Also in the early 1890s, the Dutch League acquired a new honorary secretary, W. M. H. Anten, a captain of artillery who had fallen into disgrace because of his "advanced ideas" but who added a zealous new spirit to the neo-Malthusian cause in Holland.[23] The league, domiciled in Amsterdam since its origin in 1881, and Anten moved to the Hague. The new spirit generated by the added activities and the leadership of Anten ended a period of inertia for the group.

After 1892, the league began hiring midwives to dispense information to working women in Amsterdam, the Hague, Rotterdam, Middleburg (Zeeland), Groningen, Arnheim, Utrecht, and Helder. In 1894, 640 women received advice; by 1898, the number rose to 1,741. The system worked well until it was hampered by the formation in the late 1890s of an organization of midwives against neo-Malthusianism, which excluded all women associated with the league.

Also in the late 1890s, religious and medical organizations stepped up their attacks on the Dutch neo-Malthusians. It became more and more difficult to enlist the aid of medical personnel. Doctors were not willing to risk their practices by becoming associated publicly with the neo-Malthusian cause. Consequently, in 1899, the league's newly elected secretary, Dr. Jan Rutgers, devised a plan for increasing the number of persons qualified to instruct lower-class women in contraceptive methods. He organized a system whereby he could train selected poor women themselves and others to act as advisers. He called them lay-nurses and, by 1910, had trained thirty-eight.

Dr. Jan Rutgers and his wife, Mme. Rutgers-Hoitsema, brought to the league a fresh and vigorous leadership which was to increase the membership of the organization from around 500 in 1900 to over 2,500 by 1910. Dr. Rutgers was born in 1850 and trained, in keeping with his father's wishes, for a career in the church.[24] However, a personal repugnance for theological doctrines that stressed asceticism and dualism of body and soul soon drove him to search elsewhere for a life of service to humanity. He turned to the study of medicine and established a practice in Rotterdam in 1879. He was well liked and respected in his profession and was soon elected secretary and later president of the Rotterdam Medical Association. His interests were more humane than professional, however, and he soon became absorbed in the problems of his poorer working-class patients. He studied social science and economics and was drawn to the budding socialist movement. His activities also led him to marry Maria Hoitsema, his second wife and the former headmistress of a girls' school. Together they supported the feminist, the socialist, and the family-planning movements.

The Rutgerses firmly believed that the Dutch Neo-Malthusian League "should above all endeavour to spread knowledge which would be useful of itself."[25] Dr. Rutgers considered the Malthusian doctrines, espoused by the league, a hindrance to its primary purpose because of the arguments those theories provoked. In his opinion, "all views as to the economic or other standpoints of the question were of little importance in comparison with the question of the individual."[26] It was with this conviction that he and his wife led the Dutch league in the early twentieth century, she as president until 1912 and he as secretary until 1917. The Dutch organization had already stressed practical work more than its English counterpart but never to the extent that the Rutgerses did. They emphasized getting contraceptive information and devices to as many as could be reached through lectures, literature, and private consultations in all the major cities of Holland. Nevertheless, in spite of their efforts, one Dutch neo-Malthusian lamented in

1905 that "we do not yet manage to touch one-tenth of the poor drudges who need our help."[27]

The growth of the family-limitation movement in the Netherlands prompted a clerical-minded government to take action. In 1911, the Dutch Parliament passed a law that sharply restricted the activities of the vendors of contraceptives and placed conditions on the development of Dutch birth-control organizations. "This law may greatly hamper our activity," said one neo-Malthusian worker, "but it will certainly prove unable to impede the progress of the undesired increase of families."[28] Rutgers himself took a positive view of the law. It has done much good, he observed in 1923, "because quack-advertisements do now not often offend public opinion."[29]

In 1927, a reactionary government refused to renew the Dutch league's official recognition, but the action had no effect on the organization and its work. In September 1931, the group opened its first public birth-control clinic in Amsterdam and named it the Aletta Jacobs Huis (house) in honor of Holland's first woman doctor who had taken part in the founding of the Dutch Neo-Malthusian League and who had been among the first to give free contraceptive advice to the poor mothers of Amsterdam. In the ensuing years, similar clinics were opened in other major Dutch cities.

The English Malthusian League had played an important role in bringing the Dutch organization into being. It continued to give its guidance, encouragement, and praise to its offspring even when the latter outdistanced the parent group. Membership in the Dutch league has risen to 6,000, *The Malthusian* reported in 1917. "In proportion to population our League ought to have nearly ten times this number. We heartily congratulate our Dutch friends on their progress in these difficult times."[30] C. V. Drysdale frequently cited the success of the Dutch organization as an example of the success of the neo-Malthusian movement as a whole. What he would not admit, of course, was that the progress of the Dutch group was actually evidence of the success of the family-planning movement and not of Malthusian economic doctrines. By 1931, the Dutch Neo-Malthusian League had lost all of its Malthusian vestments and, in 1946, was absorbed into the newly organized Netherlands Society for Sexual Reform.

In Germany as well, C. R. Drysdale tried to encourage individuals whom he knew to start a neo-Malthusian organization patterned on the English group. Malthusian economic doctrines, however, proved as unpopular in Germany in the late nineteenth century as in England. Drysdale enrolled G. Stille, a physician in Hanover as a vice-president of the English league in its first years. He encouraged Dr. Stille to form a similar group in Germany, but Stille reported in 1879 that "the New Malthusian faith has not yet made its way into public attention in Germany. As soon as a small number of like opinions can be united, I will do my best to found here a Malthusian Society."[31] The league's major success in Germany came through another of its vice-presidents, Max Hausmeister of Stuttgart. In 1882, Hausmeister took the lead in organizing a neo-Malthusian group called the *Sozial-Harmonische Verein* (Social Harmony Union) and a monthly journal, *Die Sozial Harmonie*.[32] The new organization was active in Stuttgart only and apparently met with little success, though it was still in existence in 1900.

As in England, the German neo-Malthusian organizers bemoaned the growth of the socialist movement in Germany and the adoption of social welfare programs by the government. In true liberal fashion, Hausmeister, himself a banker, attacked both the government for instituting welfare legislation, such as national insurance for the elderly, and the Social Democratic Party for failing to realize that the real economic problem lay in an oversupply of workers. "They did not recognise," he repeatedly maintained, "that the real cause of their unsatisfactory existence was the heavy augmentation of the population, resulting in too much competition in their own ranks."[33] Germany in the late nineteenth century, however, was going through its own industrial revolution, and economic conditions on the whole were getting better, not worse, as the Social Harmony Union often implied as part of its propaganda campaign. In 1900, even Hausmeister had to admit that the extent of trade activities in Germany seemed to diminish the importance of neo-Malthusian doctrines. Nevertheless, he said, all experience shows "that we must, ere long, have a time of great overpopulation, when work will be scarce and distress abundant everywhere. Then will be the time to establish branches throughout the whole of Germany, to teach the real remedy for poverty, prostitution, and celibacy."[34]

The Social Harmony Union probably had its greatest influence on the development of the family-limitation movement in Germany through its publication in 1895 of a practical pamphlet called *Die der Conception Vorbeugenden Mittel*. An essay on the population question filled the first half of the 36-page booklet. The remainder was devoted to various methods of contraception. The pamphlet was distributed free of charge but only to doctors and married couples who agreed to communicate the result of their experiences with the methods within two years after receiving the pamphlet. This provision undoubtedly reduced its circulation. The Social Harmony Union reported in 1899 that "a good many persons who, whilst receiving the work, had made no report on its utility."[35]

Efforts to form neo-Malthusian leagues in other parts of Germany came to naught. Drysdale had high hopes that Dr. A. Meyerhof, who wrote neo-Malthusian pamphlets under the pseudonym of Hans Ferdy, would become president of a national German Malthusian League, but such a group never materialized. Nevertheless, the family-limitation movement as a whole did rather well in Germany until the Nazi era. The organizations that promoted the movement, however, did so from the viewpoint of the health and financial benefits to be gained by individual families as opposed to the emphasis placed on economic doctrines by neo-Malthusians. As early as 1897, Dr. Bilfinger, medical officer of health in Stuttgart, undertook a lecture tour through Germany on behalf of the Social Harmony Union and expressed the opinion that "even in Catholic cities, such as Augsburg and Regensburg, the use of preventive checks was now known to be common."[36]

The English Malthusian League also enjoyed some support in France, though it was not until 1896 that a French neo-Malthusian organization was formed. The Drysdales believed that since France had a declining birthrate during much of the nineteenth century, its populace had already accepted family limitation and would therefore welcome and support the neo-Malthusian movement. Until well into the twentieth century, they praised the French peasant for his wisdom in practicing what they called conjugal prudence.

It is true that as a result of the revolution in 1789 and a redivision of the land in France, a peasant proprieter class had developed. With the institution of the Napoleonic Code in the early years of the nineteenth century, a landowner was forbidden to pass his entire holdings to one descendant. The rules of primogeniture and entail were discarded. Estates were henceforth to be divided equally among the heirs. As a result, it was prudent for the French peasant to restrict the number of his offspring. In most cases, this was the only way each child could hope to inherit enough for his needs. Even the London *Times* remarked as early as 1857, "Who can wonder at the families of these people [the French peasants], and that they carry out to the letter the teachings of Malthus and Mill, and deliberately marry with the intention of having only one or two children, or none at all?"[37]

In the late 1870s and early 1880s, C. R. and Alice Vickery Drysdale repeatedly used the example of the French peasant landholder in such a way as to imply that *all* of France, including the poor industrial working classes, practiced family limitation. "Already, owing to the prudent and praiseworthy conduct of the poorer classes in France, that country . . . [is] by far the happiest in Europe," C. R. Drysdale proclaimed in 1879.[38]

What the neo-Malthusian leaders tended to ignore was the fact that to equate the situation of a French landowner, no matter how small, with that of a French laborer in the city was not valid. Using general statistics on the decline of the French national birthrate, they hypothesized that industrial workers as well as small, rural landowners practiced family limitation. The implication was that French industrial workers were therefore economically better off than English laborers, but such was not the case. Opponents of neo-Malthusianism were quick to point out that the same crowded conditions were to be found in the few industrial areas of France as in the manufacturing centers of England. Since the class of industrial workers was so much larger in England, the problems were, of course, more apparent and perhaps more critical. It is a "gross fallacy," Henry M. Hyndman pointed out, "to suppose that New-Malthusianism is in the majority in France."[39] There is a great deal of distress, he continued, in French manufacturing centers. But the Drysdales persevered. When another socialist challenged neo-Malthusianism in 1890 saying "that the vast majority of the working classes will never put any curb on their procreative power out of regard to society and very little out of regard to their own domestic comfort," Drysdale retorted, "but surely the example of the French working classes negatives the latter part of this contention."[40]

The Drysdales assumed that statistics indicating a behavior pattern among the French peasantry indicated the same behavior among the urban working classes. As more detailed population statistics became available for the French metropolitan areas, however, it became apparent that just as in the cities of England the poor had more children than the rich, so it was in the cities of France. Even Drysdale finally admitted, "in the working classes, and above all in great cities, Malthusianism is not in fashion. . . . The working man is so unfortunate, and sees before him so little possibility of a better life, that he abandons himself without stint and without reason to the pleasures of the moment."[41] Socialists took Drysdale's statement as an admission "that comfort made people prudent as to the size of the family" and argued even more vehemently "that it would be necessary to make the people comfortable first by better distribution of wealth, before expecting to make them prudent in this matter by precept."[42]

French leaders tended to be more concerned with the decline of the birthrate in France relative to the birthrates in Germany and England than with its possible effects upon the extent of poverty in French cities. The birthrate alone, of course, tells little about population trends as a whole. It must be related to other factors, such as the death rate and the number of emigrants and immigrants, to have any real significance. The population of France, as well as of Germany and England, generally

DECLINE IN BIRTHRATE IN EUROPEAN COUNTRIES

	Decade of Highest Rate	Highest Rate	1891 to 1900	1912–1914
Germany	1871–1880	39.1	36.1	27.5 (1913)
Belgium	1871–1880	32.7	28.9	22.6 (1912)
Netherlands	1871–1880	36.4	32.5	28.2 (1914)
Italy	1881–1890	37.8	35.3	31.7 (1913)
France	1801–1810	32.2	22.1	19.0 (1913)

SOURCE: National Birth-Rate Commission, *The Declining Birth-Rate: Its Causes and Effects* (London: Chapman and Hall, Ltd., 1916), p. 27.

continued to increase in the late nineteenth and early twentieth centuries. The decline in the birthrate was somewhat more severe in France, however, than in England and Germany. A chart published by the National Birth-Rate Commission of England in 1916 gives some idea of the reason for the concern among French leaders.[43]

The Malthusian League praised the French for their prudence. National leaders lamented the situation. They were more interested in stopping the decline than in encouraging it, but first they struggled to understand what had caused the decrease. Women, as usual, came in for their share of the blame. "The expensive habits which have taken hold of French women in all ranks" draws their attention from maternal interests, one Parisian journalist suggested.[44] Heavy taxation is to blame, said a writer in the German neo-Malthusian journal, *Die Sozial Harmonie*. He claimed taxes had been stringently imposed by the French government, "for the purpose of keeping up the ideal of revenge against Germany, on account of Alsace-Lorraine."[45] Most felt, however, that the principal causes of the declining birthrate were the unlimited subdivision of land in France; the difficulties, both legal and economic, of getting married; and the general use of methods of contraception.

The French Parliament attempted to deal with the problem of the declining birthrate in the late nineteenth century. In 1885, legislative action provided a grant of £40 a year "to the seventh child of persons [with seven living children] in necessitous circumstances, when it had passed the period of primary instruction."[46] The attempt, of course, was to help parents with large families. The result, said the English Malthusian League editor, will be "to incite the poorest classes of French society to plunge themselves yet deeper into degradation and poverty."[47] A bill introduced by M. LeRoy in 1892 would have been much more comprehensive had it passed. He proposed, among other things, to: (1) simplify the legal formalities connected with marriage, including reducing from 25 to 21 the age at which a man could marry without parental consent; (2) abolish or modify the provision for equal division of property among all the children of a family; (3) imprison husbands found guilty of committing adultery; (4) require fathers of illegitimate children to shoulder financial responsibility for them; (5) have a sliding scale of taxation, to be reduced in proportion to the number of children in a family; and (6) make up the difference in tax revenue with an annually increasing levy on single men calculated on the basis of their incomes.[48]

One group of concerned and enterprising Frenchmen took it upon themselves in 1892 to form an organization for the express purpose of promoting an increase in the French population. The founders of *La Famille Française,* as they called their group, proposed to set up private insurance plans, one to provide dowries (*Assurance Dotale*) and another to provide funds for the expenses of childbirth (*Assurance Maternelle*).[49]

With the presence of such a strong national interest in increasing the birthrate, it is no wonder that neo-Malthusians made little headway in France. There were even those who implied that to promote family limitation was unpatriotic.[50] Such a charge could hardly have helped the neo-Malthusian movement in a country still smarting from national defeat in 1870, but Drysdale never wavered in his hope of seeing a French league created. Among those who sided with the movement in France was Paul Robin, director of the Prevost Orphanage at Cempuis (Oise), France.[51] As early as 1879 he arranged for Drysdale to address a working-class conference in Marseilles and continued during the 1880s to agitate in favor of neo-Malthusian doctrines whenever and wherever he could. His activities brought him censure and finally dismissal, though Drysdale claimed it was a resignation, from his post at the Cempuis orphanage in 1894.[52] Among other things, Robin was charged with teaching "the abominable and immoral Malthusian doctrines" to his female pupils, a charge he vehemently denied. "Both the general theory of population and the practical consequences which are deduced from it," he said, "are quite beyond the capacity of children."[53] He was later cleared of the charges and granted a pension by the General Council of the Seine, which had investigated the case. He was then free to promote the neo-Malthusian movement more directly and openly.

In 1896, Robin formed a French Malthusian league, *La Ligue de la Régénération Humaine* (League for Human Regeneration). Like its English counterpart, the French organization stressed theory and referred those interested in the practical side to M. O. Martinet, a pharmacist in Paris. Robin did, however, have the Dutch pamphlet, *The Means of Avoiding Large Families,* translated into French and distributed. As in Holland, Drysdale was appointed honorary president of the French organization; but Robin served as its active president. The address of the league in 1896–97 was listed as No. 6 Passage Vauconteurs, Paris. By late 1897, however, the office had been moved into Robin's home at 6 Rue Haxo. Robin started a journal for the French organization in 1897, but ill health soon forced him to relinquish all his neo-Malthusian activities. He sailed for Auckland, New Zealand, in July 1898. The league continued for a short time without him, but within a year its activities ceased.[54] By 1900, Robin was back in France ready to reestablish his defunct organization and its journal, *Régénération*. He resigned as president of the league again in 1908, however, due to ill health and dissension within the group. Nevertheless, he stayed on as vice-president until his death in September 1912.

Robin's son-in-law, Gabriel Giroud, followed him in promoting the cause of neo-Malthusianism in France. Giroud tried, for example, to get the French government to let him distribute neo-Malthusian literature to German prisoners of war in

France during World War I but was refused. Eugène Humbert and Giroud started a new neo-Malthusian periodical called *Génération Consciente* before the war but had to change its name when the government suppressed it. After this had happened several times, they chose to discontinue the journal entirely rather than risk imprisonment. Perhaps this kind of harassment explains why Giroud preferred to write under the pseudonym of G. Hardy.

Opposition to the French neo-Malthusian League began as soon as the group first organized in 1896. The Alliance Nationale was founded in the same year by Dr. Jacques Bertillon, a longstanding and vocal opponent of family limitation. "Like most French patriots," said C. V. Drysdale, Bertillon "is greatly concerned for the military power and prestige of his country."[55] Individuals like Bertillon eventually won, however, in a France more frightened of depopulation than of overpopulation. The French national assembly passed a law in 1920 forbidding publications that advocated keeping down the birthrate. In addition, the government took steps to encourage large families, including issuing a "Medal of the French Family," and instituted measures to stop abortion and the sale of contraceptives. Condoms were defined as protection against venereal disease and not as contraceptives, thus they were excluded from the ban. All of these actions had the support of the powerful French Academy of Medicine. The French birth-control movement collapsed completely in the late 1930s, "a victim of its own fossilization," says D. V. Glass, "as well as of French pro-natalist repression."[56]

The Drysdales would liked to have seen the formation of Malthusian leagues in all the countries of Europe, but their major accomplishments were in Holland, France, and Germany. In Sweden, for example, Professor Knut Wicksell and Dr. Anton Nystrom were among the few who worked for the neo-Malthusian movement. In 1910, the Swedish Parliament passed an act prohibiting the sale and circulation of birth-control information. Dr. Nystrom was arrested and fined £5 for lecturing publicly in Stockholm on methods of family limitation. But in

188

1912 the Malthusian League reported receipt of an application for the affiliation of a Swedish neo-Malthusian League. By 1922, however, they were again lamenting the lack of a Swedish organization. "There have been one or two small societies without great influence," Knut Wicksell reported, "but I think even they are now become extinct."[57] Actually the birthrate in Sweden was so low in the 1920s, second only to France, that it was difficult to arouse much public interest in the subject. The present Swedish family-planning movement got its start in the 1930s under the impetus of the National Association for Sex Education.

In 1913, the Malthusian League hailed the formation of an Italian neo-Malthusian organization and the creation of a journal to promote family planning in Italy.[58] The activities of the new organization were curtailed during World War I and were brought to a complete halt with the rise of fascism in Italy. Section 553 of the Fascist code made it a criminal offense to disseminate information about birth control. Nevertheless, the Italian birthrate fell from 38 per 1,000 in 1865–79 to 23.2 in 1936–40.[59]

In 1909, *The Malthusian* mentioned the Liga Española de Regeneracion Humana that was operating in Spain under the direction of Senor Luis Bulfi. The organization's neo-Malthusian journal, *Salud y Fuerza,* was also mentioned. Apparently the name of the journal was later changed to *El Nueva Malthusiana,* but nothing further was reported.[60] In Switzerland, a *Groupe Malthusien* was formed in Geneva in 1908 by Valentin Grandjean, with a journal, the *Bulletin Malthusien,* later called *La Vie Intime.*[61] In 1909, there were several branches throughout the country with "no less than eight Malthusian periodicals."[62] Belgium suffered from the same problem of a declining birthrate as France and was thus unfertile ground for the growth of neo-Malthusianism. A league was formed in 1906, however, under the direction of Dr. Fernand Mascaux.

In 1910, at the International Neo-Malthusian Conference held at the Hague, ten "Contributing Leagues" gave reports on

189

neo-Malthusian activities within their respective countries. Those reporting were England, Holland, France, Belgium, Switzerland, Spain, Portugal, Sweden, Germany, and Hungary. By 1914, there were also organizations reporting from Brazil, Cuba, Italy, and Algeria.[63]

In the United States, the Obscenity Law of 1873 blocked both the publication and dissemination of contraceptive information and devices until well into the twentieth century. As in other areas of the world, there were a few, however, who were willing to risk court action by printing and distributing neo-Malthusian literature. D. M. Bennett of New York, editor of a periodical called the *Truthseeker,* was imprisoned for eleven months in the late 1870s when he published a work written by Ezra Heywood. It was entitled *Cupid's Yokes.* Dr. Edward Bliss Foote, also of New York, was fined $3,000 plus almost $2,000 in court costs in 1876 for mailing one of his own publications, *Words in Pearl,* in response to a decoy letter sent from Chicago under a false name.[64] The booklet was basically a manual on contraception. Foote nevertheless continued writing and publishing other books and a periodical, the *Health Monthly,* from 1876 to 1883. In the latter venture, he was assisted by his son, Edward Bond Foote, also a doctor. The elder Foote joined the English Malthusian League and hoped to start a similar society in the United States, but he never did. Moses Harman of Chicago spent time in the Joliet (Illinois) prison and in the prison at Leavenworth, Kansas, in the late nineteenth and early twentieth centuries. His crime was publishing a bimonthly periodical called *Lucifer* in which he printed articles pleading the cause of voluntary family planning. His daughter, Lillian, carried on his work while he was in prison.

The Malthusian League on occasion sent copies of its journal to correspondents in the United States, but the periodical did not always reach its destination. The 1873 Obscenity Law provided postal authorities with the power to investigate and confiscate letters and packages suspected of being "non-mailable matter" under Section 211 of the law. In 1902, William Reynolds, the aging secretary of the league, remarked that "there were some things on which the inhabitants of the United

Kingdom might congratulate themselves as being more free than those of the democratic States of the Union."[65]

The present large and effective family-planning movement in the United States actually did not get under way until Margaret Sanger, a courageous New York nurse, took up the battle in 1914. Her first efforts to challenge the 1873 Obscenity Law by publishing a periodical called *The Woman Rebel* led to her arrest and self-imposed exile in order to avoid imprisonment. She fled first to England where she contacted the Malthusian League. She never forgot the encouragement she received from the members of the league and the friendships which she formed, especially with Alice Vickery and her son, Charles Vickery Drysdale. Mrs. Sanger differed with the Malthusian League, however, over its emphasis upon Malthusian doctrines to the neglect of the dispersal of practical information. "Not until January, 1913," she said, "did the Neo-Malthusian League begin to alter its policy toward the instruction of the working class. Lectures on theory and methods were given on street corners, but their practical leaflet could be obtained only upon written application to the League. It was the name 'Malthus,' I concluded, which kept the idea from spreading to the workers."[66] She chose the phrase "birth control" to draw attention to the family-planning movement in the United States and avoided reference to economic doctrines. She emphasized the benefits to be gained by individual families.

During her year-long European exile in 1914–15, Mrs. Sanger traveled from England to the Netherlands to learn firsthand of the latest and most practical methods of contraception from Dr. Jan Rutgers and the Dutch Neo-Malthusian League. My trip to Holland, she said, "revolutionized my ideas regarding the future of the movement. No longer could I look upon birth control knowledge as primarily a free speech fight. I realized now that it involved much more than talk, much more than books or pamphlets, no matter how widely or freely one might wish to spread pamphlets containing this information."[67] She realized the necessity to establish clinics for the dissemination of contraceptive information and appliances. Shortly after her return to the United States, she established the first birth-control clinic in America (1916). As short-lived as it was, it paved the way for the future development of a network of such clinics throughout the United States as a whole.

The Malthusian League wanted to develop programs in the Far Eastern lands as well, especially in the British colonial areas. Their funds and energy, however, were more than spent in the homeland and on the Continent. "We only wish," the leaders lamented in 1903, "that we had funds sufficient to send missionaries of our real Gospel (glad tidings) to India, China, and Japan."[68] There is, of course, a large and important family-planning movement in India today. Just what role the English Malthusian League played in its development remains to be studied. As early as 1880, the Malthusian League Council announced that efforts to combat the evils of overpopulation in India were already "bearing fruit in that distant land."[69] They were referring to the efforts of a league vice-president, Murugesa Mudalier, who published the *Philosophic Inquirer* in Madras. On 13 December 1882, another Indian neo-Malthusian, Mutha Naidu, wrote to Dr. H. A. Allbutt announcing the establishment of a Hindu Malthusian League in Madras and asking him to be "the Patron of the League." The principles and rules of the new organization, Naidu reported, were to be "the same as those of the parent League of London, to which we intend to affiliate."[70] L. Narusee was listed as secretary of the new league and Moonesawny Naiker as one of the eight members thus far enrolled. Unfortunately, *The Malthusian* gave no further news of the Madras organization.[71]

When an Indian birth-control society was formed in Delhi in 1922, however, Professor Gopalji of Ranjar College reported the news to the English neo-Malthusians and added: "Members of the Indian Birth-control Society congratulate the *parent* Society in England for organising the International Neo-Malthusian and Birth-control Conference at London on July 11–14, 1922" [Italics are mine].[72]

In 1898, Paul Robin, the French neo-Malthusian, suggested the formation of an international Malthusian league. The English organization supported the suggestion with verbal enthusiasm but took no action. So upon his return to France, Robin took the initiative in calling the International Conference of Neo-Malthusians in Paris, 4–6 August 1900. Representatives attended from Holland, Germany, France, and England eager to meet each other, exchange progress reports, and offer ideas for future programs. Robin proposed the establishment of an international federation of the neo-Malthusian league with the following program:

1. Free exchange of correspondence and of all publications issued or adopted by the various Leagues. Reciprocal right of translation of all publications in all languages. No common budget, and no central office to be formed.

2. The only point imperatively binding together the Neo-Malthusian Leagues and their members is the utility and the right of limiting births according to circumstances by artificial preventive methods.

3. The most perfect reciprocal toleration being indispensable for the prosperity and duration as well as the efficiency of the Federation, the independence of the groups and of the members is absolute in all that concerns accessory questions: such as the motives and extent of parental prudence, the sexual morality of different countries and different epochs, and speculations as to their evolution in the past and in the future, practical experiments of all kinds.[73]

Robin suggested that C. R. Drysdale should be the president "as he had been the cause of the foundation of all the Leagues in Europe," but others thought Robin himself ought to lead the group.[74] Robin declined on the basis of ill health, and Drysdale was elected unanimously.

In 1904, Alice Vickery Drysdale initiated the Women's Branch of the International Neo-Malthusian League. At the Second International Neo-Malthusian Congress held in Liege, 17–18 September 1905, some objected to the new branch claiming that such an action would divide the movement and emphasize opposition between the sexes. Dr. Vickery defended her group on the grounds that women had a special interest in the success of the movement:

Many women have learnt, many others are now learning, that only by becoming economically independent of men, by becoming politically their equal, and by controlling the production of offspring, can they obtain equally fair opportunities in life for themselves and provide for the reproduction of the race under the best possible conditions, in order to obtain the most efficient and the finest possible results.[75]

The modern feminist movement would cheer her, but in early twentieth-century England, she could stir little support among the suffragettes. They were too busy winning the vote to bother with winning control of the functions of their own bodies.

The Third International Neo-Malthusian Conference was held at the Hague in 1910. The Dutch Neo-Malthusian League was the host. Alice Vickery who replaced her deceased husband as president of the international organization presided at the meeting. During the conference, Eugène Humbert of the French league recommended the establishment of an organization that could coordinate efforts to defend individuals and groups that encountered costly legal prosecutions in their respective countries. The result was the formation of the International Bureau of Correspondence and Defense to be supported by voluntary contributions from individuals or from national neo-Malthusian leagues. C. V. Drysdale was selected as president, Dr. Jan Rutgers as secretary, and G. Hardy (Gabriel Giroud) as treasurer. Within the next three years, the new bureau came to the aid of six neo-Malthusian propagandists in Europe, subsidized the printing of a pamphlet in Yiddish, and aided in establishing a neo-Malthusian periodical in Portugal.[76]

The proceedings of the Hague conference were published not only in the national languages of the organizations present but also in Esperanto, the artificial language invented by L. L. Zamenhof, a Russian philologist, in 1887, and in Ido, a simplified version of Esperanto, devised in 1907. The attempt to develop an international language failed under the weight of twentieth-century nationalism; but during the early 1900s, the International Federation of the Neo-Malthusian Leagues supported it as a possible way to disseminate its own literature throughout the world.

In 1911, the International Federation was invited to hold a fourth meeting in Dresden in connection with the International

Hygienic Exhibition. In 1913, the American Society of Medical Sociology became the first American organization to join the International Federation of the Neo-Malthusian Leagues. Its president, Dr. W. J. Robinson, had been a staunch advocate of neo-Malthusianism for years.

The English Malthusian League itself hoped to sponsor an international conference in London. After all, the movement had started in England with T. R. Malthus. Consequently, the league planned to include an excursion to Malthus's former residence in Dorking as one of the outstanding events of the meeting. Most of the leagues in Europe were disbanded during World War I, however, leaving only the Dutch organization still in existence on the Continent in 1918. Some of the groups were never reorganized.

In 1922, the English Malthusian League sponsored the Fifth International Neo-Malthusian and Birth Control Conference in London. By that time, however, the family-planning movement in England was rapidly changing direction. The advocates of family limitation as a desirable reform in and of itself without Malthusian doctrine were beginning to form their own organizations and had infiltrated the ranks of the Malthusian League itself to the point where the Drysdales were soon to resign. Margaret Sanger came to the London international conference representing the American Birth Control League and asked why there weren't more practical clinics in England. John Maynard Keynes addressed the economic section of the conference and suggested that perhaps an oversupply of labor was not the major cause of unemployment.[77] H. G. Wells chaired the conference but had already left the Malthusian League to join Marie Stopes's Society for Constructive Birth Control.

By the time the Sixth International Neo-Malthusian and Birth Control Conference met in New York in 1925, Margaret Sanger was the undisputed leader of the worldwide birth-control movement. She remembered, however, the encouragement and friendship extended to her by the English Malthusian League during her early struggles and asked C. V. Drysdale to serve as president of the conference. Henceforth, however, the leaders of the worldwide movement looked to Mrs. Sanger for

195

guidance. Even the Birth Control International Information Centre formed in London in the early 1930s named her as its president. Nevertheless, Mrs. Sanger's own words, written in reference to Marie Stopes's debt to the Malthusian League, could be cited for her own indebtedness to the group as well: "Her path was prepared for her by years of labor of the pioneers who had preceded her."[78]

1. George Standring, "Malthusian Progress," *The Malthusian* 18, no. 8 (August 1894): 57.

2. Philip P. Poirier, *The Advent of the British Labour Party* (New York: Columbia University Press, 1958), p. 100.

3. Ibid., citing Shaw.

4. *The Malthusian* 19, no. 10 (October 1895): 76.

5. C. R. Drysdale, "International Neo-Malthusianism," *The Malthusian* 21, no. 7 (July 1897): 52.

6. Sixteenth Annual Meeting, *The Malthusian* 17, no. 6 (June 1893): 43.

7. C. R. Drysdale, "War, Pestilence, Famine, and Strikes," *The Malthusian* 22, no. 7 (July 1898): 49. Just how Drysdale explained away the American Civil War in his thinking is not clear.

8. "The Small-Family Question in Germany," *The Malthusian,* no. 18 (July 1880), p. 138.

9. C. V. Drysdale, "The Progress and Results of the Neo-Malthusian Movement," *The Malthusian* 35, no. 2 (February 1911): 11.

10. David V. Glass, *Population Policies and Movements in Europe* (London: Frank Cass and Company, Ltd., 1967, 1940), p. 161, fn.

11. The date is in dispute. One source says 1875. Heer E. Kempe, "Historical Report of the Dutch Neo-Malthusian League," *The Malthusian* 24, no. 10 (October 1900): 74. Mme. Rutgers-Hoitsema, president of the Dutch league from 1900 to 1912, says 1876. "Report of the Dutch Neo-Malthusian League," *The Malthusian* 34, no. 8 (August 1910): 65.

12. Kempe, "Historical Report," p. 69.

13. The information given here on the early Dutch organization and its members comes primarily from Mme. Rutgers-Hoitsema's report to the International Neo-Malthusian Conference in 1910, *The Malthusian* 34, no. 8 (August 1910): 64–66.

14. Mme. Rutgers-Hoitsema does not say so, but I suspect the one doctor who allowed herself to be identified was Aletta Jacobs.

15. Kempe, "Historical Report," p. 73.

16. Ibid.

17. Other pamphlets issued by the Dutch Neo-Malthusian League included: Dr. J. M. Smit, *Ons Programma,* 1882; S. Van Houten, *Darwinism and Neo-*

Malthusianism, c. 1882–83; J. A. Van der Haven, *The Dark Netherlands and the Way Out Of It,* 1890; idem, [No title.] A dialogue between two workmen, one a neo-Malthusian, in which they discuss the advantages and disadvantages of practicing family limitation; Anon. [". . . A learned economist and very distinguished statesman," says E. Kempe.], *The Combat Against Over-Population,* 1896; *What Does Neo-Malthusianism Wish For?,* 1899; *A Powerful Means of Preventing Poverty and Low Wages; Over-Population and Poverty; The Danger of Abortion; The Influence of Neo-Malthusianism Upon the Health; Is Continence Always Practicable?; Neo-Malthusianism and Morality.* In 1910, Mme. Rutgers-Hoitsema claimed a league literary organ, *The Happy Family,* published since 1904. It did not, however, appear regularly. All of the pamphlets, including an unknown number not listed above, "were sold by thousands at very low prices." Kempe, "Historical Report," p. 73.

18. C. R. Drysdale, "The Dutch Malthusian League," *The Malthusian* 16, no. 8 (August 1892): 58.

19. "Current Topics," *The Malthusian,* no. 52 (June 1883), p. 423.

20. Letter to C. V. Drysdale from Jan Rutgers, dated 26 February 1923. Private Collection of C. V. Drysdale Papers. British Library of Political and Economic Science, London.

21. C. R. Drysdale, "The Malthusian Question at Home and Abroad," *The Malthusian* 23, no. 12 (December 1899): 90, citing in full the letter written by H. Pierson.

22. The biographical material in this section comes primarily from an article by Dr. Jacobs that appeared in Norman Haire's book, *Some More Medical Views on Birth Control* (New York: E. P. Dutton and Company, Inc., 1928). The article was preceded by a very short biographical sketch of Dr. Jacobs written by Dr. Haire.

23. Letter to C. V. Drysdale from Jan Rutgers, dated 26 February 1923. C. V. Drysdale Papers.

24. Martina G. Kramers, "Dr. Jan Rutgers," *The New Generation* 3, no. 10 (October 1924): 117.

25. C. R. Drysdale, "The Malthusian Question at Home and Abroad," *The Malthusian* 23, no. 1 (January 1899): 1.

26. Ibid.

27. Martina G. Kramers, "The Dutch Neo-Malthusian League," *The Malthusian* 29, no. 3 (March 1905): 19.

28. Martina G. Kramers, "Report from the Dutch Neo-Malthusian League," *The Malthusian* 35, no. 4 (April 1911): 27.

29. Letter to C. V. Drysdale from Rutgers, dated 26 February 1923. C. V. Drysdale Papers.

30. *The Malthusian* 41, no. 3 (March 1917): 17.

31. Letter to C. R. Drysdale from G. Stille, *The Malthusian,* no. 8 (September 1879), p. 60.

32. Letter to C. R. Drysdale from Max Hausmeister dated 14 October 1892, "A Malthusian League in Germany," *The Malthusian* 16, no. 11 (November 1892): 83. *Die Sozial Harmonie* first appeared in September 1892.

33. From a report sent by Max Hausmeister to the Fifth International Neo-Malthusian and Birth Control Conference held in London in 1922. *Report*

197

of the Fifth International Neo-Malthusian and Birth Control Conference (London: William Heinemann, Ltd., 1922), p. 14.

34. C. R. Drysdale, "The Malthusian Question at Home and Abroad," *The Malthusian* 24, no. 6 (June 1900): 46, citing a report from Hausmeister.

35. C. R. Drysdale, "The Malthusian Question at Home and Abroad," *The Malthusian* 23, no. 6 (June 1899): 41, reporting on a meeting of the Stuttgart neo-Malthusian organization in 1899.

36. "The Annual Meeting of the German Malthusian League," *The Malthusian* 21, no. 9 (September 1897): 65.

37. C. R. Drysdale, *Prostitution Medically Considered With Some of Its Social Aspects.* A paper read at the Harveian Medical Society of London, January 1866 (London: Robert Hardwicke, 1866), p. 30, citing the *Times,* April 1857.

38. "The Population Question in Amsterdam." A report on C. R. Drysdale's speech before a public meeting held in connection with the International Medical Congress to promote neo-Malthusianism in Holland. *The Malthusian,* no. 8 (September 1879), p. 67.

39. James T. Blanchard, Report on a public lecture, *The Malthusian,* no. 69 (December 1884), p. 567, citing H. M. Hyndman.

40. C. R. Drysdale, "Recent Socialistic Views on the Population Question in England and France," *The Malthusian* 14, no. 8 (August 1890): 57. The socialist involved was G. A. Gaskell.

41. C. R. Drysdale, "Neo-Malthusianism in France," *The Malthusian* 17, no. 1 (January 1893): 5.

42. C. R. Drysdale, "The Cause of Poverty," A report of a lecture given by Drysdale before the National Liberal Club on 21 October 1890. The remark cited was made in the discussion that followed Drysdale's presentation. *The Malthusian* 14, no. 11 (November 1890): 91.

43. *The Declinining Birth-Rate: Its Causes and Effects.* Report of the National Birth-Rate Commission, instituted by the National Council of Public Morals (London: Chapman and Hall, Ltd., 1916), p. 27.

44. "The Recent Census in France," *The Malthusian* 25, no. 9 (September 1901): 69.

45. C. R. Drysdale, "The Malthusian Question in France and Germany," *The Malthusian* 21, no. 1 (January 1897): 2, citing *Die Sozial Harmonie,* November 1896.

46. Ninth Annual Meeting, *The Malthusian* 10, no. 6 (June 1886): 41. The deputy who introduced the act was M. Bernard Doubs.

47. Ibid.

48. C. R. Drysdale, "The Population Question in France," *The Malthusian* 16, no. 8 (August 1892): 57, citing *The Daily Chronicle,* 14 July 1892.

49. "A Strange Society," *The Malthusian* 18, no. 2 (February 1894): 12.

50. "Debate on the Population Question in Paris," *The Malthusian* 20, no. 10 (October 1896): 77. Such a remark was made at a meeting in Paris, 20 February 1896, by M. Dumont. He called neo-Malthusian propaganda "antipatriotic and anti-scientific."

51. A biography of Paul Robin was written by his son-in-law, Gabriel Giroud (Paris, 1937). D. V. Glass has called it "the best history of the French

movment." *Population Policies and Movements in Europe,* p. 39, fn. Also see: Andre Armengaud, "Mouvement Ouvrier et Néo-Malthusianisme au Début du XXᵉ Siecle," *Annales de Démographie Historique,* 1966 (Études, Chronique, Bibliographique, Documents), Société de Démographie Historique, Editions Sirey, 22, rue Soufflot, Paris, Vᵉ, 1967.

52. "Anti-Malthusian Ideas in France," *The Malthusian* 19, no. 7 (July 1895): 50.

53. "Clerical Intolerance," *The Malthusian* 18, no. 10 (October 1894): 77, citing an article in *Le Temps,* Paris.

54. C. R. Drysdale, "The Malthusian Question at Home and Abroad," *The Malthusian* 23, no. 1 (January 1899): 1. The new address of the league after Robin left was 43 Rue des Gravilliers, Paris. Listed on the committee to direct its activities were M. Eugene Fournière, deputy of L'Aisne, Dr. Meslier, J. N. Laroche, Leon Marmont, J. B. Clement, Jules Barcol, Me. Guillemand, M. Sorgue, and Me. Blanche Cobaille.

55. C. V. Drysdale, "Bertillon: La Dépopulation de la France," *The Malthusian* 36, no. 4 (April 1912): 25.

56. D. V. Glass, "Western Europe," *Family Planning and Population Programs.* Proceedings of the International Conference on Family Planning Programs, Geneva, August 1965 (Chicago: University of Chicago, 1966), p. 186.

57. Wicksell's report to the conference on progress in Sweden. *Fifth International Neo-Malthusian and Birth Control Conference,* p. 11.

58. *The Malthusian* 38, no. 2 (February 1914): 16.

59. C. V. Drysdale, "Italy and Birth Control," *The Malthusian* n.s., no. 22 (October 1951), p. 3.

60. *The Malthusian* 33, no. 7 (July 1909): 51.

61. "Our Foreign Leagues," *The Malthusian* 32, no. 5 (May 1908): 38.

62. *The Malthusian* 33, no. 7 (July 1909): 51.

63. In 1914, the following "Constituent Bodies" were listed on the cover of *The Malthusian:*

England (1877).—The Malthusian League. Periodical, *The Malthusian.*

Holland (1885).—De Nieuw-Malthusiaansche Bond. Secretary, Dr. J. Rutgers, 9 Verhulststraat Den Haag. Periodical, *Het Gellukkig Huisgezin.*

Germany (1889).—Sozial Harmonische Verein. Secretary, Herr Max Hausmeister, Stuttgart. Periodical, *Die Sozial Harmonie.*

France (1895).—*Génération Consciente.* E. Humbert, 27 Rue de la Duée, Paris XX.

Spain (1904).—Liga Española de Regeneracion Humana. Secretary, Senor Luis Bulfi, Calle Provenza 177, Pral. la, Barcelona. Periodical, *Salud y Fuerza.*

Belgium (1906).—Ligue Néo-Malthusienne. Secretary, Dr. Fernand Mascaux, Echevin, Courcelles. Periodical, *Génération Consciente,* 27 Rue de la Duée, Paris XX.

Switzerland (1908).—Groupe Malthusien. Secretary, Valentin Grandjean, 106 Rue des Eaux Vives, Geneva. Periodical, *La Vie Intime.*

Bohemia-Austria (1901).—*Zadruhy.* Secretary, Michael Kacha, 1164, Zizhov, Prague.

Portugal. *Paz e Liberdade,* Revista Anti-Militarist e Neo-Malthusiana. E. Silva, Junior, L. de Membria, 46, r/e, Lisbon.

Brazil (1905).—Seccion brasilena de propaganda. Secretaries: Manuel Moscosa, Rua de'Bento Pires 29, San Pablo; Antonio Dominiguez, Rua Vizcande de Moranguapez 25, Rio de Janeiro.

Cuba (1907).—Seccion de propaganda. Secretary, José Guardiola, Empedrado 14, Havana.

Sweden (1911).—Sallskapet for Humanitar Barnalstring. President, Mr. Hinke Bergegren Vanadisvagen 15, Stockholm Va.

Flemish Belgium (1912).—National Verbond ter Regeling van het Kindertal. President, M. L. van Brussel, Rue de Canal, 70, Louvain.

Italy (1913).—Lega Neomalthusiana Italiana. Secretary, Dr. Luigi Berta, Via Lamarmora 22, Turin. Periodical, *L'Educazione Sessuale.*

Africa.—Ligue Néo-Malthusienne, Maison du Peuple, 10 Rampe Magenta, Alger.

America (1913).—American Society of Medical Sociology. President, W. J. Robinson, M. D., 12 Mountmorris Park, W., New York. Periodical, *The Critic and Guide.*

64. Norman E. Himes, *Medical History of Contraception* (Baltimore, Maryland: The Williams & Wilkins Co., 1936), p. 277. The ruse was probably set up by the Society for the Suppression of Vice, which had been largely responsible for the Obscenity Law of 1873. Foote's publication was set in pearl type, thus the title, *Words in Pearl.*

65. Twenty-fifth Annual Meeting, *The Malthusian* 26, no. 8 (August 1902): 62.

66. Margaret Sanger, *My Fight For Birth Control* (New York: Farrar & Rinehart, Inc., 1931), p. 100.

67. Ibid., p. 116.

68. *The Malthusian* 27, no. 2 (February 1903): 10.

69. Annual Report of the Council, *The Malthusian,* no. 19 (August 1880), p. 149.

70. Letter to H. A. Allbutt from Mutha Naidu, 13 December 1882. *The Malthusian,* no. 49 (February 1883), p. 389.

71. In 1936, Norman E. Himes mentioned a Madras Neo-Malthusian League founded in 1929. *Medical History of Contraception,* p. 123. Its journal was the *Madras Birth Control Bulletin.* I don't know whether or not there was any connection between this group and the earlier one.

72. Letter to the Malthusian League from Professor Gopalji, M.S., Ranjar College, Delhi, 19 May 1922. *The New Generation* 1, no. 5 (July 1922): 5.

73. The formal title of the organization was the Fédération Universalle pour la Régénération Humaine. "The International Conference of Neo-Malthusians in Paris," *The Malthusian* 24, no. 9 (September 1900): 68.

74. Ibid.

75. "The International Neo-Malthusian Congress," *The Malthusian* 29, no. 10 (October 1905): 73.

76. "Our International Bureau," *The Malthusian* 37, no. 2 (February 1913): 11.

77. In "Some Economic Consequences of a Declining Population," *The Eugenics Review* 29, no. 1 (April 1937): 13–17, Keynes said: "We have now learned that we have another devil at our elbow at least as fierce as the Malthusian—namely the devil of unemployment escaping through the breakdown of effective demand" (p. 16).

78. Sanger, *My Fight For Birth Control,* p. 105.

7: The Final Years

Transvalue your values or perish
Thus saith Zarathustra.

Charles Vickery Drysdale, the prime mover of the Malthusian League during the twentieth century, became a staunch advocate of the Nietzschean philosophy that the weak should not be allowed to smother the strong. "Our whole course," he wrote, "has been the protection of weakness instead of fostering strength. We do not want to help the strong, but we must not put such burdens on them as to destroy their initiative."[1] And, yet, in the view of many, such as Drysdale, that was precisely what had been allowed to happen in English society. The birthrate for England and Wales had fallen steadily since the 1870s along with the death rate, such that the population continued to increase but at a slower rate, The decline had occurred, however, primarily among the upper and middle classes. The poorer classes of England had experienced a decrease in their birthrate as well but only a small one compared to the wealthier ranks of society. In London, for example, the birthrate had fallen from around 36 per 1,000 in 1877 to 24.4 in 1909.[2] A breakdown of the various sections of the metropolitan area showed that whereas the birthrate had declined to 13.6, 17.4 and 17.5 in wealthier districts, such as, Hampstead, Kensington, and Chelsea, respectively, it had declined in poorer sections such as Finsbury, St. Marylebone, and Bermondsey to 35.8, 32.1, and 31.8.[3] The death rate followed the same pattern. The trend continued until World War II, though the gap between the richer and poorer areas narrowed in the later years. In the early twentieth century, however, neo-Malthusian leaders lamented "that the people whose poverty and miserable circumstances ought to act as the greatest incentive to forethought and prudence are the very people who are the most reckless in adding to their burdens."[4]

Neo-Malthusians were not the only ones to note the differential birthrate between the rich and the poor. In December 1907, the Eugenics Education Society was founded in London primarily for the purpose of improving the quality of the English population by promoting a knowledge of the new science of eugenics. Francis Galton (1822–1911), the famous geneticist and cousin of the even more famous Charles Darwin, was selected as honorary president of the new organization. The group was divided along two lines in its approach to the problem of race improvement. The Positive, or neo-Darwinian, school proposed that the new society should work toward an increase in the "fitter types" of the population. Their objective was to select the best parents and encourage them to reproduce. They were not concerned with the problem of population numbers as a whole. The Negative school, on the other hand, advocated restricting propagation by the unfit, that is, by those having such qualities or diseases that made them unsuitable for parenthood. The Drysdales joined the latter school of thought. We neo-Malthusians, said C. V. Drysdale, "are negative eugenists to the core." We differ with them, he continued, only in that we favor "voluntary abstention from procreation on the part of the unfit to sterilisation or other compulsion, except where there is absolutely no possibility of self-control being exercised."[5] Neo-Malthusians do not agree with the positive eugenists, he said. The positivist program is designed to produce a class of "supermen," a ruling elite. The result would be either despotism or revolution, or both. It is better to encourage a decline in the birthrate of the unfit, he argued, than to encourage an increase among the fit.

Since the positive school dominated the Eugenics Society in its first years of existence, there was antagonism between the society and the Malthusian League even though both deplored the fact that the birthrate was higher among the lower classes than among the middle and upper classes. More importantly for the Malthusian League, however, was the fact that C. V. Drysdale's interest in improving the quality of the race through a negative eugenic program overshadowed his interest in promoting family limitation for the purpose of improving the quality of life for the poor. As the years passed and the success of the family-limitation movement became openly apparent, he remained committed to the aims of eugenics. "I am bound to regard better eugenic selection," he wrote in 1928, "as more important now than greater restriction of the total birth rate."[6] This change in viewpoint from the earlier emphasis of the Malthusian League on the need for a general reduction in the English birthrate as a whole to an emphasis on race regeneration played a major part in bringing the decline and final collapse of the Malthusian League after World War I. Had those within the organization who joined it to work for an improvement in the lot of the poor by persuading them to practice family limitation been able to direct the activities of the group completely, it might have become an important part of the family-planning movement that burgeoned in the 1920s and 1930s. Instead, in spite of a series of enlightened practical activities in the second and third decades of the century, the league finally floundered on the rocks of individualism, nineteenth-century classical liberalism, and eugenics.

Charles Robert Drysdale, the first president of the Malthusian League, died in December 1907 at the age of seventy-eight. He had devoted the last thirty years of his life to promoting the cause of neo-Malthusianism in the world. His efforts had brought him censure, sarcasm, and abuse except from those who saw, as he did, a population problem that could be solved only by a general acceptance and practice of family limitation. His wife, Alice Vickery Drysdale, followed her husband as president of the Malthusian League. Charles Vickery Drysdale and his wife, Bessie Ingham Drysdale, became co-secretaries.[7] C. V. assumed the editorship of *The Malthusian* as well. For a number of years, the new leaders initiated little change in the format and activities of the organization. A new campaign of monthly lectures initiated in the fall of 1906 continued as an important part of the league's program until 1910. The lecture topics remained much the same: "The High Death-Rate in France," "The Declining Birth-rate," "Poverty, Unemployment, and Population," "Should the State Discourage Large Families?" A few called for increased efforts to disseminate practical information among the poor, but the league leaders remained "convinced that the doctrine of Neo-Malthusianism will fail very largely in its ameliorative effects if it is taken up solely in its individual aspect, as lessening the burdens of each single family."[8]

In the early twentieth century, the Malthusian League adopted a flag and a symbol. Both carried the slogan "Non Quantitas Sed Qualitas" in keeping with the organization's new emphasis on improving the quality of the English population. After 1909, many of the league's publications bore the new imprint. The designer of the symbol remains unknown, but the "Betsy Ross" of the Malthusian League's flag was the daughter of Binnie Dunlop, a long-time devoted member and officer of the organization in the twentieth century.[9]

Dr. Binnie Dunlop, the son of a Glasgow physician, was one of a number of new members who aligned themselves with the Malthusian League in order to promote the cause of family limitation among the poor. Dr. Dunlop attended one of the league's lectures in 1910 and was pleasantly surprised to find an organization that espoused views he had held and written on for a number of years. He became one of the most valuable members of the organization during the remainder of its official existence. Edith How-Martyn and her husband also joined the group in 1910. She had already established a name for herself in the suffrage fight and was now ready to tackle the problem of family limitation. Since the Malthusian League was the only organization in existence at the time that advocated voluntary family limitation, she joined the group though she cared little for its economic theories. In 1911, the league acquired a general secretary who was also C. V. Drysdale's private secretary in his engineering business. Olive M. Johnson worked as C. V.'s secretary and as the league's secretary from 1911 to 1921. In 1913, she helped the organization begin a new series of activities that would bring one of its greatest periods of success. One of those acitivites was an open-air campaign in the streets of London.

C. V. Drysdale got the idea for the open-air meetings while attending such a gathering in East London in 1912 when the suffragists were supporting the candidature of George

Lansbury. Drysdale listened to a number of socialist orators trying to persuade the crowd to join their movement and decided on the spot to try the same technique in propagating neo-Malthusian doctrines.[10] Accordingly, a small band of devoted neo-Malthusians sallied forth on 21 January 1913, in spite of winter weather, in a van bedecked with rose-colored flags, lanterns, and placards advertising their meetings. The wind, rain, mud, and initially small crowds would have discouraged the fainthearted, but not this hardy group, never more than ten, who persisted in holding outdoor meetings four times a month all during 1913, except during the holiday period, August and September. In addition, they conducted an indoor meeting at the end of each month's activities in some public building near the area of the outdoor gatherings. In the early winter months of 1914, the group retreated to the warmth of the Socialist Hall in York Street, Walworth, for its meetings, but by April they were back on the streets. They continued the open-air assemblies during 1914 until the war brought an end to their activities. The London streets were darkened in the early months of the fighting due to fear of aerial attacks.[11] By November, the Malthusian League was forced to call a halt to its campaign.

The entire open-air crusade was directed to the South London areas, such as Lambeth, Bermondsey, and Southwark, where the birthrates were notoriously high. Except for a few socialist and moralistic hecklers, their efforts were well received, and the league as a whole was delighted with the results. By the end of February 1913, the meetings were attracting large enough crowds to block the roadways at some points. Sympathetic London bobbies watched over the proceedings. In the first eight meetings, the small band distributed over 12,000 handbills and leaflets.[12] "The only regret amongst nearly everybody," Drysdale reported in March, "is that we are not able to give practical information direct."[13] At every meeting, one of the league speakers, usually Dr. Binnie Dunlop as a medical man, proposed a resolution:

> That this meeting considers that a knowledge of hygienic means of restricting families ought to be available to all responsible adult

207

people in the interests of economic and race improvement, and calls upon the medical profession to provide such information when requested.[14]

The proposal invariably passed, usually unanimously, when put to a vote. But then came the requests for specific instructions on how to prevent conception. The league members were at a loss to answer the pathetic appeals except to explain that if they attempted to give such information they would thereby subject themselves to public prosecution on a charge of distributing obscene materials. When he was present, George Standring offered to send practical information to any one who applied for it, but he could not always attend. By the summer of 1913, it was clear to the league leaders that if the open-air meetings were to continue to attract an audience they were going to have to do more than just expound upon the benefits to be gained from family limitation.

At the annual meeting of the Malthusian League held at the Eustace Miles Restaurant in May 1913, the council proposed that the second objective of the league read henceforth as follows:

> To urge upon the medical profession in general, and upon hospital and public medical authorities in particular, the duty of giving instruction in hygienic contraceptive methods to all married people who desire to limit their families, or who are in any way unfit for parenthood, *and to take any other steps which may be considered desirable for the provision of such instruction.* [The italics were added by the editor of *The Malthusian* when he presented the objective in the League journal.][15]

A practical pamphlet on family limitation had already been written for the league. The council planned to publish and distribute it if the membership approved the new objective. In answer to concerned questions about the legality of such an action, council members assured the group "that the pamphlet would be issued under seal, and only to those who were of legal age, were married or about to be married, and were willing to take the responsibility for the proper use of such information."[16] By October 1913, the pamphlet was ready for distribution. Each

208

recipient was required to fill out and sign a declaration form in duplicate stating his or her age (21 or over), marital status, and agreement with the tenets of neo-Malthusianism. The forms were distributed to all league meetings and printed in *The Malthusian* (see figure). In addition, league members were provided with a supply of the forms if they wished to take part in disseminating information among the poor. "May we express the hope," Drysdale wrote in *The Malthusian*, "that this new departure will bring us renewed support, both from our present members and from those who have regarded our propaganda in the past as too academic to be worthy of support."[17]

The league's practical pamphlet was entitled *Hygienic Methods of Family Limitation*. The first edition was just a one-page leaflet printed on both sides, describing very briefly the most commonly recommended methods of contraception that could be used without the advice of a doctor. The methods mentioned were withdrawal (long prescribed by the Malthusian League), douching, and the condom.[18] These were not the most reliable techniques known at the time, but at least they were procedures that could be tried by any couple no matter how poor without the expense of medical advice at a time when there were no free clinics available. Nevertheless, there were those who objected. "Had the Malthusian League's leaflet not been so very brief as regards useful methods and so indiscriminate in its recommendation of various rather harmful ones," Marie Stopes wrote later, "I should never have written 'Wise Parenthood' [her own marriage and family-limitation manual published in 1918], but should have referred enquirers to that Society."[19]

Just who wrote the original leaflet for the Malthusian League is not clear. It may have been Binnie Dunlop since he was the most active medical doctor in the league at the time, aside from the president, Alice Vickery Drysdale. There is nothing in *The Malthusian* to reveal the identity of the pamphlet's author. It was revised in 1922, however, by Norman Haire, a young physician, recently arrived in England from Australia (1920) and active in the Malthusian League in the early 1920s. The new revised edition was nineteen pages in length and contained the rules, objects and principles of the league; sections on the necessity, morality, healthfulness, and reliability of family limitation and contraceptive methods; an explanation of how conception takes place; and, of course, an expanded description of preventive techniques. Ruled out entirely were abortion and the so-called safe period.[20] Dr. Haire recommended primarily the condom and the Dutch Mensinga pessary. The latter he called "a sure preventive" if it is well fitted. He also listed several other types of pessaries, some of which he labeled dangerous; a female sheath, unpleasant to use; a sponge or tampon, uncertain and

---

PRACTICAL METHODS OF FAMILY LIMITATION.

NOTICE.—The Council of the Malthusian League, while continuing to regard this as a matter which is strictly within the province of the medical profession, and which ought to be taken over by them, has compiled a leaflet entitled " Hygienic Methods of Family Limitation," for the benefit of those desirous of limiting their families, but who are ignorant of the means of doing so, and unable to get medical advice on the subject. This leaflet is only issued to persons over twenty-one years of age who are either married or about to be married, and who declare their conscientious belief that family limitation is justifiable on personal and national grounds. Anyone wishing to obtain a copy of this leaflet must write his or her name and address clearly upon the form of declaration below, and send it to

Mrs. B. I. Drysdale, Hon. Secretary of the Malthusian League,

124 Victoria Street, Westminster, S.W.1.

In order to encourage family limitation among the poorest classes, *no charge will be made either for the leaflet or postage*, but it is hoped that those who can afford it will enclose stamps for postage or a small donation to help the League in its work.

Under no circumstances whatever can the practical leaflet be supplied without a properly filled up declaration, nor can more than one copy be supplied to the same person. Those wishing to help others, may have additional copies of the declaration form to hand on.

If the leaflet is not received within seven clear days after posting the form, or if the seal is found broken on receipt, the Hon. Secretary should be communicated with.

Note.—The Malthusian League only advocates family limitation by prevention of conception, which is legal and is quite different from abortion, as was pointed out by the National Birth-rate Commission. The League has never advocated or given any assistance or information towards facilitating abortion.

The Malthusian League regrets that it is unable to comply with applications from the United States for this leaflet.

Instructions for filling up the Declaration Form.

NOTE.—*Please read these instructions carefully before filling up the declaration form, as mistakes involve delay and unnecessary expense, both to the applicant and to the Malthusian League.*

INSTRUCTIONS.

1. Each applicant for a copy of the practical leaflet issued by the Malthusian League must sign the declaration form himself (or herself). It is not permitted to sign a form on behalf of somebody else.

2. The signature must be written very distinctly in the applicant's ordinary handwriting.

3. The declaration form must clearly show whether the applicant is married or about to be married. If you are married, strike out the words "about to be married"; if you are about to be married, strike out the words " already married."

4. The declaration form must be filled up in ink.

N.B.—Only one copy of the leaflet can be supplied to each applicant, but additional copies of the *declaration form* to pass on to friends may be obtained from the Hon. Secretaries of the League, and will be sent with the copy of the leaflet, if so desired.

Please cut out the Application Form exactly as marked by the black lines around it.

FORM OF DECLARATION.

(*To be retained by the Malthusian League.*)

Please read carefully and fill up in ink.

I, the undersigned, hereby declare that I am over twenty-one years of age, that I am (a) already married, (b) about to be married; that I consider the artificial limitation of the family justifiable on both individual and national grounds; and that I have applied to the Malthusian League for a copy of its leaflet entitled " Hygienic Methods of Family Limitation."

And I hereby declare that I will hold myself entirely responsible for the proper use of the information therein contained, and for keeping it out of the hands of unmarried persons under twenty-one years of age.

Signed..

Address..

....

....

Date..

---

sometimes irritating; douching, but only if used with another preventive; and withdrawal. The latter method had been prescribed by the Malthusian League for decades, but Haire charged that "in many people it is followed by nervous disturbances, and we therefore do not recommend it."[21] None of the methods are "fool-proof," he concluded, but "the *Mensinga pessary is the best*" [The italics are his].[22]

During late 1913 and throughout 1914, the league issued about two hundred of its practical leaflets per month. Even during the war, applications for it continued to come in, sometimes as many as twenty a day.[23] But advertising the pamphlet was difficult. The league could find few outlets for its declaration form other than printing it in *The Malthusian* and distributing it as a handbill. Few journals or papers would publish it, even as a paid advertisement. In 1915, however, the socialist periodical, *The Clarion,* printed the information for the league and produced 1,200 requests for the leaflet; but, otherwise, the press ignored their entreaties.[24] By the end of 1926, 91,000 copies of the pamphlet had been distributed. Before its publication was suspended during World War II, the number reached 114,000.[25] The league's insistence upon a signed declaration form kept down the circulation of the pamphlet. Had they distributed it freely, the number would undoubtedly have been much higher, but they were concerned lest it fall into the hands of the young and the unmarried.

During the war, the Malthusian League, like many other organizations in England, had to curtail its activities. In the early weeks of the fighting, the league leaders drew sharp criticism when they published a leaflet called *The War* in which they urged individuals not to have any more children until the war was over and prosperity returned. A copy of the one-page tract was enclosed with the August 1914 issue of *The Malthusian*, and the unfavorable response, even from members, prompted the Drysdales to defend their stand. Some of their reasons were quite practical: "Children born now cannot be of the slightest use in this war," children prevent women from participating in the war effort, and doctors and nurses are needed for the front and in the military hospitals. Some of their other reasons, however, were indicative of the emphasis that the League leaders continued to give to the eugenic effects of family limitation. "From the eugenic standpoint this is the worst of all possible times for engendering children. The young, strong, and virile men of our country have been taken away, leaving the physically and mentally unfit, the immature, and the aged behind." Their last point was to challenge, as they had often done before, the longstanding belief that military strength and national safety demand an ever-increasing population. The only real security from war, the league leaders maintained, is "to secure international solidarity by abolishing the cut-throat competition between nations in eternal economic rivalry, caused by the futile attempt to provide for their high birth-rates."[26]

The efforts of C. V. and Bessie I. Drysdale on behalf of the Malthusian League were further curtailed by the death of their only child, Eva Mary Drysdale, in October 1914, at the age of thirteen.[27] They spent the greater part of the war out of London, especially after C. V. became ill in the fall of 1917 and later when he began work for the Anti-Submarine Division of the Admiralty. Binnie Dunlop, treasurer of the organization, minded the store in their absence and acted as editor of *The Malthusian*, at least until he was called for army medical service in late 1918.

Still another reason for a decline in the neo-Malthusian activities of the Drysdales was a revolt that had been simmering for a long time within the Malthusian League. Ever since the early years of its existence, the league had within its ranks a number of individuals who firmly believed that family limitation could bring tremendous benefits, both physically and materially, to parents who practiced it. They did not accept, however, the Malthusian economic doctrines espoused so fervently by the Drysdales and others of like mind in the organization. At the turn of the century, the group was deeply offended when the Drysdales embraced the tenets of genetics and proclaimed that "the subject of 'Eugenics' or Improvement of the Race is one which should hence forth occupy a distinct and permanent section in the columns of *The Malthusian*."[28] The change in tactics on the part of the league shortly before the outbreak of World

War I may well indicate that those favoring an emphasis upon disseminating practical information rather than upon promulgating economic theory were gaining in strength in the organization. For example, a longstanding internal debate over the name of the group and its journal was renewed in 1912. The word "Malthusian" had long been a misnomer, and by the early twentieth century the term "had been so vilified," Bessie I. Drysdale admitted, "that it would be a long time, if ever, before a paper with such a title would find a place among the general reading public, or be accepted for sale on the bookstalls."[29] But the group could reach no agreement on a new title. One member proposed "Race Control" but another provoked peals of laughter by suggesting that such a name might tempt a sportsman to buy the periodical thinking he could learn how to "find a winner."[30] Drysdale stood firm and maintained "that limitation without understanding was not altogether good." We must continue to emphasize "the theory of the subject," he said.[31] Regardless of what the other members might think, however, it was, after all, C. V. Drysdale who controlled the publication of *The Malthusian* after his father's death in 1907. Consequently, the journal continued to reflect, first and foremost, his viewpoint, at least until 1917.

Among those attracted to the Malthusian League by its aggressive, practical efforts in 1914 was H. G. Wells, the well-known author and Fabian socialist. In 1915, he agreed to be listed as a vice-president of the organization, and *The Malthusian* boasted confidently, "his adhesion to our doctrine will go far to convince the educated general public that it cannot be disregarded."[32] In the spring of 1917, however, the honeymoon came to an abrupt end. The quarrel started when Mr. F. A. Wilmer, a socialist, responded unfavorably to an article on "The Government and the War" by C. V. Drysdale (*The Malthusian*, December 1916). Drysdale countered with a lengthy article on "The Malthusianism versus Socialism Controversy" (*The Malthusian*, May 1917) in which he enumerated the many differences between the two schools of thought. The aims of socialism, he contended, are "Justice. Equality of opportunity. Suppression of competition." The aims of Malthusianism are

"Happiness. Efficiency. Race Improvement. Preservation of competition. Limitation of number of competitors."[33] He went on to list the basic assumptions underlying the two positions.

Nature and Population:

Socialism—Nature is bountiful and will provide food for all; misery is due primarily to human institutions.

Malthusianism—Nature is cruel and can never provide enough food for an unrestrained population; misery is caused by over-population and the struggle for existence resulting from it.

Competition:

Socialism—Competition is evil, wasteful and inefficient.

Malthusianism—Too many competitors is an evil, but competition is on the whole most valuable and the only satisfactory stimulus and guide to progress.

Taxation:

Socialism—Taxes should be assessed according to ability to pay.

Malthusianism—Taxation should be in proportion to the amount required for the services of protection of life and property.[34]

Drysdale concluded that "so long as these differences of outlook exist it is absolutely impossible for Socialists and Malthusians to join forces."

H. G. Wells took up the argument for socialists and made it clear that he had no stomach for Malthusian economic doctrines and felt the Malthusian League ought to stick to its primary goal of disseminating practical information. "I do not want to withdraw my name," he explained, "because I want to use whatever reputation and influence I have to help on the Malthusian propaganda," but "I cannot lend my name to back preposterous attacks on Socialism." Drysdale's article was "utterly silly," he said, and "if the Society is to go on circulating that kind of nonsense, instead of sticking to its proper task of physiological enlightenment, my membership must cease."[35] Drysdale's answer was quick and sharp. Socialists have always been our main critics, he noted, "over the whole duration of our movement."

So far is physiological enlightenment, or the teaching of the actual methods of birth control, from being the only or chief task of the

League, that it was not even among its objects until about four years ago. Its first and chief object has always been "To spread among the people, by all practicable means, a knowledge of the law of population, of its consequences, and of its bearing upon human conduct and morals." As physiological questions have never been explicitly dealt with in *The Malthusian*, it may be said that the development of the economic Malthusian doctrine and its consequences is preeminently the function of the paper, and if it leads us into conflict with other schools of economic thought we are strictly within our rights in criticising them.[36]

Drysdale came down squarely on the side of those who considered the dissemination of Malthusian economic doctrines more important than spreading practical information. "The few of us who are Darwinian Malthusians will go on in the attempt to teach a rational humanitarian philosophy of existence." As regards the league, he concluded, "we most certainly do not wish to impose our views upon it, or to cause it to lose Mr. Wells's valuable support, and Mrs. Drysdale and I have therefore tendered to the Council our resignations as Editors."[37] The membership of the league split into two conflicting groups, some aligning themselves with the Drysdales, others with Wells. The league council, however, pleaded with Dr. Drysdale to withdraw his resignation, which he did. But in September, Binnie Dunlop announced that Dr. Drysdale had been advised by his doctor to take a long holiday and that he, Dunlop, would undertake to edit *The Malthusian* and would henceforth be responsible for unsigned articles in the periodical.[38] He was called to active military duty in the fall of 1918, however, and C. V. Drysdale resumed the editorship.

The quarrel between Drysdale and H. G. Wells was only one particularly strident incident in the ongoing conflict within the Malthusian League between those who joined the organization to further the cause of family limitation as a desirable goal in itself and those who shared with the Drysdales a fervent belief in Malthusian economic doctrines now coupled with the hope of improving the race or at least saving it from further degeneration. The conflict grew more heated, however, after the Wells-Drysdale exchange. Readers of *The Malthusian* began to suggest the formation of an organization strictly devoted to

215

furthering the birth-control movement, a phrase popularized by Margaret Sanger in the United States. To suggestions that the Malthusian League itself be converted into such a society, Dunlop, like Drysdale, advised those interested in such a group to form their own organization. One reader in Glasgow subsequently wrote, "If anything should come out of the suggestion recently made in the *Malthusian* with regard to the formation of a birth control society which one could join without identifying oneself with Individualism, Puritanism, or any other ism, I should be glad to hear from you."[39] As Marie Stopes said, "The time was ripe, indeed overripe, for a consideration of the essential medical physiological factors of contraception apart from a controversial cult of economics and party politics."[40]

George Standring was among the first within the organization to take the suggestion of a new organization to heart and circulate a leaflet proposing "a society for the purpose for advocating birth control without qualification or addition thereto."[41] He received eighty favorable responses to his proposal but concluded that the number was not sufficient to ensure a viable organization. Instead he solicited support for a small birth-control journal, which he subsequently edited and published for a short time in 1919. He called the paper simply *Birth Control.*

Those who believed in family limitation without Malthusian theories were still left with no alternative but to join the Malthusian League if they wished to work within an organization for the movement. For example, C. F. Chance, who had joined the league in 1912 and had contributed handsomely in time and money, addressed a letter to the editor of *The Malthusian* in 1918 and wrote, there are "those of your members who like myself, are opposed to much of your teaching called 'Individualism' but who still support your League because it is the only organization supplying the much-needed knowledge of birth-control methods in this country."[42] It became increasingly apparent, however, that there were many others who wanted to work for the birth-control movement but who could not accommodate their own views to the Malthusian beliefs of the league leaders. "Only the other day," Drysdale admitted in late 1918, "we were told by a generous supporter of our cause that the trade unions and other working class societies are showing a disposition to take up the advocacy of birth control, but are deterred from doing so by the fear of being associated with the Malthusian doctrines and the views expressed in this paper."[43] Marie Stopes wrote, "the only society formed for public advocacy of contraception continued to be the Malthusian League. Handicapped by its 'Malthusian' economics, the advocacy of this society was very partial and voiced the views of but a small section of the public."[44]

World War I provided an unexpected boost to the family-planning movement in England as well as elsewhere. Thousands of women who had previously never seen the inside of a factory were brought into the labor force and to a clearer understanding of the value of family limitation for a working woman. Women's groups began to form within the male-dominated labor organizations. Their demands that the unions give more attention to the family-planning issue were destined to bring a lot of headaches to labor leaders in the 1920s, especially after the 1918 victory of the suffragettes. Also during World War I, the government took action to protect its soldiers from contracting venereal disease. The armed forces began issuing free condoms to service personnel in 1917, assumedly for prophylactic reasons only. The subject of voluntary family limitation became much more agreeable to the general English public, especially once the movement broke loose from its Malthusian moorings. As D. V. Glass concluded, "It is likely that the change in tenor of the birth-control movement after the ... War increased its acceptability by the public, since it was no longer basically associated with Malthusian economic doctrines which, to many people, were unpalatable."[45]

Perhaps partly in frustration at losing the lead in the movement for family limitation, C. V. Drysdale retreated more and more to a concern with race degeneration and away from the possibility of establishing a rapport with the working classes and their collectivist theories. In 1920, he wrote:

> There have been friends of our movement in this country who have deprecated our unswerving hostility to the modern Labour doctrines, and who have urged that we should conciliate Labour and induce its leaders to adopt and propagate birth control doctrines. But we have had too long and too painful an experience of these gentry to trust ourselves or our cause to their tender mercies, apart from our absolute conviction as to the error of their doctrines and methods.[46]

He was thoroughly convinced, in true Social Darwinist fashion, that any kind of collectivist system augured ill for the race as a whole. "As human evolution has been directed by the competitive struggle for existence, there is very great danger in departing from the individualistic competitive system, and thereby losing its guidance for the breeding of the future generations."[47] He was concerned, like other Social Darwinists and eugenicists, with the survival of the fittest.

On 22 February 1921, C. V. Drysdale replaced his aging mother, Alice Vickery Drysdale, as president of the Malthusian League. In his first presidential address to the membership as a whole, he redefined neo-Malthusianism in keeping with his own interest in the eugenics movement: "The neo-Malthusian idea may be briefly stated as the securing of a human race free from the evils of poverty and sex-starvation, and rapidly improving in quality through the simple expedient of general early marriage, combined with the elimination of poverty and unfitness by selective birth control."[48] Weeding out the unfit was, in his opinion, as much an objective of the Malthusian League as stamping out poverty. But who were the "unfit"? "Most certainly everyone who is unable to support himself and his family in a state of free competition is unfit from the Darwinian standpoint," Drysdale wrote. Thus the poor were, by his standards, unfit. Almost as an afterthought, Drysdale added, "In addition those who are afflicted with transmissible diseases or defects must be relegated to the category of the unfit."[49] "Not the measurement of health or intelligence but the criterion of success is the most important and the only ultimately safe standard" of who is fit.[50] Drysdale joined the Eugenics Society in 1921 and remained a member until his death in 1961.

In spite of division within the Malthusian League, 1921 proved to be a year of promise for the organization. With the opening of its first birth-control clinic in the fall and a change of format for the group by the end of the year, many in the league thought they were on the verge of a new period of progress. The members were proud of a new office that was obtained for the group at 124 Victoria Street. It occupied the top floor of a three-story building opposite Victoria Station and consisted of a large meeting room, for about sixty or seventy persons, and two smaller rooms for offices. A brass plate at the door of the building read "The Malthusian League—For Rational Birth Control."[51] During June and July, the open-air meetings that had been halted by the outbreak of war in 1914 were resumed. A three-week campaign of meetings in South London served to reemphasize for league workers the need in the poorer section of the city for having a place where working-class women could consult privately with medical personnel on contraceptive methods.

As early as 1915, the league council had had under consideration a plan for opening a birth-control clinic. Margaret Sanger, on her way home from Holland, offered to instruct nurses in the use of the method she had studied with the Dutch league. The project had to be abandoned, however, because of the war. Undoubtedly another motivation for the Malthusian League to open a clinic developed when Marie Stopes and her husband, Humphrey Verdon Roe, opened a clinic at 61, Marlborough Road, Holloway, London, on 17 March 1921.

Dr. Stopes, D. Sc., Ph.D., had already made a name for herself in the family-planning movement with the publication of two popular marriage manuals in 1918, *Married Love* and *Wise Parenthood*. Her plea for family limitation differed significantly from the Malthusian League's. In their history of the birth control movement in England, Mary Breed and Edith How-Martyn wrote: "In emphasizing the value of a harmonious sex life to married couples, the right of women to happy motherhood, and the right of children to be wanted and loved, Dr. Stopes gave a new aspect to the birth-control movement which proved more popular than the exposition of the doctrine of Malthus."[52]

219

Further, in 1921, Dr. Stopes started a new organization to promote the family-planning movement, the Society for Constructive Birth Control and Racial Progress, with herself as president and her husband as secretary. One of the vice-presidents of the new group was H. G. Wells, who had finally removed his name as an officer in the Malthusian League. In 1922, Dr. Stopes began publishing a periodical called the *Birth Control News*. Her emphasis, like Drysdale's, however, was on the need to improve the quality of the race. The motto of her organization was "Babies in the right place"; the objective of her periodical was to advocate a "joyous and deliberate motherhood, a sure light in our racial darkness."[53] Malthusian doctrine was completely unacceptable, in her opinion, because of its attachment to secularism, an association that she blamed on the Malthusian League. She retained in her own advocation of family limitation a sentiment and mysticism that alienated some but attracted others. In 1920, for example, she claimed divine guidance in the writing of her book, *A New Gospel For All People: A Revelation of God Uniting Physiology and the Religions of Man*. The publication was addressed to the bishops sitting in conference at Lambeth at the time. The antagonism and competition between the Malthusian League and Stopes provided a boost to the family-planning movement, especially in 1921–22; but to those involved and to those who watched from the sidelines, much of it seemed petty and unnecessarily hostile in view of the fact that both had much the same objectives.

The opening of the Malthusian League's birth-control clinic was made possible primarily by the financial donations of the Drysdales; Sir John Sumner, the founder of Ty-Phoo Tea, Ltd.; and Mr. A. K. Bulley of Neston, Cheshire. C. V. and Bessie Drysdale contributed £1,000 in early 1921 to sustain the league's periodical and launch new activities. Part of this went into the opening of the clinic, but John Sumner of Birmingham provided the location by purchasing a building at 153a East Street, Walworth, and renting it to the league for a trifling sum. Mr. Bulley provided £350 for the first year's expenses.[54] In spite of Mrs. Drysdale's ill health, necessitating a severe operation on 1 October, the East Street Welfare Centre for Pre-Maternity,

Maternity and Child Welfare opened its doors on 9 November 1921 at the corner of East Street and South Street, Walworth, not far from the Elephant and Castle. London had many welfare clinics that provided advice and medical treatment to poor mothers and children, but the Walworth Women's Welfare Centre, as it was later called, provided contraceptive advice as well. The league leaders hoped that the center would serve as a model for the establishment of other such clinics.

In the first months, the Walworth Centre was open two after-noons a week, one afternoon for providing the usual child-welfare and maternity services and the other primarily for dispensing contraceptive advice. Dr. Norman Haire, who had already established himself as a well-known gynecologist in his Harley Street practice, served as the medical officer in charge of the clinic until 1923; he was assisted by a registered nurse. Attendance was sparse in the first months. Records indicate only two women sought advice in November 1921; in January 1922, only eight. By January 1923, however, attendance was up to 258; and by 1953, the clinic was serving between 1,500 and 2,000 persons each year.[55] In addition, from 1923 to 1936, the center served as a training school for doctors and nurses in-terested in learning about birth-control methods. After World War II, medical schools gradually began to include such instruc-tion in their own curriculums.

In 1922, the Malthusian League was forced to relinquish its affiliation with the Walworth Centre. The expenses of main-taining it were too great. Around £550 per annum were required to keep the clinic open, and as early as February 1922 *The Malthusian* announced the "danger of having to close . . . [the center] in the near future unless more funds are forthcoming."[56] Alice Vickery Drysdale and her son, C. V., were each donating £10 a month to the League in 1921 and 1922 and making loans to it when necessary; otherwise, however, donors were few in number. Within a year after its opening, the Walworth Centre was placed in the hands of a special committee set up to take on the responsibility. In 1923, the committee became the Society for the Provision of Birth Control Clinics, and by 1928 it had twelve clinics in operation, three in London, seven in the provinces, and two in Scotland.[57] The National Birth Control Association absorbed the Society in 1937 and later was itself renamed the Family Planning Association. There were, of course, other groups and even private individuals who began to open centers and dispense contraceptive information by the mid twenties. The era of birth-control clinics was at hand; nevertheless, Marie Stopes and the Malthusian League were first. The next step was to get the English government to permit its own vast network of welfare centers to give contraceptive advice.

Meanwhile, the Malthusian League went on with its propaganda efforts with a new program of open-air meetings in South London during the fall of 1921 and conducted a series of fortnightly lectures at the new clinic, sometimes for men only, other times for both men and women. Even more importantly for the future of the league itself was the attempt made in 1921–22 to change the image of the organization in keeping with suggestions and criticisms that had become increasingly more insistent since the war. For example, the ongoing debate over a new name for the league periodical gained in intensity during 1920–21. Readers of *The Malthusian* were prolific with suggestions for a new title: *Birth Control, Happy Families, The Population Journal, Matrimonial Economy, Hope* (A Crusade against Poverty), *Motherhood, The Voice of Reason.* The Drysdales gave ground gradually but grudgingly to those in the organization pushing for a new title. "We ourselves are very reluctant to make a change as our paper has appeared under its present title for forty years, and we have not the slightest intention to lower our flag or change our policy." The title of the journal might change, the name of the organization might change, but Drysdale made it quite clear that he would not. "Our interpretation of the Malthusian theory has led us to a strongly individualistic doctrine which offends many advocates of birth control, and even those who are Malthusians in the sense of admitting the law of Malthus, but who believe that much may be done for human improvement by Socialistic measures." He and his wife, he proclaimed, would continue to be "totally and irreconcilably opposed to [such a] . . . view."[58]

As a compromise, Drysdale suggested the league enlarge its journal and divide it into two sections, one with a new title carrying news of all aspects of the birth-control movement and the other with the old title continuing the longstanding policies of the organization. The suggestion, as he well knew, was impracticable unless they could achieve a much larger circulation of the periodical than previously. But after the king's physician, Lord Dawson of Penn, defended the practice of voluntary family limitation in a speech before a church congress in October 1921, newsagents were more willing to carry birth-control periodicals on their open racks. The possibility of increasing *The Malthusian's* circulation became a reality. This further spurred the league to change the name of its journal. In the last issue of the journal under the old title, C. V. Drysdale commented, "The title of the *Malthusian* has always been somewhat of a misnomer owing to its advocacy of early marriage and the employment of contraceptive devices, and as the title neo-Malthusian is unlikely to be understood or popular, it has been thought advisable to make a complete change."[59]

In keeping with a suggestion from Mrs. Drysdale, *The Malthusian* became *The New Generation*, subtitled *For Rational Birth Control*, in January 1922. "It will not be committed to any sectarian or political doctrine," Editor Drysdale promised in the first issue.[60] But by May, critics on the Left were already complaining, "Apparently, *The New Generation* is only to be 'The Malthusian' over again, larger and better printed." Eden and Cedar Paul, both outspoken advocates of communism in England in the 1920s, said, "Our case is Communism *and* Birth Control; just as Dr. Drysdale's case is Individualism *and* Birth Control." They emphasized that, "if *The New Generation* continues to identify itself with bourgeois economics exclusively, if it continues to ignore or deride proletarian economics, it will inevitably continue to alienate class-conscious proletarians."[61] That the editors, C. V. and Bessie Drysdale, would print such criticisms is evidence of their sincerity in saying they felt the new journal should reflect all viewpoints within the birth-control movement, but they were undoubtedly offended by such direct attacks.

The change in title and format of the journal did, however, seem to provoke new interest in the Malthusian League. During the first three months that *The New Generation* was in circulation, the League enrolled 108 new members. So encouraged were the leaders of the organization that at the Fifth International Neo-Malthusian and Birth Control Conference held in London, 11–14 July 1922, Bessie Drysdale announced that the Malthusian League would henceforth be known as the New Generation League. The change was obviously made in an attempt to draw the much-needed support of those in English society who now approved of birth control but for reasons little akin to those of the Drysdales. "There has been a strongly expressed general wish made within recent times," Mrs. Drysdale continued, "that we should have a Society that would bring in that very large body of popular and public opinion in favour of Birth Control on various terms and from various points of view, but at least in favour of Birth Control."[62]

The Drysdales continued to hold the key offices of the organization with C. V. as president and his wife, Bessie, as secretary. In addition, they served as coeditors of *The New Generation*, and as a consequence, the journal continued its antilabor tone. During the election of 1922, Mrs. Drysdale wrote an editorial opposing the election of a Labour-controlled government:

> If it were only a question of class interest, we should have no objection whatever to a Labour Government. The wage earners form the great majority of the community, and, on our principle of the greatest happiness of the greatest number, we should cordially endorse their right to govern, *if they only knew what was best for themselves*. But unfortunately, it is not so, and we must regretfully endorse Mr. [Winston] Churchill's contention that Labour is not fit to govern. [The italics are hers.][63]

Her use of the pronoun "we" was perhaps unfortunate because although she probably meant only C. V. and herself the implication was that the entire organization adhered to her position. It was soon apparent that was not the case. H. Jennie Baker, a member of the New Generation League but also a leader in organizing working women, expressed the anger of labor members:

> The "Malthusian" was so anti-Labour that I could not take it, or would have found it impossible to belong to the Malthusian League. I understood *The New Generation* was to be entirely non-political,

but I find the editorial stigmatising Labour as "unfit to govern," and stating, as if it were a matter allowing of no question, that Labour "doctrines are unscientific and erroneous."

Such remarks make it entirely impossible for me to pass on the paper to others, as one would like to do by way of propaganda in the cause of birth control, and if the paragraphs are to be taken as expressing the attitude of the League, as well as of the Editor of its paper, it will be necessary for me to resign my membership, as it is impossible for me to be publicly associated with a body holding anti-Labour views.[64]

It was becoming more and more apparent that name changes meant little as long as the leadership remained the same. The Drysdales, too, were tiring of the struggle to maintain a place for their Malthusian economic theories with the increased agitation against them within the organization. At the Forty-fourth Annual Meeting in July 1922, the league council nominated Harold Cox, a well-known economist and former member of Parliament, as president of the New Generation League instead of C. V. Drysdale, who undoubtedly had suggested the change himself. Mr. Cox declined the nomination, however, and C. V. was reelected.

In spite of the highly successful Fifth International Conference arranged primarily by the Drysdales and held in London in July 1922, an extraordinary session of the members of the New Generation League was called on 16 January 1923, at which time C. V. and Bessie Drysdale announced their resignations. Mrs. Drysdale had never fully recovered her strength after her illness in 1921 and needed a prolonged rest. They were also weary of giving time and money to a movement that was so obviously becoming more and more antagonistic to their way of thinking. I realize, said Dr. Drysdale when the council asked him to continue as president, that I am "not an acceptable apostle to the working classes, among whom the movement is now spreading."[65] And so, "for the first time in nearly seventy years," the new editor of *The New Generation* proclaimed, "England has a Birth Control movement without a Drysdale at the head."[66] Whether active or not, however, C. V. continued to be listed as president of the organization.

The new editor and secretary of the New Generation League was Robert Bird Kerr, a Fabian socialist who had already had a long career as a lawyer in Canada. He was born in 1867 in Scotland and attended Edinburgh University.[67] He developed an early aversion to Christianity and became absorbed in radical ideas while studying for a short time at Bonn University. It was in Germany, Kerr said, that he was converted to the family-limitation movement when he picked up a German copy of George Drysdale's *Elements of Social Science* on a Munich bookstall in the early 1890s.[68] He returned to Edinburgh and joined G. B. Shaw and the Webbs in the youthful Fabian Society. But feeling uncomfortable with his new ideas in staid Victorian Edinburgh, he migrated to North America in 1893 to practice law first in Phoenix, Arizona, then Victoria, and finally in Kelowna, British Columbia. He retained his socialistic ideas but lived quietly and frugally for thirty years practicing law and writing. After retiring at age 55, he returned to England in 1922 and took up residence in London. Kerr had been in contact with the Malthusian League since the first decade of the century. From the beginning, however, it had been apparent he was in favor of family limitation but not of Malthusian doctrines. He wrote to C. R. Drysdale in 1906: "It is useless to tell a man that if he and ten million others will have small families, he will gain something. The thing to do is to show him how *he* will gain by *having a small family himself,* no matter what the others do."[69] This was the viewpoint he brought to the league when he became an active member in January 1923. Until his health failed in January 1951, Kerr remained as the editor of *The New Generation* which in 1949 was renamed *The Malthusian.*

Meanwhile, the work of the New Generation League continued, primarily in the form of public meetings. Now, however, every shade of opinion was represented on the speakers' platform, "from the communist who considers birth control a purely individual matter to the individualist who believes it should be brought about by collective action."[70] Speaking for the league at its public meetings during the mid twenties were such diverse personalities as communists like F. W. Stella Browne and Dr. Eden Paul; Fabian socialists, such as, R. B. Kerr and Bertrand

226

Russell; former or current members of Parliament like John M. Robertson, Harold Cox, and Ernest Thurtle; women labor leaders, such as, H. Jennie Baker; and, of course, individualists like the Drysdales. The membership of the league increased during the first half of 1923 from 616 to over a thousand primarily because of its new practical tone.

At the annual General Meeting in May 1925, however, the members voted to rename their organization the Malthusian League. The change was initiated by Dr. Drysdale. The vote on his motion, only one against, is perhaps indicative of the extent to which he and his supporters had recaptured control of the group. The name and policy of the league had been changed in 1922 with a view to popularizing it. "This, however, was now felt to have been a mistake," Drysdale explained, "because there were other societies available for people who desired a mainly popular propaganda, and there was needed a society which upheld the fundamental principles of Malthus and Darwin, and thereby provided a sound social philosophy." So the group returned to Malthus, though Drysdale assured them that reassuming the old name "would not mean any slackening of the League's practical propaganda."[71]

Bessie Drysdale also renewed her activities on behalf of the Malthusian League in 1925. She came out of retirement to initiate and lead a motor campaign to publicize the drive to get the Ministry of Health to allow government welfare centers to dispense contraceptive information and devices. With the financial help once again of its generous benefactor John Sumner, and of Dr. Alice Vickery Drysdale, the league printed a million leaflets urging voters to write to the minister of health demanding birth-control instruction for poor mothers. Mrs. Drysdale's plan was for two or three ladies and a driver to tour England by motor car, draft local help along the way, and distribute 1,200 to 1,300 leaflets daily. They actually gave out about 5,000 per day. The little group was given a "send-off" from the league office on Sunday, 28 June, at 10 A.M. They planned to start their campaign in Birmingham, the home of the current minister of health, Neville Chamberlain, and of their generous supporter, Mr. Sumner. The tour lasted until 10 October, a total of 105 days, and the ladies, ten or so, who took turns at distributing the leaflets handed out 460,000 of them in fifty-seven communities. As they moved from town to town, they found support among the various labor organizations, the Labour party, the Independent Labour party, co-operative societies, women's guilds, and working men's clubs and were encouraged by the friendly attitude of most local medical officers of health and the local constabularies. There was, of course, some opposition. The *Catholic Times* wrote:

> The Malthusian League has adopted a new method of propagating its repulsive doctrines. From correspondents we learn that it is being carried out in several places. . . . The League and its propaganda is regarded with absolute abhorrence by thousands of Christians, lettered and unlettered alike. The spread of its pernicious teaching can only subvert public morals. Its actions will have to be watched and countered.[72]

Distribution of the remaining leaflets continued throughout the winter of 1925–26, primarily in the Greater London area.

Results of such a campaign are, of course, practically impossible to calculate, but the fact remains that the issue of birth-control information in welfare centers waxed hot during the late 1920s, even in the Houses of Parliament. On 6 February 1926, Mr. Ernest Thurtle, Labor member of Shoreditch, introduced a bill in the House of Commons to authorize local authorities to spend money in giving birth-control information to married women who requested it. The bill was defeated by 169 to 84, a fairly good showing for a first attempt.[73] On 28 April, Lord Buckmaster, a vice-president of the Malthusian League and former lord chancellor, moved in the House of Lords that the government withdraw all instructions that prevented the giving of birth-control information at welfare centers. The motion carried by a vote of 57 to 44. "The House of Lords," the league proclaimed proudly, "is thus the first legislative body in the history of the world to express approval of birth control."[74] The efforts of the Malthusian League and of all the other organizations and individuals who had worked for the same objective were crowned with at least partial success in 1930. A Labour-controlled Ministry of Health issued Memorandum 153/M.C.W. that allowed the dispensation of contraceptive advice at Maternity and Infant Welfare Centres but only where a doctor judged that further pregnancy would be detrimental to the health of the mother. The memorandum was less a victory for the Malthusian League, however, than it was for a number of other organizations that had developed in the 1920s primarily for the purpose of pressuring the government into accepting birth control as a public policy. Such groups as the National Union of Societies for Equal Citizenship, the Society for the Provision of Birth Control Clinics, the Women's National Liberal Federation, and the Workers' Birth Control Group joined in the fight to get government health officials to recognize the desirability of assuring that medical information on methods of birth control was available to married people who needed and wanted it. The Malthusian League itself, meanwhile, officially ceased to exist in December 1927.

On 26 July 1927, at 8 P.M., almost two hundred people gathered over filet de sole and vol-au-vent in the Holborn Restaurant to celebrate the fiftieth anniversary of the Bradlaugh-Besant trial and the founding of the Malthusian League. Among those present in the crowd were John Maynard Keynes, who chaired the after-dinner proceedings, Annie Besant, Mrs. Hypatia Bradlaugh Bonner and her husband, Dr. and Mrs. C. V. Drysdale, A. B. Moss (one of the last of the living charter members of the League), H. G. Wells, Professor Julian Huxley, John Sumner, and a host of other friends of the Drysdales, of Mrs. Besant, and of the league.[75] The entire group rose to cheer Annie Besant when she replied to a toast in honor of "The Pioneers" of the birth-control movement. She was still a Theosophist but testified that she had long believed in the benefits to be gained from family limitation. Dr. Alice Vickery Drysdale was still living but was unable to attend the dinner (she died in 1929). J. M. Keynes, R. B. Kerr, H. G. Wells, and John Sumner all spoke briefly and glowingly of the progress of the neo-Malthusian movement. Dr. C. V. Drysdale concluded the evening with his own account of the activities of the Malthusian League.

On 16 December 1927, the league held its last annual meeting at which time Dr. Drysdale declared the work of the organization complete. In 1877, he said, the birthrate stood at 36 per thousand; in 1927, it was under 18 per thousand. Even the birthrates of the rich and the poor were rapidly being equalized. He moved, therefore, that the Malthusian League cease its activities except for publication of *The New Generation;* distribution of the practical pamphlet, *Hygienic Methods of Family Limitation;* and meetings of the league council as needed:

> The Malthusian League records with the greatest satisfaction that in the fifty years which have elapsed since the Bradlaugh-Besant trial and the formation of the League, the neo-Malthusian doctrine and the practice of birth control have been accepted throughout the civilized world to such an extent that their complete adoption is absolutely assured. It expresses its great pleasure at the formation of numerous organizations in this and other countries for the carrying on of this propaganda and wishes them every success, and feels that the propaganda may now be left in their hands. It therefore resolves to discontinue its propaganda leaving the Council to resume activity should necessity arise.[76]

1. A scribbled note found among the private collection of the C. V. Drysdale Papers, Box 5, contained this statement and the quotation from Friedrich Nietzsche's *Thus Spake Zarathustra.* They are indicative of Drysdale's conservative, individualistic philosophy that determined his actions and views until his death in 1961. British Library of Political and Economic Science, London.

2. "Vital Statistics of London," *The Malthusian* 34, no. 4 (April 1910): 26.

3. Ibid. In 1909, the birthrates and death rates for the various areas of London were as follows:

Area	Birth-rate	Death rate	Area	Birth-rate	Death rate
County of London	24.4	14.0	Camberwell	23.2	13.4
Finsbury	35.8	19.2	Hammersmith	23.0	14.3
St. Marylebone	32.1	14.6	Battersea	22.9	13.0
Bermondsey	31.8	18.8	Islington	22.8	14.0
Stepney	31.5	15.3	Greenwich	22.5	12.2
Shoreditch	30.5	19.0	Woolwich	22.4	11.9
Bethnal Green	30.5	16.8	St. Pancras	22.2	14.8
Poplar	29.3	16.3	Lewisham	21.9	10.3
Southwark	27.2	16.8	Paddington	19.1	12.9
Holborn	26.8	15.6	Stoke Newington	18.3	11.3
Lambeth	26.1	14.1	Chelsea	17.5	14.4
Deptford	25.8	13.6	Kensington	17.4	12.9
Fulham	23.9	12.0	City of Westminster	15.0	13.1
Hackney	23.6	12.6	Hampstead	13.6	8.9
Wandsworth	23.4	11.9	City of London	13.2	20.3

4. C. R. Drysdale, "Opponents of the Latter-Day Gospel of Parental Prudence," *The Malthusian* 26, no. 11 (November 1902): 82.

5. C. V. Drysdale, "The 'Eugenics Review' and the Malthusian League," *The Malthusian* 33, no. 12 (December 1909): 90.

6. Letter to the Editor of *The New Generation,* R. B. Kerr, from C. V. Drysdale, *The New Generation* 7, no. 7 (July 1928): 82.

7. Charles Vickery Drysdale was born 8 July 1874. He prepared for an engineering career at the Finsbury and Central Technical Colleges. His first position was as associate head of the Department of Electrical Engineering and Applied Physics, Northampton Institute, 1896–1910. In 1898, he married Bessie Ingham Edwards (1871–1950), a teacher at Stockwell College. He was also an examiner for the Spectacle Makers' Company (1902–1929) and a member of the Jury Electrical Section at the St. Louis Exhibition in 1904. During World War I, he served in the Anti-Submarine Division of the Office of the Admiralty and became director of scientific research in 1929, a post he held until his retirement in 1934. In addition to a number of publications on electricity (e.g., *The Foundations of Alternate-Current Theory* and *Electrical Measuring Instruments*), he has been credited with the invention of a number of scientific instruments. For his service to the British government in the Office of the Admiralty, he was awarded the O.B.E.

8. "Notes," *The Malthusian* 33, no. 1 (January 1909): 6.

9. The flag first appeared in the second decade of the twentieth century and is now housed at the Family Planning Association, 27/35 Mortimer Street, London. It was given to the association in 1962 by Mr. R. G. Morton, the last treasurer of the Malthusian League. The banner is 6 x 4 feet and is made of pink sateen with the symbol of the league and the words "The Malthusian League: A Crusade Against Poverty" worked on it in black silk and silk cord.

10. C. V. Drysdale, "A Retrospect," *The Malthusian* 45, no. 5 (May 1921): 34.

11. *The Malthusian* reported in November 1914: "Owing to the darkening of the streets the League has held no open-air meetings in South London for the last three weeks, and may suspend them until the fear of aerial attacks has passed." 38, no. 11 (November 1914): 81.

12. "Our South London Campaign," *The Malthusian* 37, no. 3 (March 1913): 17.

13. Ibid.

14. "Malthusian League Meetings," *The Malthusian* 37, no. 3 (March 1913): 18.

15. "Annual General Meeting of the Malthusian League," *The Malthusian* 37, no. 6 (June 1913): 41.

16. Ibid.

17. "Our New Departure," *The Malthusian* 37, no. 9 (September 1913): 66.

18. Marie Stopes referred to the original Malthusian League pamphlet as a "single sheet" and mentioned the methods it recommended in her book on *Contraception: Its Theory, History, and Practice* (London: John Bale, Sons & Danielsson, Ltd., 1923), p. 312, fn. To my knowledge, there is no extant copy of the original pamphlet.

19. Ibid., p. 317.

20. Diverse opinion had developed by the early 1920s as to when the "safe period" occurred in the menstrual cycle. The two major opinions as to when it occurred were in direct conflict with each other. No wonder Haire concluded that the procedure was unreliable.

As the female egg cell is generally believed to pass into the womb about the time of the monthly flow, it has been very commonly supposed that there is a safe period (most generally thought to be the middle fortnight between the monthly periods, or, according to other writers, the three days immediately before a period) during which intercourse can take place without conception resulting. Couples who do not like to abstain entirely or to use preventives may possibly succeed in this way. But as it is known that the sperm cells can remain alive in the wife's body for several weeks, waiting to fertilise an egg when it comes along, *there is no reliance whatever to be placed on this method of prevention,* and the writer cannot recommend it. [Italics are his.] Norman Haire. *Hygienic Methods of Family Limitation* (London: Malthusian League, 1922), p. 8.

21. Ibid., p. 14.

22. Ibid., p. 15.

23. "Applications More Numerous Than Ever," *The Malthusian* 39, no. 2 (February 1915): 12.

24. Bessie Drysdale, "Business (More Than) As Usual," *The Malthusian* 39, no. 4 (April 1915): 26.

25. *The New Generation* 19, no. 1 (January 1940).

26. "Why the Malthusian League Has Advised Against Having Children in War Time," *The Malthusian* 38, no. 12 (December 1914): 31.

27. C. V. and Bessie Ingham Drysdale apparently adopted a son, Eric, probably after Eva's death. Eric visited his adoptive parents in 1950 shortly before Mrs. Drysdale died. He was living in Brazil at the time with his wife, Marilyn.

28. The statement was actually written by Arthur P. Busch in "The Malthusian League: A New Departure," *The Malthusian* 23, no. 3 (March 1899): 20, but the editor, C. R. Drysdale, added, "We are thoroughly in accord with Mr. Busch."

29. Bessie Drysdale, "London Members' 'At Home,'" *The Malthusian* 36, no. 4 (April 1912): 27.

30. Ibid., p. 28.

31. Ibid.

32. "Our New Vice-Presidents," *The Malthusian* 39, no. 2 (February 1915): 9.

33. C. V. Drysdale, "The Malthusianism versus Socialism Controversy," *The Malthusian* 41, no. 5 (May 1917): 37.

34. Ibid., pp. 37–38. This by no means exhausts Drysdale's points of contrast (he lists fifteen in all), but the tone throughout is much the same.

35. Letter to the Editor of *The Malthusian* from H. G. Wells, *The Malthusian* 41, no. 6 (June 1917): 43–44.

36. C. V. Drysdale, "Mr. H. G. Wells and Socialism," *The Malthusian* 41, no. 6 (June 1917): 41–42.

37. Ibid., p. 43.

38. "Foreword by the Honorary Secretary," *The Malthusian* 41, no. 9 (September 1917): 70.

39. *The Malthusian* 42, no. 8 (August 1918): 63.

40. Stopes, *Contraception,* p. 318.

41. "Projected Birth Control Society," Letter to the Editor from George Standring, *The Malthusian* 43, no. 8 (August 1919): 60.

42. Letter to the Editor from C. F. Chance, *The Malthusian* 42, no. 11 (November 1918): 86.

43. C. V. Drysdale, "Practice v. Theory," *The Malthusian* 42, no. 10 (October 1918): 74.

44. Stopes, *Contraception,* p. 312.

45. D. V. Glass, *Population Policies and Movements in Europe* (London: Frank Cass and Company, Ltd., 1967, 1940), p. 60. fn.

46. C. V. Drysdale, "Suppression of Neo-Malthusian Propaganda in France," *The Malthusian* 44, no. 10 (October 1920): 79.

47. C. V. Drysdale, "Neo-Malthusianism and Democracy," *The Malthusian* 44, no. 7 (July 1920): 50.

48. C. V. Drysdale, *The Neo-Malthusian Ideal and How it Can Be Realised* (London: The Malthusian League, 1921), p. 4. Presidential address delivered by Dr. Drysdale to the Forty-fourth Annual General Meeting of the Malthusian League, later printed as a pamphlet.

49. *The New Generation* 1, no. 6 (June 1922): 15.

50. *The Malthusian* 44, no. 8 (August 1920): 60.

51. [Bessie Drysdale], "Notes from the Honorary Secretary," *The Malthusian* 45, no. 6 (June 1921), 41.

52. Mary Breed and Edith How-Martyn, *The Birth Control Movement in England* (London: John Bale, Sons & Danielsson, Ltd., 1930), p. 14.

53. Ibid., p. 22.

54. "The New Clinic," *The Malthusian* 45, no. 8 (August 1921): 60. These same gentlemen had come to the aid of the league earlier in 1921 with contributions of £100 each, primarily for outfitting and maintaining the new office in Victoria Street.

55. N. Wright, "Early Days at Walworth," *Family Planning* 1, no. 4 (January 1953): 7.

56. "Clinics," *The New Generation* 1, no. 2 (February 1922): 16.

57. Wright, "Early Days at Walworth," p. 7. The three in London were the Walworth Women's Welfare Centre; the North Kensington Welfare Centre, opened in November 1924; and the East London Centre, opened in June 1926.

58. "Suggestions for a New Title," *The Malthusian* 44, no. 2 (February 1920): 11.

59. "The Last Number of 'The Malthusian,'" *The Malthusian* 45, no. 12 (December 1921): 97.

60. "Our Message," *The New Generation* 1, no. 1 (January 1922): 2.

61. Eden and Cedar Paul, "'The New Generation' Starts Prancing," *The New Generation* 1, no. 5 (May 1922): 3.

62. Speech by Bessie I. Drysdale, *Report of the Fifth International Neo-Malthusian and Birth Control Conference,* London, 11–14 July 1922 (London: William Heinemann, Ltd., 1922), p. 211.

63. Bessie I. Drysdale, "The Political Situation," *The New Generation* 1, no. 4 (April 1922): 1–2.

64. H. Jennie Baker, "A Protest," Letter to the Editor, *The New Generation* 1, no. 5 (May 1922): 15.

65. *The New Generation* 2, no. 2 (February 1923): 17.

66. R. B. Kerr, *The New Generation* 2, no. 2 (February 1923): 17.

67. Hilda D. Romanes, "Obituary: The Late R. B. Kerr, M.A., LL.B.," *The Malthusian,* n.s., no. 19 (May–June 1951), p. 4.

68. *The New Generation* 2, no. 2 (February 1923): 17.

69. Letter to the Editor from R. B. Kerr, *The Malthusian* 30, no. 9 (September 1906): 65.

70. *The New Generation* 2, no. 4 (April 1923): 42.

71. Forty-seventh Annual Meeting, *The New Generation* 4, no. 7 (July 1925): 76.

72. "Passing Comments," *The New Generation* 4, no. 10 (October 1925): 109, citing the *Catholic Times,* 5 September 1925.

73. *The New Generation* reported the vote as follows:

For:	54 Conservatives	Against:	114 Conservatives
	27 Labour		44 Labour
	3 Liberal		10 Liberal
			1 Prohibitionist

The New Generation 5, no. 3 (March 1926): 25.

74. *Forty-eighth Annual Report of the Malthusian League for the Year Ending March 31st, 1926.* Published separately by the Malthusian League, 120, Victoria Street, Westminster, London, p. 2.

75. The list of guests was included in "Our Successful Jubilee Dinner," *The New Generation* 6, no. 8 (August 1927): 87.

76. "Malthusian League Meets," *The New Generation* 7, no. 1 (January 1928): 6.

8: The Postmortem Period

The Malthusian League suspended its official activities in December 1927 but maintained a shadowy existence for another thirty-four years. R. B. Kerr continued to edit the league's periodical, *The New Generation,* with the help of a few generous donors; and C. V. Drysdale continued to be listed as president of the organization. The council met on a regular basis in the first few years after the league's official demise, and there was even occasionally talk of reviving the group. In 1931, Edith How-Martyn suggested the founding of an annual lecture dinner in honor of Malthus and the league, but Kerr discouraged the idea. He labeled it unprogressive and said one dinner honoring the dead was enough, referring to the Jubilee celebration in 1927. "We should prefer a dinner for the purpose of stimulating thought and original research on population problems, with a view to the production of future Malthuses."[1] Nevertheless, Mrs. How-Martyn and a number of other ladies initiated a Malthusian ball in 1933 to highlight public acceptance of the Malthusian theory "that a limited birth rate is indispensable to the prevention of war and poverty."[2] The affair served to chronicle the respectability that the birth-control movement had gained in England by the 1930s, a movement in which Mrs. How-Martyn had been active for many years. The guest list read like the register of the English coats of arms: the Countess of Athlone, the Marchioness of Carlsbrooke, the Earl of Feversham, the Earl of Listowel, the Countess of Warwick, Viscount Moore, Lord Brougham, Baroness Ravensdale, Lady Muriel Beckwith, and so forth. Also invited, of course, were individuals who had devoted time and money over the years to propagating neo-Malthusian doctrines, such as the Drysdales, Harold J. Laski, Julian Huxley, and H. G. Wells.

Even a second world war didn't destroy the shadow of the league entirely. *The New Generation* was reduced in size to cut costs, but the council carried on as usual. In July 1946, Binnie Dunlop died after serving as treasurer for the organization since 1927. The secretary, Olive Johnson, assumed both offices until Mr. R. G. Morton, a council member since 1944, was persuaded to accept the position of treasurer. Following World War II, interest in world population problems increased. Food shortages, created in many areas by the ravages of war, prompted a revival of the Malthusian prognosis of inevitable doom for the poorer sections of the population. C. V. Drysdale thought he saw in the renewed interest in Malthus and his population theories a need for a regeneration of the old Malthusian League.

Consequently, in 1949, Drysdale initiated "A New Educational Campaign." The resulting burst of activity, however, was more like the last convulsive movements of an organism before drawing the final breath of life. The league council met regularly during 1949 to map out a strategy for the campaign. *The New Generation* resumed its old name *The Malthusian* in October, and a major objective for the revitalized league was defined:

> The Object of The Malthusian League is to promote understanding of the economic and evolutionary doctrines of Malthus and Darwin and of the necessity for restricting reproduction, especially of the least healthy and capable individuals, in order to render it possible to secure sufficiency of all the necessaries and comforts of existence for all the inhabitants of the world and a high and more nearly uniform quality of the human race, and to eliminate social and international antagonism and wars.[3]

All mention of the necessity of spreading practical information was omitted, but the eugenic concern remained an integral part of the league's doctrines, as evidenced in a set of new principles designed for the organization. The principles were printed on the inside back cover of *The Malthusian* in October 1949 and read as follows:

1. That unrestrained reproduction has led, and must inevitably lead, to insufficiency of food and therefore to poverty, famine, disease and war.

2. That a high average standard of health and efficiency of the human race can only be secured and maintained by reducing the reproduction of all individuals who suffer from serious hereditary disease or defects, or who are incapable of supporting themselves and their offspring.

Drysdale's plan was to revitalize the league journal and add to it monthly installments of his own article, "The Scientific Path to Peace and Prosperity." The journal would be circulated on college and university campuses in the hope of attracting young people to the doctrines of the organization. Drysdale was encouraged in his plans by the fact that a few students had already formed a group for studying and discussing the population question and had written to the league for information. In early 1950, Dr. Drysdale addressed a student meeting at Sheffield University, but by April, he was already suggesting another reorganization of the league. He proposed that it be made an international organization with headquarters in the United States under Mrs. Sanger's presidency and that the English group remain as a British association to distribute literature.[4]

As usual, the group was plagued with money problems. The cost of *The Malthusian* was 8d. per copy; they sold it for 6d. and gave away many free copies. Donors made up the difference. The league received a legacy of over £407 in May 1950 that allowed the small group to carry on unperturbed by financial worries.

Old age with its attendant illnesses became the final executioner of what remained of the organization. Bessie Drysdale had two serious operations during the 1940s and lived out her life as an invalid much dependent upon her husband's care. She died on 6 September 1950. In many respects, the shadow of the league died with her. No further council meetings were held after the summer of 1950. The only remnant was *The Malthusian*. R. B. Kerr suffered a paralytic stroke in January 1951 and died the following April. Miss Olive Johnson, Mr. Herbert Cutner (a long-time member of the league), and C. V. Drysdale managed to maintain the journal for a short time with great effort since all three were quite elderly. They conserved their energy by combining issues; for example, the last issue of *The Malthusian* covered a four-month period, June to September

239

1952. The publication still carried, however, an application form for membership in the Malthusian League. C. V. went to live with Olive Johnson in May 1951 and remained with her till she died in December 1958. He lived out his last years with his nephew in Sussex.[5]

After all of its financial woes over the years, the Malthusian League still had over £1,400, primarily from bequests, in the bank when its last president died on 8 February 1961. R. G. Morton, a member of the league since before World War I and its last treasurer, was left with the task of clearing up the final business of the organization. He tried to find enough members to call a meeting in 1961 but couldn't. With the help of T. Murray Mills, one of C. V. Drysdale's coexecutors (the other was his nephew), Mr. Morton proceeded to distribute the remaining funds of the Malthusian League to various organizations that had objectives similar to those of the league. Eight hundred and fifty pounds went to the Family Planning Association, £350 to the International Planned Parenthood Federation, £141 9s. 10d. to the Abortion Law Reform League, and £100 to the Simon Population Trust.[6] He gave the Malthusian League banner, which had been entrusted to his care in 1939, to the Family Planning Association in London.

The Malthusian League had begun its long history of activities in 1877 with two objectives: (1) to agitate for the abolition of all penalties on the public discussion of the population question, and to obtain such a statutory definition as shall render it impossible, in the future, to bring such discussions within the scope of the common law as a misdemeanor and (2) to spread among the people, by all practicable means, a knowledge of the law of population, of its consequences, and of its bearing upon human conduct and morals. Courts still struggle, of course, with the question of how to define "obscenity." It is one of the category of questions with which each generation must struggle. Obscenity, like beauty, is in the eye of the beholder; and what is obscene to one generation may not be to another. Certainly the type of material for which Charles Bradlaugh and Annie Besant were prosecuted would lift few, if any, eyebrows today. The league's first objective was achieved as voluntary family limitation became acceptable to almost all segments of

English society. At least some credit for the change in attitude should go to the league, for it is through the efforts and determination of such individuals and organizations that new ideas are disseminated.

Social and economic conditions, however, undoubtedly played the major role in prompting the various segments of English society to accept and practice family limitation during the late nineteenth and twentieth centuries, but groups, such as the Malthusian League, contributed to the process by popularizing the idea. Their reticence in distributing practical information, however, probably reduced the extent to which they could have been effective. By the early twentieth century, the league leaders realized full well that they had not reached the poorer classes whom they would most liked to have influenced. "The League has made its appeal with success to the thoughtful and provident classes," George Standring commented in 1909, "but it has as yet lamentably failed to win the ear of those [to] whom its message has been primarily addressed—to the poor and suffering."[7] The league's propaganda had not been acceptable to the lower classes. The kind of economic theory that the league espoused was an anathema to many of those in the working classes who bothered with doctrines. The philosophy of the organization was the liberal nineteenth-century ideology of the English middle class. Little wonder that C. V. Drysdale admitted before the Birth-Rate Commission in 1913 that the Malthusian League had failed to reach the lower classes. "There have been too many obstacles to our doing it on anything like a large scale."[8] The league blamed the obstinacy of the ruling classes in blocking birth-control information from being disseminated among the lower classes. "All we could do," Drysdale said, "was continually to direct all our movement to convincing the educated classes of the necessity of so extending it; but they allowed it to stop at themselves, and did not let it go any further."[9] He was reluctant to admit that it was the attachment of Malthusian economic theories to the practice of family limitation that caused many workers to scorn league propaganda.

In 1930, the National Birth Control Council was formed to coordinate the activities of all organizations working to promote family planning in England. It included among its members

241

many who had been active in the Malthusian League in earlier years, such as C. V. Drysdale, J. Maynard Keynes, Bertrand Russell, and H. G. Wells. In 1939, the council was renamed the Family Planning Association, an active and viable organization in present-day England. As Professor Julian Huxley proclaimed in 1937, "It is now almost forgotten, save by a few experts, that the idea of consciously controlling our numbers in the world was once associated with an austere philosophy which bore the portentous name of 'Neo-Malthusianism.'"[10]

1. "Proposed Annual Dinner," *The New Generation* 10, no. 9 (September 1931): 107.

2. "The Malthusian Ball," *The New Generation* 12, no. 4 (April 1933): 37.

3. Taken from the inside back cover of *The Malthusian,* n.s., no. 1 (October 1949).

4. Letter to R. B. Kerr from Olive Johnson, 15 April 1950. Palmer Collection, London.

5. C. V. and Bessie Drysdale are buried in a family plot at Brookwood Cemetery south of London. Their daughter, Eva, and Charles Robert and Alice Vickery Drysdale are also buried there in a section of the cemetery reserved for "nonbelievers."

6. Letter to Mrs. Eileen Palmer from R. G. Morton, 30 October 1962. Palmer Collection, London.

7. George Standring, "Obstacles in Our Path," *The Malthusian* 33, no. 3 (March 1909): 17.

8. C. V. Drysdale testifying before the National Birth-Rate Commission. *The Declining Birth-Rate: Its Causes and Effects* (London: Chapman and Hall, Ltd., 1916), p. 125.

9. Ibid.

10. "Passing Comments," *The New Generation* 16, no. 8 (August 1937): 85, citing J. Huxley.

Bibliography

COLLECTIONS

C. V. Drysdale Papers: The British Library of Political and Economic Science, Houghton Street, London, W.C.2, has in its archives a collection of C. V. Drysdale's papers. The collection contains manuscript fragments and some correspondence.

Palmer Collection: The major source of information on the Malthusian League and its many years of activities is primarily the organization's own journal called *The Malthusian* from February 1879 through 1921 and from October 1949 until its demise in 1952. From January 1922 to August 1949, the journal was published under the title, *The New Generation*. The only complete set I know of in existence is in the private collection of Mrs. Eileen Palmer, London, to whom I am indebted for its use. Mrs. Palmer also has some of the correspondence of individuals who were prominent in the Malthusian League in its last years.

MALTHUSIAN LEAGUE PUBLICATIONS

Pamphlets published in the first years of the league:

No. 1   C. R. Drysdale. *The Principle of Population.* 1877. 4 pp.
No. 2   C. R. Drysdale. *The Struggle for Enjoyable Existence.* 1877. 8 pp.
No. 3   *The Limitation of Families.* A discussion at the London Dialectical Society in 1868. 1877. 8 pp.
No. 4   H. A. Allbutt. *Evils of Over-Childbearing and Over-Lactation.* 1878. 4 pp.
No. 5   C. R. Drysdale, ed. *Great is Truth, and It Will Prevail.* 1878. 4 pp.
No. 6   C. R. Drysdale. *Presidential Address.* Delivered 18 July 1878. 8 pp.
No. 7   *The Bondsmen of These Our Days.* 1879. 8 pp.
No. 8   J. K. Page. *The Cause of Poverty.* 1879. 4 pp.
No. 9   C. R. Drysdale. *Large Families and Over-Population.* Presidential Address, 1879. 12 pp.
No. 10 Annie Besant. *The Social Aspects of Malthusianism.* 1880. 8 pp.

Leaflets published between 1877 and 1880:

No. 1   *J. S. Mill on Small Families.* 1877.

No. 2   C. R. Drysdale, ed. *What Parents May Do, and Ought To Do, for the Sake of Their Children.* 1877.

No. 3   C. E. Cairnes. *Low Wages and Over-Population.*

No. 4   *Matthew Arnold on the Prosperity of the French Peasant.*

No. 5   *Low Wages and Dear Food* (An Address to Working People).

No. 6   *The Propriety of Not Having More Children Than We Can Keep.*

Six additional leaflets were published by 1907:

No. 7   *The Cry of the Poor.* 2 pp.

No. 8   *How to Raise Wages.* 2 pp.

No. 9   *Extracts From a Judgment Delivered in the Supreme Court of New South Wales,* by Mr. Justice Windeyer, Senior Puisine Judge. 2 pp.

No. 10   [Collection of Quotations on the Population Question.] 1893. 2 pp.

No. 11   *Extract from the Club and Institute Journal.* A statement of recognition of the work of the Malthusian League. 2 pp.

No. 12   *Christianity and Parental Prudence.* By J. K. P[age]. 2 pp.

The following were published in the early twentieth century. They are unnumbered but clearly marked as Malthusian League leaflets:

L. C. C. Elections: Progressive or Moderate? 2 pp. Appeared in *The Malthusian* 31, no. 2 (February 1907): 9.

Parental Prudence: The Only Road to Social Reform. Two issues: 3 pp. and 2 pp. Colonel R. G. Ingersoll.

The Semi-Starvation of the Human Race. 4 pp.

To Working Men and Women. 2 pp. Bessie I. Drysdale.

Unemployment. First appeared in *The Malthusian* 32, no. 11 (November 1908): 83. Bessie Drysdale.

Why Are We Not Better Off? 2 pp. Appeared in *The Malthusian* 31, no. 12 (December 1907): 90.

The following publications are not marked as leaflets, but their length and content would indicate their purpose was the same:

A New Commandment. 2 pp.

Labour Unrest. 2 pp.

During the first months of World War I, the league published several new leaflets, again unnumbered:

Should Working Men and Women Be Urged to Have Large Families at the Present Time? 2 pp. Bessie Drysdale.

To Working Men and Women! Get Rid of Poverty by keeping your family to the size you can bring up well. 2 pp. Bessie Drysdale.

244

The War. 2 pp.

War Babies. 2 pp. Bessie Drysdale.

Some examples of Malthusian League pamphlets published in the twentieth century:

A Private Letter From E. B. to J. S. on the Birth-Rate Question. First appeared as a series in *The Malthusian,* September 1904 to March 1905.

A Women's Malthusian League. First appeared in *The Malthusian* 28, no. 9 (September 1904): 67–69. Alice Drysdale Vickery.

Our Manifesto: Unemployment: Its Cause and Remedy. First appeared in *The Malthusian* 32, no. 11 (November 1908): 81–83. 8 pp. C. V. Drysdale.

Reasons Why You Should Become a Member of the Malthusian League. 3 pp.

This Outspoken Article on the Burden of Large Families Among the Poor Is Reprinted by the Malthusian League With Kind Permission From 'John Bull.' 2 pp. Margaret McGregor, M.A.

Wanted—Beautiful Babies. 4 pp. Bessie Drysdale.

PUBLICATIONS BY THE DRYSDALES

Drysdale, Charles Vickery (does not include his technical writings):

"The Birth Control Movement: Its Scientific and Ethical Bases." *The Eugenics Review* 20, no. 3 (October 1928): 173–78.

Can Everyone Be Fed? A reply to Prince Kropotkin.

Diagrams of International Vital Statistics.

The Empire and the Birth-Rate. A paper read before the Royal Colonial Institute, March 1914.

The Fallacies of Henry George. London: The Malthusian League [n.d., probably published after World War I]. First appeared as a series of articles in *The Malthusian,* 1917–18.

Freewomen and the Birth-Rate.

The Malthusian Doctrine and Its Modern Aspects. First appeared as a series in *The Malthusian,* 1916–17.

Neo-Malthusianism and Eugenics. 31 pp.

The Neo-Malthusian Ideal and How It Can Be Realised. Presidential Address delivered by C. V. Drysdale to the 44th Annual General Meeting of the Malthusian League, 1921. 16 pp.

The Small Family System: Is It Injurious or Immoral? London: A. C. Fifield, 1913.

Wages and the Cost of Living. A paper written for the Economics and Statistical Section of the British Association Meeting at Birmingham in September 1913 and rejected by the Organising Committee, 1913; reprinted in 1921. 48 pp.

BIBLIOGRAPHY

Drysdale, Charles Robert:

Medical Opinions On the Population Question. London: George Standring, 1901.

The Nature and Treatment of Syphilis and the Other So-called 'Contagious Diseases.' 4th ed. London: Baillière, Tindall, and Cox, 1880 [First edition, 1863].

Prostitution Medically Considered With Some of Its Social Aspects. A paper read at the Harveian Medical Society of London, January 1866. London: Robert Hardwicke, 1866.

Drysdale, George:

The Elements of Social Science: or Physical, Sexual and Natural Religion. An Exposition of the True Cause and Only Cure of the Three Primary Social Evils: Poverty, Prostitution and Celibacy. 35th ed. London: G. Standring, 7/9 Finsbury Street, E. C., 1905.

Evils of a Hereditary Aristocracy. 1869.

The Irish Land Question. 1867.

Logic and Utility. 1866.

The Political Economist and Journal of Social Science, nos. 1–15 (January 1856–April 1857). A journal edited by George Drysdale.

Population Fallacies: A Defence of the Malthusian or True Theory Of Society. 1867.

State Measures for the Direct Prevention of Poverty, War and Pestilence. 1885.

State Measures for the Direct Prevention of Poverty, War and Infectious Diseases. 1905.

The State Remedy for Poverty. 1904.

ORIGINS OF THE MALTHUSIAN LEAGUE

Bradlaugh's abortive attempt to start a Malthusian league in the early 1860s:

The National Reformer 2 (1861). This volume of the periodical published by Charles Bradlaugh contains a number of articles pertaining to Bradlaugh's attempt to start a league in 1861. It also contains Bradlaugh's series of articles entitled *Jesus, Shelley, and Malthus; or, Pious Poverty and Heterodox Happiness.* The series was later reprinted as a pamphlet.

Bradlaugh, Charles. "Editorial," *The National Reformer* 3, no. 95 (8 March 1862): 5.

The background, events, and consequences of the Bradlaugh-Besant trial:

Banks, J. A., and Olive Banks. "The Bradlaugh-Besant Trial and the English Newspapers." *Population Studies, A Journal of Demography* 8, no. 1 (July 1954): 22–34.

Besant, Annie. *The Law of Population: Its Consequences, and Its Bearing Upon Human Conduct and Morals*. London: Freethought Publishing Co., [1877].

In the High Court of Justice: Queen's Bench Division, June 18th 1877: The Queen v. Charles Bradlaugh and Annie Besant. London: Freethought Publishing Co., 28, Stonecutter Street [1877]. A stenographic report of the trial as published by Besant and Bradlaugh.

Knowlton, Dr. [Charles]. *A History of the Recent Excitement in Ashfield*. Part 1. Ashfield, Mass., 1834. Part 2 appeared as a letter from Knowlton in the *Boston Investigator* 5, no. 27 (235), 25 September 1835 [p. 1], cols. 2–3.

The Law Reports. Queen's Bench Division. II, 1876–77. XL. Victoria. "The Queen v. Charles Bradlaugh and Annie Besant," 28 June 1877. London: William Clowes & Sons, 1877. Pp. 569–74.

The Law Reports. Queen's Bench Division. III, 1877–78. XLI. Victoria. In the Court of Appeal, 12 February 1878. "Charles Bradlaugh and Annie Besant v. the Queen." London: William Clowes & Sons, 1878. Pp. 607–42.

The National Reformer 29 (1877). This volume contains many valuable articles on activities before, during, and after the Bradlaugh-Besant trial, including the founding of the Malthusian League.

Watts, Charles. *A Refutation of Mr. Bradlaugh's Inaccuracies and Misrepresentations*. London, 1877.

Edward Truelove's trial:

In the High Court of Justice: Queen's Bench Division, February 1, 1878: The Queen v. Edward Truelove, for Publishing the Hon. Robert Dale Owen's 'Moral Physiology' and a Pamphlet Entitled 'Individual, Family, and National Poverty.' London: Edward Truelove, 256, High Holborn, 1878.

Owen, Robert Dale. *Moral Physiology; Or, a Brief and Plain Treatise On the Population Question*, "A New Edition." London: E. Truelove, 256, High Holborn [1870]. First edition, New York, 1830.

Life of Annie Besant:

Besant, Annie. *Annie Besant: An Autobiography*. London: T. Fisher Unwin, 1893.

Nethercot, Arthur H. *The First Five Lives of Annie Besant*. Chicago: University of Chicago Press, 1960.

———. *The Last Four Lives of Annie Besant*. Chicago: University of Chicago Press, 1963.

West, Geoffrey [Wells, Geoffrey Harry]. *Mrs. Annie Besant*. London: Gerald Howe, Ltd., 1927.

Life of Charles Bradlaugh:

BIBLIOGRAPHY

Arnstein, Walter L. *The Bradlaugh Case*. Oxford: The Oxford University Press, 1965.

Bradlaugh Bonner, Hypatia, and John M. Robertson. *Charles Bradlaugh: A Record of His Life and Work*, 2 vols. 5th ed. London: T. Fisher Unwin, 1902.

LABOR AND THE LEAGUE

Cairnes, J. E. *Some Leading Principles of Political Economy Newly Expounded*. London, 1874.

Hyndman, Henry M. "The Iron Law of Wages." *Justice* 1, no. 9 (15 March 1884): 3.

————. *The Record of An Adventurous Life*. New York: The Macmillan Company, 1911.

"Mainly About People." *The Star,* no. 227 (9 October 1888), p. 1.

Quelch, Harry. "Thrift: From a Worker's Point of View." *Justice* 1, no. 36 (20 September 1884): 4.

Ricardo, David. *The Works and Correspondence of David Ricardo*. Vol. 1, *On the Principles of Political Economy and Taxation,* edited by Piero Sraffa. Cambridge: Cambridge University Press, 1951.

Webb, Sidney. *The Decline in the Birth-Rate*. Fabian Tract no. 131. London: The Fabian Society, March 1907.

———— and Beatrice Webb. *Industrial Democracy*. London: Longmans, Green and Co., 1902.

THE ALLBUTT TRIAL

Allbutt, Henry Arthur. *Artificial Checks to Population: Is The Popular Teaching of Them Infamous?* An address delivered at Leeds, Bradford, Pudsey, and Morley in February, March, and April 1888. First edition. London: R. Forder, 1889.

————. *The Wife's Handbook: How A Woman Should Order Herself During Pregnancy, in the Lying-in Room, and After Delivery. With Hints On the Management of the Baby, and on Other Matters of Importance Necessary to be Known by Married Women.* 2nd ed. London: W. J. Ramsey, 28, Stonecutter Street, E. C., 1886.

Minutes of the General Medical Council, of Its Executive and Dental Committees, and of Its Three Branch Councils, For the Year 1887, 24. London: Spottiswoode & Co., 1888.

THE ENGLISH PROFESSIONS

Doctors:

The Lancet. "About Children." 8 January 1887, p. 88.
"A Horrible Trade." 1 February 1896, pp. 336–37.
"Class Mortality Statistics." 30 April 1887, pp. 887–89.
General Medical Council. 26 November 1887, pp. 1085–86.

"The Religious Newspaper and Immoral Advertisements." 18 January 1896, p. 183.

"The Wail of a French Philanthropist." 29 February 1896, pp. 564–65.

Peel, John. "Contraception and the Medical Profession." *Population Studies, A Journal of Demography* 18, no. 2 (November 1964): 133–45.

Routh, Charles Henry Felix. *The Moral and Physical Evils Likely To Follow If Practices Intended to Act As Checks to Population Be Not Strongly Discouraged and Condemned.* London: Baillière, Tindall, & Cox, 1879.

Clergymen:

Aquinas, Thomas. *Summa Theologica.* Secundae 2 ae, Ques. 154, Article I.

Fiske, Reverend Charles. "The Church and Birth Control." *The Atlantic Monthly* 146 (November 1930): 598–605.

Whatham, Reverend A. E. *Neo-Malthusianism, A Defence.* 10th ed. Walthamstow, England: J. King & Co., 1907.

Politicians:

Russell, Bertrand, and Patricia Russell, eds. *The Amberley Papers: The Letters and Diaries of Lord and Lady Amberley.* 2 vols. London, 1937.

St. John-Stevas, Norman. *Life, Death and the Law.* Bloomington, Indiana: Indiana University Press, 1961.

GENERAL SOURCES

Armengaud, André. "Mouvement Ouvrier et Néo-Malthusianisme au Début du XXe Siecle." *Annales de Démographie Historique,* 1966 (Études, Chronique, Bibliographique, Documents). Société de Démographie Historique. Editions Sirey, 22, rue Soufflot, Paris, V^e, 1967.

Banks, J. A. *Prosperity and Parenthood: A Study of Family Planning Among the Victorian Middle Classes.* London: Routledge & Kegan Paul Ltd., 1954.

Breed, Mary, and Edith How-Martyn. *The Birth Control Movement in England.* London: John Bales, Sons & Danielsson, Ltd., 1930.

Brown, Ford K. *Fathers of the Victorians.* Cambridge: Cambridge University Press, 1961.

Carlile, Richard. *Every Woman's Book; or, What Is Love? Containing Most Important Instructions for the Prudent Regulation of the Principle of Love and the Number of a Family.* 4th ed. London: R. Carlile, 62, Fleet Street, 1828.

Christie, W. D. *John Stuart Mill and Mr. Abraham Hayward, Q. C.* London, 1873.

BIBLIOGRAPHY

Eversley, D. E. C. *Social Theories of Fertility and the Malthusian Debate.* London: Oxford University Press, 1959.

Family Planning and Population Programs. Proceedings of the International Conference on Family Planning Programs, Geneva, August 1965. Chicago: University of Chicago Press, 1966.

Field, James Alfred. *Essays on Population and Other Papers.* Compiled and edited by Helen Fisher Hohman. Chicago: University of Chicago Press, 1931. Reissued by Kennikat Press, 1967.

————. "The Early Propagandist Movement in English Population Theory," *Bulletin of the American Economics Association,* 4th ser. 1, no. 2 (April 1911): 207–36.

Forty-second Annual Report of the Malthusian League. 1920.

Forty-eighth Annual Report of the Malthusian League. 1926.

Fryer, Peter. *The Birth Controllers.* New York: Stein and Day, 1965.

————. *British Birth Control Ephemera, 1870–1947.* The Collis Collection, Vol. 1. Leicester, Eng.: The Barracuda Press, 1969.

Glass, David V. *Population Policies and Movements in Europe.* 2d ed. London: Frank Cass and Company, Ltd., 1967.

Haire, Norman. *Hygienic Methods of Family Limitation.* London: The Malthusian League, 1922.

————. *Some More Medical Views on Birth Control.* New York: E. P. Dutton & Co., Inc., 1928.

Heilbroner, Robert L. *The Worldly Philosophers.* New York: Simon and Schuster, 1953.

Himes, Norman E. *Medical History of Contraception.* Baltimore: The Williams & Wilkins Company, 1936.

————. "Notes on the Origin of the Terms Contraception, Birth Control, Neo-Malthusianism, Etc." *Medical Journal and Record* 135, no. 10 (May 1932): 495–96.

Holmes, J. R. *True Morality; or, The Theory and Practice of Neo-Malthusianism.* 2nd ed. Hanney, Wantage, Berkshire, Eng: J. R. Holmes, 1892 [1st ed., 1891].

Keynes, J. Maynard. "Some Economic Consequences of a Declining Population." *The Eugenics Review* 29, no. 1 (April 1937): 13–17.

The Labour Standard, no. 9 (2 July 1881), p. 5.

The Malthusian Handbook, Designed to Induce Married People to Limit Their Families Within Their Means. London: W. H. Reynolds, New Cross, S.E., 1893.

Marcus, Steven. *The Other Victorians: A Study of Sexuality and Pornography in Mid-Nineteenth-Century England.* New York: Basic Books, Inc., 1966.

Micklewright, F. H. Amphlett. "The Rise and Decline of English Neo-Malthusianism." *Population Studies, A Journal of Demography* 15, no. 1 (July 1961): 32–51.

250

Mill, John Stuart. *Principles of Political Economy*. New York: D. Appleton and Co., 1887.

National Birth-Rate Commission. *The Declining Birth-Rate: Its Causes and Effects*. Report of and the chief evidence taken by the National Birth-Rate Commission, instituted, with official recognition, by the National Council of Public Morals—for the Promotion of Race Regeneration—Spiritual, Moral and Physical. London: Chapman and Hall, Ltd., 1916.

The National Reformer 32 (1878) and 33 (1879). These volumes contain information on the Malthusian League's activities in its first years.

Pamphlets on Malthusianism, 1879–1916. University of London. The Goldsmith's Library.

Pearsall, Ronald. *The Worm in the Bud. The World of Victorian Sexuality*. London: Weidenfeld & Nicolson, 1969. Also available in Penguin Books, 1974.

Peel, John. "Birth Control and the British Working-Class Movement: A Bibliographical Review." *Bulletin of the Society For the Study of Labour History*, no. 7 (Autumn 1963), pp. 16–22.

Place, Francis. *Illustrations and Proofs of the Principle of Population*. Being the First Work on Population in the English Language Recommending Birth Control. Introduction by Norman E. Himes. 2nd ed. New York: Augustus M. Kelley, 1967 [first published in 1822].

Poirier, Philip P. *The Advent of the British Labour Party*. New York: Columbia University Press, 1958.

Report of the Fifth International Neo-Malthusian and Birth Control Conference, Kingsway Hall, London, 11–14 July 1922. Edited by Raymond Pierpoint. London: William Heinemann, Ltd., 1922.

Robinson, Victor. *Pioneers of Birth Control in England and America*. New York: Voluntary Parenthood League, 206 Broadway, 1919.

Sanger, Margaret. *My Fight For Birth Control*. New York: Farrar & Rinehart, Inc., 1931.

Smith, Kenneth. *The Malthusian Controversy*. London: Routledge & Kegan Paul Ltd., 1951.

Standring, George. "Dr. C. R. Drysdale." *The Republican* 12, no. 4 (July 1886): 25–26.

———. "Ourself." *The Republican* 11, no. 2 (May 1885): 1.

Stopes, Marie. *Contraception: Its Theory, History, and Practice: A Manual for the Medical and Legal Professions*. London: John Bale, Sons & Danielsson, Ltd., 1923.

Wheeler, J. M. *A Biographical Dictionary of Freethinkers of All Ages and Nations*. London: Progressive Publishing Company, 1889.

Wright, N. "Early Days at Walworth." *Family Planning* 1, no. 4 (January 1953): 7.

Index

Abortion and abortifacients, 43, 124, 126, 132; English law on, in 1880s, 162–63 n.28, 188, 196–97 n.17, 210

Abortion Law Reform League, 240

Aldred, Guy Alfred (1886–1963), 159

Allbutt, Clifford (cousin of Henry A.), 140

Allbutt, Henry Arthur (1846–1904), 128, 131–41, 192

Allbutt, Lawrence (brother of Henry A.), 138

Alliance Nationale (1896), 188

Amberley, John Russell, Viscount (1842–76), 149

American Birth Control League, 195

American Society of Medical Sociology, 195

Anten, W. M. H., 178

Aquinas, Saint Thomas (ca. 1225–74), 144

Autobiography (Besant), 47, 108

Aveling, Edward Bibbins (1851–98), 93, 99

Baker, H. Jennie, 112, 224–25, 227

Banks, J. A., 117 n.31

Banks, J. A., and Olive, xvi, 45–46

Bax, Ernest Belfort (1854–1926), 93

Bedborough, George, 157

Belgium, and neo-Malthusianism, 189

Bennett, D. M., 190

Bentham, Jeremy (1748–1832), 6

Bergeret, Louis François Étienne, 123

Bertillon, Jacques, 188

Besant, Annie (née Wood) (1847–1933), 18–19, 25, 28–29, 32, 43, 105–7, 153; and Charles Brad-laugh, 46, 48, 100–101; and the Malthusian League, 49–51, 63–64, 99–100, 229; and socialism, 93, 100–101; and Theosophy, 48, 108–9; biographical information on, 46–48; *Law of Population,* 42–45, 68–71; trial of, and Charles Bradlaugh, xx, 36–37. *See also* Bradlaugh-Besant trial

Birth control, xvi; origin of term, xiv–xv, xxi–xxii n.8, 191. *See also* Family limitation; Family planning movement; Neo-Malthusianism

Birth Control International Information Centre, 196

Birth Control News (1922–46), 220

Birth rate: in England, 170, 203; in European countries, 185; in France, 184–85; in Italy, 189; in London, 203, 230 n.3; in Sweden, 189

Blavatsky, Helena Petrovna (1831–91), 48, 108

Bohn, Henry George (1796–1884), 61

Bonser, Thomas Owen (1844–99), 65, 72, 74–75, 77, 170–71

Bradlaugh Bonner, Hypatia (daughter), 31, 35, 48, 229

Bradlaugh-Besant trial, xvii; party responsible for, 33–35; in court, 36–37; effect of, 40–41, 45; and the newspapers, 45–46, 47, 53 n.30, 170

Bradlaugh, Charles (1833–91), 18–19, 31, 153–54; and Annie Besant, 46, 48, 100–101; biographical information on, 26–27; and the Malthusian League, xvii, xix–xx, 25, 51, 64–65, 98–99, 121, 160; trial of, and Annie Besant, 36–37

British Medical Association, 122, 128–30, 138

British Medical Journal, 138

Browne, Frances Worsley Stella (ca. 1881–1955), 119 n.81, 226

Buckmaster, Stanley Owen, first viscount (1861–1934), 228

Bulletin Malthusien (La Vie Intime), 189

Bulley, A. K., 220

Burke, Edmund, 3

Burns, John (1858–1943), 92, 155

Burrows, Herbert (1845–1922), 73, 93–94, 102, 106, 138

Cairnes, John E. (1823–75), 88

Campbell Act. *See* Obscene Publications Act of 1857

Carlile, Richard (1790–1843), 8, 26

Chamberlain, Neville, 227

Champion, Henry Hyde, 93

Chance, C. F., 216

Christian Evidence Society, 33

Christianity, and family limitation, 142–49, 176

Church of England, 146–47

Clarion, The (1891–1932), 211

Cockburn, Alexander James Edmund (Lord Chief Justice) (1802–80), 35–36, 38–39, 46

Code Napoléon. See Napoleonic Code

Coitus interruptus (withdrawal), 16, 43, 124, 133, 209

Collins, W. W., 156

Condom (sheath), 16, 43, 69, 133–34, 188, 209, 217

Conservative party, 121

Contagious Diseases Acts (1864, 1866, 1869), 43, 60

Contraception: Its Theory, History, and Practice (Stopes), 231 n.18

Conway, Moncure Daniel (1832–1907), 100, 146

Cook, Henry, 29–30

Cox, Harold (1859–1923), 159, 225, 227

Criminal Law Amendment Act, 163 n.32

Cutner, Herbert, 21 n.16, 82 n.17, 239

Darwin, Charles, 227

Dawson, Reverend Leonard, 145

Dawson of Penn, Bertrand Dawson, first viscount (1864–1945), 161, 223

Declining Birth-Rate, The, Fabian Tract no. 131 (1907), 103

Democratic Federation. *See* Social Democratic Federation

Diaphragm (Dutch cap), 69, 134, 177–78, 210

Disraeli, Benjamin, 151

Douche, 16, 43, 133, 209

Drysdale, Bessie Ingham (née Edwards) (Mrs. Charles Vickery) (1871–1950): antilabor tone of, 224; and Malthusian League, 58, 64, 78, 205, 225, 227, 229; personal information on, 220, 231 n.7, 232 n.27, 239

Drysdale, Charles Robert (1829–1907), 6, 91, 98, 102–3, 109–10, 127–30, 152, 154, 183–84; biographical information on, 58–60, 81–82 n.17, 205; and Bradlaugh-Besant trial, 35–36, 61; favors state control of population, 150, 166 n.83; and international interests, 171–72, 187, 193; in Malthusian League, 51, 57, 65, 78; and medical profession, 121–22; on prostitution and venereal diseases, 14, 59–61; on women's rights, 60

Drysdale, Charles Vickery (son of Charles Robert) (1874–1961), xvi–xvii, xix, 6, 91–92, 98, 150, 191, 194–95, 203, 230 n.1, 242; antilabor tone of, 111, 217–18; biographical information on, 231 n.7, 232 n.27, 240; and eugenics, 204–5, 218; and H. G. Wells, 213–15; in Malthusian League, 58, 78, 205–7, 218, 225, 227, 229, 237–39; on socialism, 115–16, 213–14

Drysdale, Eric (son of Charles Vickery), 232 n.27

Drysdale, Eva Mary (daughter of Charles Vickery), 212

Drysdale family, 150–51, 242 n.5; and Malthusian League, 57–58, 80, 220–21

Drysdale, George (brother of Charles Robert) (1825–1904), xvii, 11, 15, 21–22 n.21, 22 n.29, 226; biographical information on, 9–11; and Charles Bradlaugh, 26–28, 32–33; *Elements of Social Science,* 9, 11–17; and international interests, 171–72; on methods of contraception, 15–16; as the philosopher of the Malthusian League, 8, 57; picture, 10

Dunlop, Binnie (1874–1946), 63–64, 78, 206–9, 212, 215, 238

Dutch Neo-Malthusian League (Dutch Nieuw-Malthusiaansche Bond), 137–38, 191, 194, 196–97 n.17; and Jan Rutgers, 178–79; membership of, 179–80; origin and history of, 173–81

Dutch cap. *See* Diaphragm

Dutch Nieuw-Malthusiaansche Bond. *See* Dutch Neo-Malthusian League

East London Centre (1926), 233 n.57

East Street Welfare Centre for Pre-Maternity, Maternity, and Child Welfare. *See* Walworth Women's Welfare Centre

E. Lambert and Son (London), 134, 157–58

Elements of Social Science (George Drysdale), 9, 11, 18–20, 26–27, 33, 107, 226; description of, 11–18

Ellis, Henry Havelock (1859–1939), 5, 124, 157

Esperanto, 194

Essay on The Principle of Population (T. R. Malthus), xii

Eugenics, 149, 204, 218

Eugenics Education Society. *See* Eugenics Society

Eugenics Society, 204–5, 218

Eversley, D. E., xii

Fabian News, 73

Fabian Society, 73, 106, 226; and family limitation, 100–104

La Famille Française (1892), 186

Family limitation, 5, 103–4, 141, 180, 182; and Christianity, 142–49; and the medical profession, 121–42. *See also* Family planning movement; Neo-Malthusianism

Family Planning Association (England), 22 n.24, 231 n.9, 240, 242

Family planning movement, xv–xvi, xx. *See also* Family limitation; Neo-Malthusianism

Fascism, 189

Fédération Universalle pour la Régénération Humaine, 200 n.73

Ferdy, Hans. *See* Meyerhof, A.

Field, James Alfred (1880–1927), xvi, xxii n.12, 8, 160

Foote, Edward Bliss (U.S.) (1829–1960), xiv, 190, 200 n.64

Foote, Edward Bond (son of Edward Bliss) (1854–1912), 190

Foote, G. W., 31

Forder, Robert, 25

France, 124, 154, 182–88

French Academy of Medicine, 188

Free love, 18

Freethought Publishing Company, 32, 48, 54 n.55, 78

Free trade, 95, 169

Freud, Sigmund, 5

Fruits of Philosophy, The (Knowlton), 29, 31, 33, 37, 41, 61

Fryer, Peter, xviii

Galton, Francis W. (1822–1911), 104, 204

Garibaldi, Guiseppe, 36

General Council of Medical Education and Registration. *See* General Medical Council

General Medical Council, 135–40, 163–64 n.36, 164 n.47

Génération Consciente, 188

George, Henry, 89–92, 116 n.10

Germany, and neo-Malthusianism, 181–82

Gerritsen, Carl Victor, 64, 128, 173–74

Giroud, Gabriel [pseud. G. Hardy], 187, 194

Gladstone, William Ewart (1809–98), 7–8, 151

Glasier, J. Bruce, 93

Glass, David V., xvi–xviii, 68, 172, 188, 217

Godwin, William (1756–1836), 4, 89

Grandjean, Valentin, 189

Groupe Malthusien (Switzerland), 189

Haire, Norman (1892–1952), 221, 232 n.20; *Hygienic Methods of Family Limitation,* 209–11

Hardie, Keir, 109, 155

Hardy, G. *See* Giroud, Gabriel

Harman, Lillian (daughter of Moses), 190

Harman, Moses (U.S.) (1830–1910), 190

Hasse, Karl or C. *See* Mensinga, Wilhelm Peter Johannes

Hausmeister, Max, 181

Hayward, Abraham (1801–84), 7

Headlam, Stewart D., 91, 102, 146

Heldt, H. B., 173

Hember, Robert G., 51, 63

Himes, Norman Edwin (1899–1949), xvi–xvii, 33

Holmes, J. R., 30, 52 n.13, 158

Holyoake, Austin (1826–74), 29

Holyoake, George Jacob (1817–1906), 29, 31

Hoskyns, Reverend Edwyn, 106–7

Howarth, Edmund, 159

How-Martyn, Edith (née How) (1875–1954), 206, 219, 237

Humbert, Eugène, 188, 194

Huxley, Julian, 229, 237, 242

Huxley, Thomas, xv

Hygienic Methods of Family Limitation (1913), 72, 209, 230

Hyndman, Henry Mayers (1842–1921), 32, 73, 90, 92, 99, 103, 116 n.10, 184

Ido, 194

Indecent Advertisements Act (1889), 157

Independent Labour party, 109, 115, 228

India, and neo-Malthusianism, 192

Indian Birth-Control Society (1922), 192

Individual, Family and National Poverty (J. H. Palmer), 38

Inge, Very Reverend William Ralph (1860–1954), 148

International Bureau of Correspondence and Defense, 158, 194

International Congress of Hygiene (Paris, 1878; Turin, 1880), 128

International Federation of Neo-Malthusian Leagues, 193

International Medical Congress: Amsterdam (1879), 123, 172; London (1881), 129

International Neo-Malthusian [and Birth Control] Conferences: First, Paris (1900), 193; Second, Liege (1905), 193; Third, Hague (1910), 189, 194; Fourth, Dresden (1911), 194; Fifth, London (1922), 195, 224; Sixth, New York (1925), 195

International Planned Parenthood Federation, 240

International Population Year (1974), xi

Italy, and neo-Malthusianism, 189

Jacobs, Aletta Henriette (1854–1929), 69, 176–78, 180, 196 n.14

Jewson, Dorothy, 113–14

Johnson, Olive M., xix, 206, 238–40

Joynes, J. L., 93–95, 99

Kerr, Robert (1867–1951), 78–80, 112, 226, 229, 237, 239

Keynes, John Maynard, first baron (1883–1946), 159, 195, 201 n.77, 229, 242

Knowlton, Charles (1800–1850), 16, 29, 41, 52 n.10, 61

Krafft-Ebing, Richard von, 124

Labor movement, and the Malthusian League, 105–11

Labour party, 109, 111–15, 121, 228

Labour Representation Committee, 109

Lambeth Conferences of Bishops: (1908), 146; (1920), 146, 220; (1930), 147; (1958), 166 n.73

Lancet, The, 122–23, 125–26

Land reform, xiii, 44, 153

Lane, Sir William Arbuthnot, 159

Laski, Frida (Mrs. Harold J.), 113

Laski, Harold J. (1893–1950), 237

Law of Population, The (Besant), 54 n.55, 108, 156; description of, 42–45; and the Malthusian League, 68, 70–71

Lawton, Frederick, 144–45

League for Human Regeneration. See Ligue de la Régénération Humaine, La

Leeds Vigilance Society, 135, 140, 163 n.32

Levy, J. H., 94, 100

Liberal party, 119 n.81, 121

Liga Española de Regeneracion Humana (1909) (Spain), 189

Ligue de la Régénération Humaine, La (League for Human Regeneration), 187, 199 n.54

Loader, Henry, 156–57

Lyttelton, Honorable A., 144–45

MacDonald, James Ramsay (1866–1937), 92–93, 114, 147

Madras Birth Control Bulletin, 200 n.71

Madras Neo-Malthusian League, 200 n.71

Madras Secular Society, 137

Malthus, Reverend Thomas Robert (1766–1834), xii–xiii, 3–4, 88–89, 150, 161, 195

Malthusian, origin of term, xiv–xv

Malthusian ball (1933), 237

Malthusian Handbook, The (Standring), 69, 71

Malthusian League, xvii–xx, 4, 15–17, 44, 75–77, 87, 91, 95, 97–98, 107–8, 148, 152–54, 158–59, 169–170, 177, 191, 204–8, 210–12, 219, 226–30, 231 n.11, 240–41; and Henry A. Allbutt, 131–32, 137, 139; and Annie Besant, 99–100; and Charles Bradlaugh, 98–100; and Christianity, 141–49; conflict within, 212–13, 215–17, 222–24, 227; distributes practical information on contraception, 208–11; and family limitation movement, xiii–xvi, xviii, xx, 216–17, 240–41; financial support for, 220, 227, 233 n.54, 239; foreign branches of, 172–76, 178–82, 187–90, 192, 199–200 n.63; and international neo-Malthusianism, 192–96; and labor movement, 105–11; Medical Branch of, 128–29; membership in, 52, 62; opens Walworth Women's Welfare Centre, 220–21; origin and early organization of, 20, 49–52, 64–65; philosophy of, 3, 17–18, 87;

Malthusian League (*continued*)
principles and objectives of, xiii,
65–66, 238–41, publications of,
67–68; requests for practical information from, 69–72; and socialism,
xii, 15, 89–105, 110–11; and Marie
Stopes, 196, 220; techniques of
propaganda of, 67, 77–78, 155; and
Edward Truelove, 39–40; and Sidney and Beatrice Webb, 102–4

Malthusian League banner, 231 n.9,
240

Malthusian literature, 82 n.20

Malthusian, The (1879–1921, 1949–
52), xviii–xix, 6, 11, 21–22 n.21, 65,
68, 73, 87, 137, 150, 170–71, 213,
239–240; distribution and circulation of, 79–80; editors of, 78, 205,
215; name changes of, 222–23, 238;
origin and format of, 78–79

Mann, Tom, 92, 103

Married Love (Stopes), 219

Marx, Eleanor (Mrs. Edward Aveling)
(1856–1898), 93

Marx, Karl, 92

Mascaux, Ferdinand, 189

Mayer & Company (Leeds), 134

*Means of Preventing Large Families,
The,* 174–75, 187

Medical Act of 1815, 164 n.47

Medical Act of 1858, 138, 164 n.47

Medical Branch (of Malthusian
League), 128–29

Medical History of Contraception
(Himes), xvi

Medical journals, 122–23

Medical profession, and family limitation, 121–42

Medical Society of London, 126

Memorandum 153/M.C.W. (1930),
228–29

Mensinga, Wilhelm Peter Johannes
("Karl" or "C. Hasse"), 69, 134, 177

Meyerhof, A. [pseud. Ferdy, Hans],
182

Millard, Charles Killick (1870–1952),
81 n.17

Mill, James, 5

Mill, John Stuart, 6–8, 60, 150

Moral Physiology (Owen), 38, 45

Morris, William, 93

Morton, R. G., 231 n.9, 238, 240

Moss, A. B., 229

Mudalier, Murugesa, 64, 192

My Fight For Birth Control (Sanger),
xiv–xv

Naidu, Mutha, 192

Naiker, Moonesawny, 192

Napoleonic Code (*Code Napoléon*),
154, 183

Narusee, L., 192

National Association for Sex Education (Sweden), 189

National Birth Control Council, 113,
222, 241–42

National Birth-Rate Commission, 98,
147–48, 185

National Council of Public Morals,
147–48

National Labour Women's Conference: (1924), 112; (1925), 113;
(1927), 114; (1928), 115

National Reformer (1860–1893), xix,
11, 25–28, 31, 41, 48–49, 65, 78,
101, 130

National Secular Society, 25, 31, 40,
46, 72, 87, 137

National Union of Societies for Equal
Citizenship, 229

Neo-Malthusian, origin of term, xiv,
xxi n.6

Neo-Malthusianism, 25, 108–9, 131,
194, 205, 242; in Belgium, 189; in
Germany, 181–82; in Holland,
172–81; in India, 192; in Italy, 189;
in Spain, 189; in Sweden, 188–89; in
Switzerland, 189; and Charles
Bradlaugh, 27–28, 52 n.9; and

eugenics, 204, 218; and socialism, 73, 89. *See also* Family limitation; Family planning movement

Neo-Malthusianism: A Defence (A. E. Whatham), 145, 165 n.68

Netherlands Society for Sexual Reform, 181

New Generation, The (1922–49), xviii, 79, 223–24, 230, 237–38

New Generation League (1922–25), xviii, 79, 224, 226–27

North Kensington Welfare Centre (1924), 233 n.57

Nystrom, Anton, 188

Obscenity Law of 1873 (U.S.), 190–91

Obscene Publications Act of 1857 (Campbell Act), 28, 32, 155

Onanism, 143–44

Owen, Robert Dale (1801–77), 38, 41, 45

Page, J. K., 51, 63, 65, 95–96, 128, 132, 154

Paley, William, xii

Palmer, Eileen, xix

Palmer, J. H., 38

Parris, Touzeau, 25, 36, 64–65, 93

Paul, Eden, 226

Paul, Eden and Cedar, 223

Peel, John, 123

Pitt, William (the Younger), xii

Place, Francis (1771–1854), xvi, xviii, 7, 16

Political Economist; and Journal of Social Science, The (George Drysdale, ed.), 19–20

Politicians, and family limitation, 121, 149–55, 160–61, 234 n.73

Population: as sign of national strength, xii, 149; debate on, xi–xiii,4

Post Office Protection Act of 1884, 157, 167 n.103

Principles of Political Economy (J. S. Mill), 6

Progress and Poverty (H. George), 90, 92

Prosecutions, 156–60

Prostitution, 14, 59–60, 80 n.7

Queen *vs.* Charles Bradlaugh and Annie Besant, 29–33

Queen *vs.* Edward Truelove, 37–39

Quelch, Harry, 110

Ramsey, William J., 25, 134

Rendell, Walter John, 134

Reynolds, William Hammond (1844–1911), 25, 51, 63, 65, 72, 74–78, 170, 190–91

Rhythm method (safe period), 148, 210; physiologically inaccurate in nineteenth century, 13, 15–16, 22 n.24, 43, 83 n.28, 125, 133, 232 n.20

Ricardo, David (1772–1823), 3, 94, 97, 117 n.22, 150

Robertson, John Mackinnon (1856–1933), 99, 151, 227

Robin, Paul, 186–87, 192–93, 198–99 n.51

Robinson, Victor (son of William J.), 81 n.17

Robinson, William Josephus (U.S.) (1867–1936), 81 n.17, 195

Roe, Humphrey Verdon (1878–1949), 219

Rothwell, John, 97

Routh, Charles Henry Felix (1822–1909), 122–25, 127

Royal College of Physicians (Edinburgh), 131, 135–40, 164 n.42

Russell, Bertrand Arthur William, third earl, 159–60, 226–27, 242

Russell, Dora (née Black) (Mrs. Bertrand A. W.), 111–14, 159

Rutgers-Hoitsema, Maria (née Hoitsema), 175–76, 179, 196 n.11

Rutgers, Johannes (Jan) (1851–1924), 175–76, 178–79, 191, 194

Safe period. *See* Rhythm method

Sanger, Margaret (née Higgins) (1883–1966), xiv–xv, 89, 159, 191–92, 195–96; coins term "birth control", xiv–xv, xxi n.8, 216; and Malthusian League, 191, 196, 219; pays tribute to Drysdales, 58

Shaw, George Bernard (1856–1950), 99–100, 103, 170

Sheath. *See* Condom

Simon Population Trust, 240

Smit, J. M., 173

Smith, Adam, xii, 3, 17, 87, 110, 117 n.22, 124, 161

Social Darwinism, 44–45, 218

Social Democratic Federation (Democratic Federation), 92–93, 100, 106–7, 109–10

Social Harmony Union (Sozial-Harmonische Verein), 181–82

Sozial-Harmonische Verein. *See* Social Harmony Union

Socialism, 15, 73, 89, 175, 184; and the Malthusian League, xii, 89–105, 110–11, 213–14

Socialist League, 93, 106

Society for Constructive Birth Control and Racial Progress (1921), 113, 195, 220

Society for the Provision of Birth Control Clinics, 221, 229

Society for the Suppression of Vice (U.K.), 35, 37–38, 53 n.29

Society for the Suppression of Vice (U.S.), 200 n.64

Society of Apothecaries (London), 131, 135–36, 139–40

Spain, and neo-Malthusianism, 189

Standring, George (1855–1924), xix, 73, 83 n.28, 83 n.43, 150, 160, 216, 241; biographical information on, 72–73: *Malthusian Handbook*, 68–69; and the Malthusian League,

25, 51, 65, 72–74, 78–79, 169–70, 208

Stead, William Thomas (1849–1912), 163 n.32

Stille, G., 181

Stopes, Marie Charlotte Carmichael (1880–1958), 29, 113, 131, 142, 195–96, 209, 216–17, 219–20, 231 n.18

Sumner, Sir John (1856–1934), 220, 227, 229

Sweden, and neo-Malthusianism, 188–89

Switzerland, and neo-Malthusianism, 189

Symes, J., 25

Syphilis, 14, 59

Theosophy, 48, 108

Thorne, Will, 92

Thurtle, Ernest, 114, 227–28

Truelove, Edward, 11; and the Malthusian League, 25, 51, 65; prosecution of, 35–41, 45

True Morality, or the Theory and Practice of Neo-Malthusianism (J. R. Holmes), 158

United Nations (UN), xi

Utilitarianism, 3, 6, 8, 44

Vaginal sponge, 16, 43, 133

Van Houten, Samuel (1837–1930), xiv, xxi n.6, 35, 64, 173, 176, 196–97 n.17

Varenholz, C. F., 117 n.27

Vickery, Alice (Mrs. Charles Robert Drysdale) (1844–1929), 90–91, 109–10, 150, 152–53, 183, 193–94; as a feminist, 62; at Bradlaugh-Besant trial, 62; biographical information on, 61–62, 81–82 n.17; and the Malthusian League, 51, 57–58, 64, 205, 227, 229; and Margaret Sanger, 191

Walworth Women's Welfare Centre, 220–21, 233 n.57

War, The (Malthusian League), 211–12

Watson, James (1799–1874), 29, 38

Watts, Charles (1836–1906), 29, 30–32

Watts, James, 36

Wealth of Nations, xii

Webb, Sidney James, Baron Passfield (1859–1947), 102–3

Webb, Sidney, and Beatrice (née Potter) (1858–1943), 88, 102–4

Wedgwood, Mrs. Josiah C., 113

Wells, H. G., 159, 195, 220, 229, 237, 242; conflict between Charles Vickery Drysdale and, 213–15

Whatham, Arthur E., 145

Wheatley, John (1869–1930), 111

White, James, 158–59

Wicksell, Knut, 188

Wife's Handbook, The (Allbutt), 71, 75, 156; circulation of, 141; description of, 132–34; publication of, 83 n.40, 135; role of, in Allbutt case, 134–36, 138

Williamson, Joseph, 72, 75–77

Wise Parenthood (Stopes), 209, 219

Withdrawal. See *Coitus interruptus*

Women's National Liberal Federation, 229

Words in Pearl (E. B. Foote), 190, 200 n.64

Workers' Birth Control Group, 112–13, 229

World Population Conference, Bucharest (1974), xi–xiii, 4

Young, Henry S., 156